By the authors (with Gloria Kaufer Greene)

Don't Tell 'Em It's Good for 'Em
Eat Your Vegetables!

SOUP'S ON

Nancy Bagget
&
Ruth Glick

A Bobbs-Merrill Book
Macmillan Publishing Company
New York
Collier Macmillan Publishers
London

641.8

FEB 3 '86

Macmillan Publishing Company
866 Third Avenue, New York, N.Y. 10022
Collier Macmillan Canada, Inc.

Coordinating Editor: Rosalyn T. Badalamenti

Library of Congress Cataloging-in-Publication Data
Baggett, Nancy, 1943–
Soup's on.
"A Bobbs-Merrill book."
Includes index.
1. Soups. I. Glick, Ruth, 1942– . II. Title.
TX757.B34 1985b   641.8'13   85-18786
ISBN 0-02-505200-4

Macmillan books are available at special discounts for bulk purchases for sales promotions, premiums, fund-raising, or educational use.
For details, contact:

Special Sales Director
Macmillan Publishing Company
866 Third Avenue
New York, N.Y. 10022

10 9 8 7 6 5 4 3 2 1

Printed in the United States of America

To Roc and Norman, who never turn
down a good bowl of soup

Acknowledgments

Heartfelt thanks go to the following:

To Rosalyn T. Badalamenti, whose professional expertise, coordinating skills, and dedication once again proved so invaluable.

To Linda Hayes, whose help and encouragement we can always count on.

To Cornelia Guest, Bonnie Ammer, and John Woodside, who lent valuable support and assistance along the way.

To Kathy Jensen, Pricilla Moore, Holly Nickerson, Leslie Ziegler, and Nancy Thomas, who helped us test recipes and offered many constructive suggestions.

Contents

INTRODUCTION 1

1 GETTING STARTED 5

2 SOUPS FROM AROUND THE WORLD 15

3 MEAT AND POULTRY SOUPS 47

4 FISH AND SHELLFISH SOUPS 79

5 VEGETABLE SOUPS 109

6 BEAN AND GRAIN SOUPS 147

7 VEGETARIAN SOUPS 167

8 CROCK POT SOUPS 183

9 QUICK SOUPS 201

10 ELEGANT SOUPS 223

11 COLD SOUPS 253

12 FRUIT SOUPS 273

13 STOCKS AND CLEAR SOUPS 293

14 THE FINAL TOUCH 313

LIST OF MAIN-DISH SOUPS 321

INDEX 327

INTRODUCTION

A kettle of hearty soup simmering on the back of the stove has irresistible appeal. It's the perfect way to warm the soul on a cold and blustery day. It fills the house with tantalizing aromas. It's delicious, nourishing, and oh-so-satisfying. And it calls to mind a simpler era when meals were routinely prepared from garden-fresh ingredients.

Yet, while almost everyone recognizes the pleasures of soup, most cooks have only a few recipes in their repertoires. *Soup's On* can change all that by introducing a whole array of additional possibilities. Included among the more than two hundred recipes are soups as diverse as Tomato Bisque with Thyme and Bacon, Beefy Minestrone, spicy Shrimp and Chicken Gumbo, cold Cucumber Soup, Greek Avgolemono, aromatic Indian Mulligatawny, savory Potage Vert, and old favorites like Split Pea and Ham and Chicken Noodle Soup.

From long experience at the soupmaker's art, we've discovered some basic principles that guarantee delicious results. For example, we rely mainly on fresh ingredients. But we've also discovered that certain prepared products, such as canned tomatoes and chicken broth, can work well when seasoned properly. In addition, soupmaking is one culinary area where creativity really pays off. Sometimes it's the addition of wine to the mixed vegetable potage or the tarragon to the cabbage soup that brings out the flavor of the finished dish. Other times it's a subtle but surprising blend of ingredients that magically works together, as in our Oyster and Mushroom Soup Florentine. And, then again, it may be something so basic as the richness of the stock, as with our Favorite Oxtail Soup.

As an added bonus, we've developed many of our soups with more than taste appeal in mind. We're also concerned about good nutrition—in a low-key, unobtrusive fashion. We've found that soups are one of the most delicious and appealing ways to incorporate healthful vegetables, beans, and grains into the diet. What's more, it's possible to make wonderfully satisfying and rich soups without overloading them with high-calorie ingredients, such as heavy cream and butter. We use only enough butter to provide satisfying flavor. And we've found that heavy cream is rarely necessary to produce wonderfully rich and creamy soups. In almost every case, half-and-half or light cream give excellent results.

Since the majority of cooks want to make the most of their time in the kitchen, we've designed our recipes to be as simple and easy to use as possible. The instructions in *Soup's On* are designed to be clear and specific. Most require only everyday kitchen equipment, such as an assortment of saucepans, large pots, and wooden spoons. Also particularly useful in soupmaking are a blender and food processor. The former is wonderful for puréeing, and the latter is a great time-saver for chopping and grating ingredients.

As a rule we avoid esoteric or tricky techniques in *Soup's On* —unless these yield clearly superior results. If we ask you to go to the trouble of sieving a soup, for example, it's because that's the only way to obtain the velvety texture desired. If we include an instruction to brown soup bones, it's because the step adds a great deal to the rich taste of the finished product.

You'll notice, too, that our recipes are designed with kitchen cleanup in mind; we don't call for five pots when one or two will do!

We've also taken convenience into consideration. For example, we have a quick chapter which features delicious soups that can be made in under 30 minutes. Many others throughout the book can be prepared in less than an hour. Those like meat and bean soups, which require longer cooking, are often very simple to put together. If you prefer homemade stocks to commercial broths, as we do, these can always be prepared in advance and stored in the refrigerator or freezer. Also included in *Soup's On* is a special crock pot chapter for cooks who like soup but need to be away from the kitchen all day.

Finally, you'll notice that recipes often include suggestions for garnishing and serving. That's because we feel it's worth some extra effort to make food look as good as it tastes.

1
GETTING STARTED

Happily, most of the skills required in soupmaking are pretty basic. Mankind, after all, has been cooking flavorful ingredients together in liquid since the dawn of civilization.

Of course, soupmaking has undergone a lot of refinements through the ages. But even today, the novice cook can turn out delicious soups with a minimum of equipment and hardly any fuss and bother.

The recipes in this book have been carefully tested and retested so that they will yield wonderful soup every time. The information which follows will help you duplicate our results.

TECHNIQUES AND EQUIPMENT

Chopping, Dicing, and Slicing

The way vegetables and other ingredients are cut up affects not only cooking time but also the look and texture of the final dish. Moreover, the size of the cut pieces also determines the volume when ingredients are measured. Therefore, we are careful to specify how this should be done in each recipe.

In the large majority of our soups containing vegetables, these are chopped. When we specify "finely chopped" we mean small pieces roughly ⅛ to ¼ inch square. "Coarsely chopped" refers to pieces that are about ½ inch square. If directions simply say "chopped," the size should be between these two. In all cases, the pieces need not be particularly even.

Some recipes also call for dicing. By dicing we mean cutting into small cubes about ¼ inch square. In this technique, the emphasis is on neat, even cutting.

Many soups also call for slicing vegetables. In this case, we often specify the thickness. However, when we simply call for "thinly sliced" ingredients, cut them about ⅛ inch thick. The food processor is not recommended for this procedure because the slices will be paper thin. When directed to "coarsely slice," cut ingredients into approximately ¼- to ⅜-inch-thick slices.

Sautéing

Many of the recipes in *Soup's On* begin with instructions to lightly cook onions, garlic, and, sometimes, other vegetables in butter or oil. This technique, known as sautéing, helps bring out the flavor of the ingredients. The idea is to briefly cook the vegetables until they are tender, not to brown them.

Browning or Roasting

In a few recipes, soup bones are roasted in the oven or browned in oil on the top of the stove as the first preparation step. This classic French technique helps bring out the meaty flavor and should not be omitted. Often, this process yields little brown bits of meat and juices in the bottom of the pan. These, too, contribute to the rich taste and should not be discarded.

Simmering

You'll notice that the large majority of recipes in *Soup's On* call for bringing the ingredients to a boil and then lowering the heat and simmering. Technically, simmering means that the mixture is cooking at about 185 to 205 degrees Fahrenheit. However, practically speaking, simmering means the bottom of the soup should be at a very low boil with bubbles continuously, but gently, breaking the surface. If the soup boils harder, too much liquid may evaporate and the bottom may burn. On the other hand, if a simmer is not maintained, the ingredients may not cook in the specified time.

Long-cooking soups should be checked frequently. As the temperature of the stove, pot, and even the air in the kitchen rises, the soup will boil more briskly. This means the heat setting will probably have to be adjusted downward several times to maintain the gentle simmering desired. (By the way, if you can hear the soup bubbling, it's probably cooking too hard.)

Stirring

Most recipes also call for stirring at least occasionally as the soup cooks. The idea is not simply to wave a spoon around in the top of the liquid, but to reach down into the pot with the utensil and redistribute the contents on the bottom so that the soup does not stick and burn.

Stirring is even more important in recipes featuring a *roux*— the combining of butter and flour into a smooth paste. Here, it's important to be sure the flour is thoroughly incorporated and then cooked slightly before liquid is added. Then the liquid should be added gradually and the mixture stirred vigorously and continuously until it is completely smooth.

Straining and Sieving

Directions to strain or sieve ingredients appear in a recipe only when the texture or appearance of the soup is significantly improved by taking this extra step. Often the technique is employed to quickly remove large quantities of seasoning ingredients from a stock which is then used as the foundation for a soup. In *Soup's On* sieving is not used in place of puréeing, because the blender or food processor can quickly accomplish this job.

Temperamental Ingredients

Some ingredients—particularly milk, cream, eggs, and cheese —need to be handled carefully in soupmaking. Milk is generally stable when added to hot liquids; however, when it is not fresh, it may curdle. (If the milk is not actually sour, the soup will still taste good, even though the appearance will be affected.)

In a few recipes where milk is the sole liquid in the soup, where it will be cooked for a long period of time, or when it will be added to an acid mixture (such as one featuring tomatoes), a bit of extra care should be taken. In these cases, we've called for scalding the milk first, because this step increases its stability. Scalding means to heat milk (or cream) just to the boiling point. The pan should then be quickly removed from the heat so that the liquid doesn't foam up over the top.

Cream is a bit more temperamental than milk. Once cream has been added to hot soup, it's best not to boil the mixture because it may curdle.

Eggs are even more likely to curdle. Sometimes this tendency is capitalized upon in recipes, such as in the classic Chinese recipe, Hot and Sour Soup, where small bits of egg are desired. More often, eggs are used to provide creaminess and to thicken soups slightly. In this case, follow the recipe directions exactly and never allow the soup to boil (or even come to a simmer) once the eggs have been added.

For the same reason, also follow instructions carefully when adding cheese to soup. To achieve the desired smoothness in a cheese soup, the proportion of cheese to starch and liquid is critical. So be sure to add the amounts called for. Likewise, carefully observe directions for heating the soup, as boiling can cause cheese to separate out. (Again, only the appearance is affected. The soup will still taste fine.)

Pots and Pans

Throughout *Soup's On* when we don't specify pot and pan sizes by quarts, we refer to them as small, medium, and large. By this we mean:

Small saucepan—1½ quarts or less
Medium-sized saucepan—2 to 3 quarts
Large saucepan—4 or more quarts
Dutch oven or small pot—4 to 5 quarts
Large pot—6 to 7 quarts
Very large pot—8 quarts or larger

Blenders and Food Processors

Blenders and food processors are two of the most useful tools in modern soupmaking. The blender is very convenient for puréeing ingredients when a smooth texture is desired. However, particular care must be taken when blending mixtures which have just been cooked. Always cool them slightly first and start the blending process on *low speed* until the mixture is partially puréed. Then raise the speed to medium or high. As an added precaution, do not fill the container more than about half full. To be extra safe, when working with hot liquids, we cover the top of the blender container with a dish towel or cloth and hold the lid down firmly.

The food processor can also be used to purée some soups, but it is not as efficient at this task. Puréeing will take considerably longer, and the mixture will probably not be quite as smooth. Keep this in mind when recipes give a choice of these appliances.

On the other hand, the food processor chops uncooked ingredients quickly and is excellent for shredding and grating vegetables and cheese.

INGREDIENTS

Throughout *Soup's On* we've tried to be as specific as possible about what ingredients to use. Following are some additional comments which may answer questions that come up.

BOUQUET GARNI: Many cookbooks frequently call for a *bouquet garni* or *sachet d'épice* in soup recipes. Basically, these terms refer to herbs and spices bound in a cheesecloth bag so that they can be easily removed from the soup after cooking. Where possible, we have avoided calling for this because few home cooks really want to go to the trouble. In cases where it's important to the look of the soup to remove the herbs, we generally call for straining the broth instead.

BROTH AND BOUILLON: While we like to make soup with homemade stock, it is sometimes convenient to substitute a commercial product. There is a wide selection available, including canned broth, canned bouillon, and bouillon cubes and granules. Some stores also carry commercial beef and chicken broth bases. Here's a rundown of what we've found works well.

Good-quality canned broth, such as College Inn, Swanson, or Progresso, makes a satisfactory substitute for homemade stock. Some cooks also like Campbell's Beef Bouillon, but we find the taste a bit strong. In addition, this particular product is sold "double strength," so be sure to dilute it with an equal amount of water when using it in our recipes.

Particularly when a small amount of beef or chicken "stock or broth" is called for, bouillon cubes or granules reconstituted in water make an acceptable substitute.

Commercial bases were formerly available only to restaurants but are now offered in some supermarkets. If you make soup often, you may want to experiment with these.

Substitutes for vegetable stock include bouillon powders, granules, pastes, and cubes. The powders, sold by such manufacturers as MBT, are available in supermarkets. Health food stores sell vegetable bouillon cubes, pastes, and granules. Often these have a lower salt content than the supermarket offerings. Some are even salt-free. If these latter are used, you may want to adjust the amount of salt called for in our recipes.

CANNED TOMATOES: There's a vast difference between tomatoes and tomatoes! Lower-priced brands may seem like a bargain, but often they are so pale and tasteless that they contribute little to a soup. In cases where a full-bodied tomato flavor is essential, we call for imported Italian (plum) tomatoes or Italian-style tomatoes. On the other hand, there are some less expensive canned tomatoes that are perfectly satisfactory for most soupmaking. You may want to shop around and try several different brands.

CHEESE: The most accurate way to measure cheese is by weight, so in *Soup's On* we always call for a specific number of ounces. However, for your convenience, an approximation is also given in cups. In general, ¼ cup of lightly packed shredded or grated cheese is roughly equivalent to about 1 ounce.

CLAM JUICE: This commercial product may be found in the canned and bottled juice department or with the canned fish in supermarkets. In some fish and seafood soups we use it as a ready made stock. However, because it is quite salty, we don't usually recommend it where large quantities of fish stock are required in a recipe.

COUNTRY HAM: A number of recipes call for country ham. Don't substitute ordinary boiled ham, since the results will not be the same. Country ham (sometimes called Virginia ham or "Smithfield" ham) is a smokier, saltier, drier product. Small amounts lend wonderful flavor to bean and hearty vegetable soups. Packages of presliced and pretrimmed country ham are available in the meat departments of many grocery stores and in specialty food shops.

CREAM: Throughout *Soup's On* where cream is called for, we normally give a choice of "light cream" or "half-and-half," which is half milk and half light cream. Light cream has about 20 percent butterfat and is sometimes called "table cream." (There are only a few recipes that require "heavy" or "whipping" cream, which has over 30 percent butterfat.)

When we give a choice, either light cream or half-and-half will yield perfectly satisfactory results.

LEEKS: Many American cooks are just becoming familiar with this subtle-tasting member of the onion family. However, leeks add wonderful flavor to soups. If there's a choice, avoid very large, dry looking leeks, because these may be tough.

As they grow, leeks tend to trap grit between the cylindrical leaf layers and, therefore, must be cleaned carefully before using. The easiest way to do this is to split the leek lengthwise, separate the layers, and wash carefully under cool running water. Then repeat the process until the leek is grit-free. (In recipes where leeks are a featured ingredient, detailed cleaning instructions are included.)

OLIVE OIL: The rich, fruity taste of high-quality olive oil contributes significantly to the flavor of some soups. While it's not necessary to buy the most expensive brands or grades, don't pick the least expensive ones either, as these have very little flavor.

ONIONS: These are a mainstay of soupmaking. Unless some particular type is specified, use standard yellow cooking onions.

PARSLEY: Dry parsley is never suggested as a substitute for fresh in *Soup's On.* When dried, parsley loses its flavor and, therefore, contributes nothing, except a little color, to a recipe. If only a small amount of fresh parsley is called for, and none is available, simply omit it.

PEPPER: Freshly ground pepper has a very distinctive and, we feel, appealing taste, which is why we express a preference for it in our recipes. You will also notice that some recipes call for "white pepper." In light-colored soups, this is often for the sake of appearance. However, white pepper, which is harvested when less mature than black, also has a slightly different flavor, and this may be the reason it's specified. In some areas, white pepper is available only in specialty food shops.

POTATOES: Potatoes can be a very important ingredient in soupmaking. They not only flavor soups but also help thicken broths. Sometimes we specifically call for "boiling potatoes," thin red or brown rounded potatoes with firm, waxy flesh. If these are unavailable, substitute "all-purpose" potatoes. "Baking potatoes" are not satisfactory. In recipes which simply call for "potatoes," either boiling potatoes or all-purpose potatoes may be used.

SALT: Normally we suggest how much salt is needed to season a soup. However, consider this as simply a guide. The amount of salt in canned broths and tomato products, and even in fresh vegetables, varies a great deal. If a range is given, start with the small amount and then, if necessary, adjust to suit your taste.

VEGETABLE OIL: In recipes that call for vegetable oil, we usually use corn oil, although an all-purpose vegetable oil will be satisfactory. In some cases, we do prefer peanut oil because it lends a rich, distinctive taste to the dish. However, if peanut oil is unavailable, regular vegetable oil may be substituted.

WINE: Unless a specific type is called for, any pleasant, inexpensive table wine can be used. Do not substitute "cooking wine" of the sort sold in supermarkets. It is usually much too salty and often too strong and sour as well. Similarly, in recipes that specify "sherry," use an inexpensive dry or medium-dry sherry; "cooking sherry" is not satisfactory. (Unlike wine, sherry keeps well for several months at room temperature after it has been opened.)

2
SOUPS FROM AROUND THE WORLD

Of the kitchen arts, soupmaking is among the most ancient and widely practiced. Peoples everywhere prepare and find comfort in the simple, nourishing food called soup. Despite its universality, however, all soup is not the same!

This chapter is the happy result. The recipes included here showcase the diverse culinary tastes and traditions of nations around the world. Many recipes also demonstrate the creative use of indigenous foodstuffs by native cooks. The aromatic Indian soup Mulligatawny, for example, combines a wealth of vegetables with fruit, chicken, and the distinctive blend of spices known as curry powder. Entirely different in character is Scotland's hearty traditional soup Scotch Broth, which features barley, sturdy root vegetables, and meat from the lambs that flourish in the rugged Highland terrain. Albondigas, or Mexican meatball soup, is a zesty, festive-looking creation, accented with sweet red and green peppers, green chilies, and ground coriander. And there are numerous other recipes that are as different from one another as they are from these.

The recipes in this chapter represent a wonderful way to broaden your culinary horizons and add interest to menus. Another excellent reason to try them is that they are very good soups.

√ Goulash Soup

Paprika, beef, and caraway are the key elements in this robust and zesty Middle European soup. It makes a gratifying and warming meal on a cold day.

    2 tablespoons butter or margarine, divided
    2 tablespoons vegetable oil, divided
    2 large onions, finely chopped
    1 large celery stalk, including leaves, finely chopped
    1 large garlic clove, minced
    1½ pounds lean stew beef, trimmed and cut into ½-inch
        cubes
    3 cups water

1½ cups tomato juice
½ cup dry red wine
3 tablespoons paprika, preferably imported sweet paprika
1 teaspoon sugar
1 bay leaf
1½ teaspoons caraway seeds
1½ teaspoons dried marjoram leaves
½ teaspoon dried thyme leaves
¼ teaspoon celery seeds
½ to ¾ teaspoon black pepper, preferably freshly ground
2 large boiling potatoes, peeled and cut into ½-inch cubes
¾ to 1 teaspoon salt

Combine 1 tablespoon of the butter and 1 tablespoon of the oil in a large Dutch oven or pot over medium-high heat. Add the onions, celery, and garlic and cook, stirring, for 5 to 6 minutes, or until the onions are limp. Using a slotted spoon, transfer the vegetables to a bowl and set them aside. Add the remaining butter and oil to the Dutch oven. Raise the heat to high. When the mixture is hot but not smoking, add the beef cubes, stirring. Cook the cubes, stirring, for 7 to 8 minutes, or until lightly browned on all sides. Stir in the water, the reserved vegetables, and all remaining ingredients, *except* the potatoes and salt. Bring the mixture to a boil; then lower the heat and simmer, covered, for 1 hour and 20 to 30 minutes.

Stir in the potatoes and continue simmering, covered, for 25 to 30 minutes longer, or until the potatoes and beef are tender; stir occasionally to prevent the potatoes from sticking to the bottom of the pot. Discard the bay leaf and add the salt.

Makes 5 to 7 servings.

√Corn and Bean con Carne Soup

Tortilla chips make a nice accompaniment to this hearty Tex-Mex soup.

1 pound lean ground beef
1 large onion, finely chopped
1 garlic clove, minced
2½ cups beef stock, brown stock, broth, or bouillon
3 cups tomato juice
2 16-ounce cans tomatoes, including juice
1 15-ounce can red kidney beans, well drained
2 cups loose-pack frozen corn kernels
1 4-ounce can chopped green chilies, well drained
2 to 3 teaspoons chili powder, or to taste
2 teaspoons sugar
¼ teaspoon salt, or to taste
½ teaspoon ground cumin
¼ teaspoon black pepper, preferably freshly ground

In a large saucepan or small Dutch oven, combine the ground beef, onion, and garlic. Cook over medium-high heat, stirring frequently and breaking the ground beef up with a large spoon, for 5 to 6 minutes, or until it is browned. Drain off and discard the fat from the pan. Add the beef stock, tomato juice, and tomatoes, breaking up the tomatoes with a large spoon. Stir in the kidney beans, corn, and chilies. Add all the remaining ingredients and stir to mix well. Bring the soup to a boil. Cover the pan, lower the heat, and simmer the soup for about 45 minutes, or until the flavors are well blended.

Makes 5 to 7 servings.

Note: For an easy variation, sprinkle grated Cheddar or Monterey Jack cheese on top of this soup just before serving.

Albóndigas (Mexican Meatball Soup)

Loaded with colorful, savory vegetables and well-seasoned meatballs, this traditional Mexican soup makes a zesty meal.

Meatballs

1 pound very lean ground beef
1 large egg, lightly beaten
¼ cup fresh white bread crumbs (prepared in a food processor or blender)
3 tablespoons finely chopped onion
3 tablespoons drained chopped green chilies from a 4-ounce can (Reserve the remainder of the can for use in the soup.)
1 teaspoon ground coriander
¼ teaspoon dried thyme leaves
Generous ¼ teaspoon black pepper, preferably freshly ground
Generous ¾ teaspoon salt

Soup

3 tablespoons vegetable oil
½ cup finely chopped onion
2 garlic cloves, minced
1 cup diced celery
⅔ cup diced sweet green pepper
⅔ cup diced sweet red pepper
1 cup diced carrot
6 cups chicken stock or broth
2 bay leaves
Generous ¼ teaspoon dried thyme leaves
Generous ¼ teaspoon black pepper, preferably freshly ground
⅛ teaspoon ground coriander
1 cup drained chopped canned tomatoes, preferably Italian-style (plum) tomatoes
Remainder of the drained chopped green chilies from the 4-ounce can

1 to 2 drops Tabasco sauce, or more to taste

Salt to taste

2 tablespoons finely chopped green onions (scallions), including green tops, or chopped fresh chives for garnish

To prepare the meatballs: Combine all the meatball ingredients in a medium-sized bowl. With your hands or a fork, mix together the ingredients until thoroughly blended and smooth. Shape the mixture into smooth 1-inch-diameter meatballs, using about 1 tablespoon for each. Reserve the meatballs on a tray or platter. Cover and refrigerate until needed. (If desired, the meatballs may be prepared up to 8 hours in advance.)

To prepare the soup: Combine the oil, onion, garlic, and celery in a large pot. Cook over medium-high heat, stirring, for 4 to 5 minutes, or until the onion is limp. Stir in the sweet peppers and carrot and cook, stirring, for 3 minutes longer. Add the stock, bay leaves, thyme, black pepper, and coriander. Bring the mixture to a boil; then lower the heat and simmer, covered, for 10 minutes.

Gently add the meatballs and simmer, covered, for 10 minutes more. Stir in the tomatoes and green chilies and continue simmering, covered, for about 5 minutes longer, or until the meatballs are cooked through and the vegetables are tender. Stir in the Tabasco sauce and salt. Discard the bay leaves. Sprinkle the soup with the green onions and serve.

Makes 5 to 6 servings.

Danish-Style Oxtail Soup with Dumplings

A very robust and satisfying soup. Be sure to ask the butcher to saw the oxtails into short lengths.

    4 to 5 medium-sized leeks (about 2½ pounds total weight)
    ¼ cup vegetable oil
    4 to 4½ pounds oxtails, sawed into 2- to 2½-inch lengths
    1¼ pounds meaty shin beef, including bone
    12 cups water
    6 large carrots, coarsely sliced, divided
    3 medium-sized parsnips, peeled and coarsely sliced, divided
    ⅓ cup coarsely chopped fresh parsley leaves
    3 large bay leaves
    1¼ teaspoons whole black peppercorns, coarsely crushed
    1 teaspoon dried thyme leaves
    2 to 2¼ teaspoons salt

Dumplings

    6 tablespoons butter or margarine
    ½ cup all-purpose white flour
    ½ teaspoon salt
    Pinch of ground nutmeg
    Scant ½ cup water
    2 large eggs

Trim off and discard the root and the top 3 inches of the leek green parts. Pull off and discard the tough outer two or three leaves. Wash the leeks under cool running water; then drain them. Cut off the leek green parts and coarsely chop them. Transfer the chopped green parts to a colander. Very thoroughly rinse them under cool running water to remove all traces of grit. Drain and set aside. Set the leek white parts aside separately.

Heat the oil in a very large soup pot over high heat until hot, but not smoking. Lower the heat to medium-high and, in batches, brown the oxtails and shin beef. Brown the bones well on all sides, turning frequently to prevent them from burning.

Add the water, leek green parts, about a third of the carrots, about half of the parsnips, the parsley, bay leaves, pepper, and thyme. Bring the mixture to a boil; then cover the pot, lower the heat, and simmer for 2½ hours.

Meanwhile, rinse the leek white parts under cool water. Cut them crosswise into very thin slices. Transfer them to a colander. Very thoroughly rinse the slices under cool running water; then drain them well and set them aside.

When the soup has simmered for 2½ hours, turn it out into a large colander set over a large bowl; let it stand until all the stock drains into the bowl.

Rinse out and dry the pot previously used. Strain the reserved stock through a fine sieve into the pot previously used. Skim off and discard any fat on the surface. Add the remaining carrots and parsnips and the sliced leek white parts to the stock. Add the salt. Bring the soup to a boil once more. Cover the pot and gently boil the soup for about 25 minutes, or until the carrots are almost tender.

Meanwhile, when the oxtails and shin bones are cool enough to handle, remove the meat and cut it into bite-sized pieces; set it aside. (Discard the cooked vegetables.)

Prepare the dumpling dough as follows: Melt the butter in a small heavy saucepan over medium-high heat. Using a wooden spoon, stir in the flour, salt, and nutmeg until well blended and smooth. Cook, stirring, for 1½ minutes. Add the water, stirring vigorously, until the mixture thickens and becomes smooth. Remove the pan from the heat and continue stirring for 1 minute. Add the eggs, stirring vigorously until they are thoroughly incorporated and the mixture is very smooth and well mixed. Cover and set aside.

When the carrots are almost tender, stir the reserved meat into the pot. Using two teaspoons, shape the dumpling dough into ¾- to 1-inch-diameter dumplings and gently slip them into the pot one at a time. Simmer the soup for 7 to 9 minutes longer, or until the dumplings are cooked through and the carrots are tender. Sprinkle the soup with finely chopped fresh parsley and serve. It is also very good reheated.

Makes 6 to 8 servings.

Spanish-Style Vegetable Soup

On a recent trip to Spain, one of us enjoyed several versions of this tasty vegetable-meat soup. For American cooks, the combination of ingredients is unusual, but they yield very flavorful results.

    2 tablespoons olive oil
    1 large onion, finely chopped
    2 large garlic cloves, minced
    1 medium-sized leek, white part only, well washed and
        chopped (see page 13)
    12 cups water
    2 pounds beef soup bones
    ½ pound veal stew meat, cut into ½-inch cubes
    1 8-ounce package country ham, trimmed of all fat and cut
        into bite-sized pieces
    ½ cup dry lima beans or navy beans, sorted and washed
    3 large romaine lettuce leaves, coarsely shredded
    ½ cup finely chopped fresh parsley leaves
    2 medium-sized carrots, thinly sliced
    2 large celery stalks, including leaves, thinly sliced
    2 large bay leaves
    1 teaspoon dried thyme leaves
    ½ teaspoon salt, or to taste
    ¼ teaspoon black pepper, or to taste, preferably freshly
        ground
    ½ pound bony chicken pieces, such as wings or backs
    2 large boiling potatoes, peeled or unpeeled, cut into ¾-
        inch cubes
    6 to 7 medium-sized fresh asparagus spears, cut crosswise
        into 1-inch pieces, tips and tender green parts only
    1½ cups 1-inch fresh green bean pieces

   In a large soup pot, combine the olive oil, onion, garlic, and leek. Cook over medium-high heat, stirring frequently, for about 5 to 6 minutes, or until the onion is tender. Add the water, beef bones, veal, ham, lima beans, lettuce, parsley, carrots, celery, bay leaves, thyme, salt, and pepper. Bring the mixture to a boil. Lower the heat, cover, and simmer for about 40 minutes. Add the chicken and simmer 1 hour longer. Remove the chicken pieces and reserve. Add the potatoes, asparagus, and green beans. Simmer for an additional 30 to 40 minutes, or until the vegetables and beans are tender.

When the chicken is cool enough to handle, remove any meat from the bones and return it to the soup. At the end of the cooking period, remove and discard the beef bones and bay leaves. With a large shallow spoon, skim the fat from the top of the soup and discard it.

Makes 9 to 11 servings.

Scotch Broth

The traditional vegetable-meat soup of Scotland relies on inexpensive cuts of lamb for its rich flavor. Riblets yield the best results. However, if they are used, you may want to make the soup a day ahead and refrigerate it so that the fat can be easily removed from the surface. The soup tastes wonderful reheated.

3 tablespoons vegetable oil (approximately)
4½ to 5 pounds lamb riblets or neck shoulder slices (or a combination of both)
2 large lamb shanks (about 2 pounds total weight)
10 cups water
¼ cup pearl barley
½ cup dry yellow split peas, sorted and washed
2 large carrots, thinly sliced
2 large celery stalks, thinly sliced
2 medium-sized turnips, peeled and diced
2 large onions, finely chopped
2 garlic cloves, minced
2 bay leaves
1 teaspoon dried thyme leaves
½ cup finely chopped fresh parsley leaves

½ to ¾ teaspoon black pepper, preferably freshly ground
2 teaspoons to 1 tablespoon salt, or to taste

In a large heavy soup pot, combine the 3 tablespoons of oil and half of the lamb riblets. Lightly brown the meat over medium-high heat, stirring frequently. With a slotted spoon, remove the meat and reserve it in a medium-sized bowl. Add the remaining riblets and brown them, stirring frequently. Add more oil if necessary. Scrape up any browned bits from the bottom of the pot. Add the lamb shanks, reserved riblets, and water to the pot. Bring to a boil over high heat. Cover the pot, lower the heat, and simmer for 1 hour and 15 minutes.

Add all the remaining ingredients. Bring the soup to a boil again. Simmer for about 1 hour and 30 minutes longer, or until the barley and split peas have thickened the soup slightly. Remove the pot from the heat. Remove and discard the bay leaves.

Using a slotted spoon, remove the meat and bones and reserve them. With a large shallow spoon, carefully skim the fat from the surface of the soup (unless it is to be chilled and reheated. In that case, remove the fat after it has solidified.) When the meat from the shanks is cool enough to handle, cut it into bite-sized pieces and return it to the soup. If desired, also cut some of the meat from the riblets into bite-sized pieces and return them to the soup. Simmer the soup for an additional 5 or 6 minutes before serving.

This soup thickens on standing and may need to be thinned with a little water before reheating.

Makes 7 to 9 servings.

Chinese Pork and Watercress Soup

In this recipe, the watercress is barely cooked at all, which helps retain its bright color and fresh, peppery taste.

3½ ounces fresh pork loin, well trimmed and cut into very thin 1-inch-long strips
½ small garlic clove

¼-inch-thick slice peeled gingerroot
5½ cups chicken stock or broth
4 to 5 green onions (scallions), including 1 inch of green
    top, quartered lengthwise and cut into 1-inch lengths
1 tablespoon dry sherry
½ teaspoon soy sauce
1½ cups lightly packed fresh, tender watercress sprigs
⅛ to ¼ teaspoon salt (optional)

Combine the pork strips, garlic clove half, and ginger-root in a small saucepan. Add ½ cup of the stock and bring the mixture to a simmer over medium-high heat. Simmer, covered, for 6 to 7 minutes, or until the pork is cooked through. Remove the pan from the heat. Using a slotted spoon, transfer the pork strips to a colander. Rinse the pork thoroughly under cool water to remove any scum; set aside to drain. Strain the broth used to cook the pork through a very fine sieve into a 2- to 3-quart saucepan; discard the garlic and gingerroot.

Add the remaining 5 cups of stock, the green onions, sherry, soy sauce, and pork to the sieved broth. Bring the mixture to a boil. Then lower the heat and simmer, covered, for 2 minutes. Stir in the watercress. Add the salt, if needed. Remove the pan from the heat and let stand for 30 seconds, or until the water-cress is wilted but not cooked. Serve immediately.

Makes 4 to 5 servings.

Frankfurt Bean Soup

This hearty, well-flavored soup is a popular regional specialty from the Frankfurt area of West Germany. Yes, Frankfurt Bean Soup does contain frankfurters (or *wurst* as the Germans call them)! Served along with buttered slabs of dark, coarse-grained bread, it makes a satisfying cool-weather meal.

3½ cups dry Great Northern beans, sorted and washed
    (about 1⅓ pounds)
2 tablespoons vegetable oil, divided

2 tablespoons butter or margarine, divided

1 pound imported German bockwurst *or* rindswurst sausages *or* American frankfurters, cut into ¼-inch-thick slices

2 large onions, chopped

2 large carrots, finely chopped

¼ cup chopped fresh parsley leaves

1 large celery stalk, finely chopped

1 medium-sized parsnip, peeled and finely chopped (optional)

8 cups water

2 medium-sized smoked pork hocks (about 1¼ pounds total weight)

2 large bay leaves

½ teaspoon dried thyme leaves

½ teaspoon dried marjoram leaves

Generous ½ teaspoon black pepper, preferably freshly ground

1 cup finely diced lean country ham

½ to ¾ teaspoon salt, or to taste

1 to 2 teaspoons finely chopped fresh parsley leaves for garnish (optional)

Cover the beans with about 2 inches of cold water in a very large soup pot. Bring the water to a boil over high heat. Boil the beans, uncovered, for 2 minutes. Turn off the heat and cover the beans; let them stand at room temperature for 1 hour.

Turn out the beans into a colander and drain them well. Rinse out and dry the pot. Combine 1 tablespoon of the oil and 1 tablespoon of the butter in the pot. Place over high heat until the butter melts and the fat is very hot but not smoking. In two batches, add the sliced sausages and cook, stirring constantly, for 5 to 6 minutes, or until they are browned on all sides. Using a slotted spoon, transfer the browned sausages to a large bowl; cover and refrigerate them.

Add the remaining 1 tablespoon each of oil and butter to the pot and lower the heat to medium-high. Stir in the onions, carrots, parsley, celery, and parsnip (if used). Cook the vegetables, stirring, for 4 to 5 minutes, or until the onions are limp.

Add the water, pork hocks, bay leaves, thyme, marjoram, and pepper. Return the beans to the pot. Bring the mixture to a boil over medium-high heat. Lower the heat and simmer, covered, for 1 hour and 25 to 30 minutes, or until the beans are tender.

Discard the bay leaves. Let the mixture cool slightly. In batches, if necessary, scoop about 4 cups of the beans and a little liquid from the pot and transfer to a food processor or blender. (If a blender is used, blend for 10 seconds on low speed. Then raise speed to high.) Process or blend until puréed; return the purée to the pot. Stir in the ham and reserved browned sausage slices and continue simmering for about 25 to 30 minutes longer, stirring occasionally. Add the salt. Sprinkle the soup with chopped parsley, if desired.

The soup is excellent reheated. However, it does thicken upon standing. If necessary, thin it with a bit of water, and reheat over low heat, stirring occasionally, to prevent the bottom from scorching.

Makes 5 to 6 servings.

Cock-a-Leekie

An ancient soup much loved in Scotland, Cock-a-Leekie pairs —what else?!—chicken and leeks. The combination works wonderfully well.

Traditionally, the soup is garnished with prunes, although no one seems sure how this somewhat odd custom came about. We don't find that the prunes do any harm, but at the same time, they don't seem to add a great deal either. So, if you prefer, we suggest that they simply be omitted from the recipe.

8 to 9 small leeks (about 2 to 2¼ pounds total weight)
4- to 4½-pound frying or roasting chicken, quartered
3 cups water
3 cups chicken stock or broth
1 small bay leaf
2 whole cloves

Pinch of ground mace
Generous ¼ teaspoon black pepper, preferably freshly
ground
6 to 7 pitted prunes (optional)
1¼ to 1½ teaspoons salt, or to taste

Trim off and discard the root and the top 3 inches of
the leek green parts. Pull off and discard the tough outer two
or three leaves. Wash the leeks under cool running water; then
drain them. Cut off the leek green parts and coarsely chop
them. Transfer the chopped green parts to a colander. Very
thoroughly rinse them under cool running water to remove all
traces of grit. Drain and set them aside. Cut the leek white parts
in half lengthwise. Rinse the white parts under cool water, separating the layers to remove any grit trapped among them.

Combine the chicken, water, stock, chopped leek green parts,
bay leaf, cloves, mace, and pepper in a large soup pot. Bring
the mixture to a boil over medium heat. Lower the heat and
simmer, covered, for 1 hour and 10 to 15 minutes, or until the
chicken is tender.

Meanwhile, coarsely chop the leek white parts. Transfer
them to a colander. Very thoroughly rinse them under cool
running water; then drain them well and set them aside.

When the chicken is tender, remove it from the pot and set
it aside to cool. Using a large shallow spoon, skim off and discard any fat on the broth surface. Discard the bay leaf and
cloves. Stir in the reserved leek white parts and prunes and
continue simmering, uncovered, for about 12 to 13 minutes, or
until the leeks are tender.

When the chicken is cool enough to handle, remove the meat
from the bones and cut it into large bite-sized pieces. Return
the chicken meat to the pot. Add the salt. Simmer for about 3
minutes longer, or until the soup is heated through.

Divide the soup among large soup plates or bowls, including
1 prune with each serving.

Makes 5 to 7 servings.

Chicken and Vegetable Soup Provençal

This colorful, aromatic soup is usually served with croûtes (well-toasted slices of French bread) which are placed in the bottom of soup plates before the soup is added. The soup can be garnished with a sprinkling of grated Parmesan cheese or enlivened with the traditional Provençal seasoning paste known as pistou. (For the recipe, see page 319.)

6½ cups chicken stock or broth
½ cup dry white wine
3 medium-sized leeks, green parts very well washed and coarsely chopped, and white parts reserved (see page 13)
⅓ cup coarsely chopped fresh parsley leaves
1 ⅛-inch-thick orange slice
1 teaspoon whole black peppercorns
2 large bay leaves
½ teaspoon dried thyme leaves
Generous ¼ teaspoon saffron threads, very finely crumbled
¼ teaspoon fennel seeds
Generous ⅛ teaspoon dried basil leaves
Generous ⅛ teaspoon dried crushed red (hot) pepper
3¼ to 3½ pounds meaty chicken pieces
3½ tablespoons olive oil
2 large garlic cloves, minced
1 medium-sized carrot, cut into 1-inch-long and ⅛-inch-thick julienne (matchstick strips)
1 small sweet green pepper, cut into 1-inch-long and ¼-inch-thick strips
1 small sweet red pepper, cut into 1-inch-long and ¼-inch-thick strips (If unavailable, substitute 1 4-ounce jar sliced pimientos, well drained.)
2 small zucchini, cut into 1-inch-long and ¼-inch-thick julienne (matchstick strips)

3 canned Italian-style (plum) tomatoes, well drained and
chopped
½ to ¾ teaspoon salt, or to taste
⅛ teaspoon white pepper, preferably freshly ground
About 1 tablespoon finely chopped fresh parsley leaves for
garnish (optional)
4 to 6 croûtes for garnish (see page 316)
Pistou (see page 319) *or* about 3 or 4 tablespoons grated
Parmesan cheese for garnish

Combine the stock, wine, leek green parts, parsley, orange slice, peppercorns, bay leaves, thyme, saffron, fennel
seeds, basil, and dried red pepper in a large soup pot. Add the
chicken and bring to a boil over medium-high heat. Lower the
heat and simmer, uncovered, for 1 hour.

Meanwhile, rinse the leek white parts and slice them in
eighths lengthwise. Rinse the leek lengths, separating the leaves
to remove any grit trapped among the layers. Cut the lengths
into 1-inch-long pieces. Transfer the pieces to a colander and
rinse once more; set them aside to drain.

When the mixture has cooked for 1 hour, remove the
chicken using tongs or a slotted spoon and set it aside to cool.
Strain the broth through a very fine sieve into a large bowl;
press down hard on the solids to force through as much liquid
as possible. Discard the solids.

Rinse out the pot previously used and add the olive oil, garlic,
leek white pieces, and carrots to it. Cook over medium-high
heat, stirring, for 5 to 6 minutes, or until the leeks are soft.
Add the sweet green pepper and red pepper (if used). (If pimiento is substituted for the sweet red pepper, do not add it
now. Instead, stir it into the pot with the salt and white pepper
just before the soup is served.) Cook the mixture, stirring, for
2 minutes longer. Return the strained broth to the pot. Bring
the mixture to a boil. Lower the heat to medium-high and
simmer, covered, for 3 minutes. Add the zucchini and tomato
and continue simmering for 4 to 5 minutes longer, or until the
vegetables are just tender. Add the salt, white pepper, and
parsley, if desired.

To serve the soup, lay the croûtes, one each, in soup plates or large bowls. If garnishing the soup with pistou, stir 3 or 4 generous tablespoons of it into the pot and cook, stirring, for about 30 seconds. Ladle the soup over the croûtes and serve immediately. Pass the remainder of the pistou at the table so diners can add more to their soup if desired. Or, if garnishing the soup with grated Parmesan, pass a small bowl of it at the table so diners can sprinkle some over their soup.

Makes 4 to 6 servings.

Waterzooi (Belgian Chicken and Vegetable Soup)

Lemon, bay leaves, and white wine enhance succulent chunks of chicken and tender vegetables in this traditional soup from Belgium. It makes an unusual and somewhat elegant one-dish meal.

6 small leeks (about 1½ pounds total weight)
4½ to 5 pounds meaty chicken pieces
5 cups chicken stock or broth
2 cups water
⅓ cup dry white wine
3 large bay leaves
1 teaspoon whole black peppercorns
¼ teaspoon dried thyme leaves
⅛ teaspoon ground nutmeg
3 medium-sized carrots, cut into ⅛-inch-thick slices
3 medium-sized celery stalks, cut into ⅛-inch-thick slices
1¼ cups small cauliflower flowerets
2 tablespoons butter or margarine
3 tablespoons all-purpose white flour
2 tablespoons fresh lemon juice
3 egg yolks
½ cup light cream or half-and-half
⅛ to ¼ teaspoon salt, or to taste

About 1 tablespoon finely chopped fresh parsley leaves for
   garnish
Lemon wedges for garnish (optional)

Trim off and discard the root and the top 3 inches of
the leeks. Pull off and discard the tough outer two or three
leaves. Wash the leeks under cool running water; then drain
them. Cut off the leek green parts and coarsely chop them.
Transfer the chopped green parts to a colander. Very thoroughly rinse them under cool running water to remove all
traces of grit. Drain and set aside. Cut the leek white parts
crosswise into ⅛-inch-thick slices. Swish them around in a bowl
of cool water to loosen any grit trapped in the layers. Turn out
the slices into a colander. Very thoroughly rinse them under
cool running water; then drain them well.

Place the chicken pieces on a broiler pan under a preheated
broiler element and broil for 6 to 8 minutes, or until the pieces
are well browned *but not* charred. Turn over the chicken pieces
and broil on the second side for 5 to 6 minutes, or until well
browned *but not* charred.

Transfer the chicken pieces to a very large pot, along with
the chicken stock, water, wine, chopped green leek parts, bay
leaves, peppercorns, thyme, and nutmeg. Bring to a boil over
medium-high heat. Then lower the heat and simmer the mixture, covered, for 1 hour.

Remove the chicken pieces to a bowl to cool. Strain the pot
liquid through a fine sieve and return it to the pot; discard the
solids. Add the carrots and celery to the pot. Return it to the
heat and continue simmering, covered, for 20 minutes. Stir in
the reserved leek white parts and the cauliflower and continue
simmering, covered, for 20 minutes longer.

Drain 3 cups of liquid from the pot and reserve it. Remove
the chicken from the bones and cut it into bite-sized pieces.
Return them to the pot.

In a medium-sized saucepan over medium heat, melt the
butter. Using a wooden spoon, stir in the flour until well
blended and smooth. Cook, stirring, for 2 minutes. Stir in the
reserved 3 cups of liquid until thoroughly incorporated and
smooth. Add the lemon juice. Using a fork, beat the egg yolks

and cream together until well blended. Stir the cream-yolk mixture into the saucepan. Cook over medium heat, stirring constantly, until the mixture thickens slightly and coats the spoon, about 5 minutes; *do not* allow it to come near a simmer or it may curdle. (If the mixture begins to overheat, immediately lift the pan from the heat, stirring, until it is slightly cooler.) Transfer the thickened mixture to the large pot and stir to incorporate it. Stir in the salt.

Ladle the soup into soup plates or large bowls. Garnish each serving with a light sprinkling of parsley and a lemon wedge, if desired.

Makes 5 to 6 servings.

Tortilla Soup

There seem to be many versions of this colorful soup around today, and little wonder, since it is very good. The name comes from the fact that the soup is garnished with crisp, freshly fried tortilla strips.

3 tablespoons peanut or vegetable oil, divided
1 large garlic clove, minced
4 green onions (scallions), including green tops, finely chopped
7 cups chicken stock or broth
2 small (bone-in) chicken breast halves, skin removed
¾ to 1 teaspoon Tabasco sauce
1½ teaspoons dried oregano leaves
1½ teaspoons dried marjoram leaves
¼ to ½ teaspoon black pepper, preferably freshly ground
6 corn tortillas, halved and cut crosswise into ¼-inch-thick strips
2 tablespoons grated mild Cheddar cheese
1 cup drained and chopped canned Italian-style (plum) tomatoes
1 tablespoon finely chopped fresh parsley leaves

Combine 1½ tablespoons of the oil, the garlic, and green onions in a 3- to 4-quart soup pot or saucepan over medium-high heat. Cook, stirring, for 4 to 5 minutes, or until the green onions are limp. Add the chicken stock, whole chicken breast halves, Tabasco sauce, oregano, marjoram, and black pepper and bring the mixture to a boil. Lower the heat, cover the pot, and simmer the mixture for 12 to 15 minutes, or until the chicken breasts are cooked through.

Meanwhile, in a very large frying pan or sauté pan over high heat, heat the remaining 1½ tablespoons oil to hot but not smoking. Lower the heat slightly and add the tortilla strips, stirring. Fry the strips, stirring constantly, for 3 to 4 minutes, or until they are crisp and very lightly browned. With a slotted spoon, transfer the strips to paper towels, spreading them out in an even layer. Immediately sprinkle the strips with the grated cheese.

When the chicken breasts are just cooked through, remove them from the pot and set them aside until they are cool enough to handle. Add the tomatoes to the soup, and let it return to a simmer. Cut the chicken meat into bite-sized pieces and return it to the pot. Continue cooking until the chicken is just heated through, 2 to 3 minutes longer. Stir the parsley into the soup.

Ladle the soup into individual serving bowls. Sprinkle some of the tortilla strips over each bowl and serve immediately.

Makes 6 to 7 servings.

Mulligatawny

Colorful and lightly spiced with curry powder, this popular soup originated in India. Today, however, versions can be found all over—from the British Isles to the Bahamas.

2½ tablespoons peanut or vegetable oil
2 large onions, coarsely chopped
2 large celery stalks, coarsely chopped
1 large garlic clove, minced

2 large Winesap or other tart, flavorful apples, peeled and
   coarsely chopped
1 large carrot, coarsely chopped
1 small turnip, peeled and coarsely chopped
¼ cup coarsely chopped fresh parsley leaves
2 tablespoons coarsely chopped sweet red pepper (If unavailable, substitute sweet green pepper.)
2¾ cups chicken stock or broth
2 cups water
1 large bay leaf
2¼ teaspoons curry powder
½ teaspoon chili powder
¼ teaspoon ground allspice
¼ teaspoon dried thyme leaves
¼ teaspoon black pepper, preferably freshly ground
Pinch of dried crushed red (hot) pepper
2 to 2½ pounds bony chicken pieces (wings, backs, etc.)
1 cup chopped canned tomatoes, including juice
⅓ cup light cream or half-and-half
1 to 1¼ teaspoons salt, or to taste
About 1 tablespoon finely chopped fresh parsley leaves for
   garnish (optional)

Combine the oil, onions, celery, and garlic in a large
pot. Cook over medium-high heat, stirring, for 4 to 5 minutes,
or until the onions are limp. Add the apples, carrot, turnip,
parsley, and sweet pepper and cook, stirring, for 3 to 4 minutes
longer. Stir in the stock, water, bay leaf, curry powder, chili
powder, allspice, thyme, pepper, and dried red pepper. Add
the chicken. Bring the mixture to a boil; then lower the heat
and simmer, covered, for 1 hour and 5 to 10 minutes.

Remove the pot from the heat. Remove the chicken from the
pot and set it aside to cool. Skim off and discard any fat on the
surface of the soup, using a large shallow spoon. Discard the
bay leaf. Scoop about 2 cups of the vegetables from the pot and
transfer them to a blender or food processor. Blend or process
until the mixture is completely puréed. Return the purée to the
pot, along with the tomatoes.

When the chicken is cool enough to handle, remove the meat

from the bones and cut it into bite-sized pieces. Return the meat to the pot, and bring the mixture to a simmer over medium-high heat. Stir in the cream, and continue heating until the soup is piping hot *but not* boiling. Stir in the salt. Garnish the soup with parsley, if desired.

Makes 4 to 6 servings.

√ Malaysian Chicken and Green Onion Soup

An unusual blend of seasonings gives this light soup its distinctive aroma and appealingly exotic flavor.

5½ cups chicken stock or broth, divided
2 tablespoons coarsely chopped gingerroot
1 garlic clove, minced
1 ¼-inch-thick lemon slice
Generous ½ teaspoon anise seeds
½ teaspoon coriander seeds
¼ teaspoon cumin seeds
¼ teaspoon whole black peppercorns
2 medium-sized skinless and boneless chicken breast halves, cut into 1-inch-long by ¼-inch-thick strips
1 cup coarsely shredded green onions (scallions), including green tops
1 to 2 tablespoons coarsely chopped fresh coriander leaves for garnish (optional)

Combine 5 cups of the stock, the gingerroot, garlic, lemon slice, anise, coriander, cumin, and peppercorns in a 2-quart saucepan. Bring the mixture to a boil over medium-high heat. Then lower the heat and simmer the mixture, covered, for 25 to 30 minutes.

Meanwhile, in a small saucepan, combine the remaining ½ cup stock and the chicken pieces and bring to a simmer over medium-high heat. Lower the heat and gently simmer, covered, for 2 to 3 minutes, or until the chicken pieces are just cooked through. Turn out the chicken into a colander, discarding the stock. Thoroughly rinse the chicken pieces to remove any scum and set them aside to drain.

When the stock and seasoning ingredients have simmered for 25 to 30 minutes, strain the broth through a very fine sieve; discard the seasoning ingredients. Rinse out the large saucepan previously used and return the strained broth to it. Bring the broth to a simmer over medium-high heat. Add the green onions and simmer for 2 minutes. Stir in the reserved chicken pieces and simmer for 1 minute longer.

Serve in small bowls or soup cups, garnished with fresh coriander, if desired.

Makes 5 to 6 servings.

Soupe au Pistou

Soupe au Pistou—which means "soup with pesto" in French—is the popular French rendition of a delightful bean and vegetable soup that originated in Genoa, Italy. So, what we have here is our slightly Americanized version of the French version of an Italian soup!

Pistou is a zesty, herbed seasoning paste redolent of basil and garlic. Prepare it while the beans for the soup cook. (See page 319 for the recipe.)

¾ cup dry navy or Great Northern beans, sorted and washed
8½ cups water
¼ teaspoon white pepper, preferably freshly ground
2 tablespoons good-quality olive oil
2 medium-sized onions, finely chopped
2 large garlic cloves, minced
¼ cup chopped fresh parsley leaves
2 medium-sized celery stalks, diced
1 medium-sized leek

1½ cups 1-inch fresh green bean pieces
2 medium-sized boiling potatoes, peeled and diced
1 cup unpeeled diced zucchini
1 cup chopped fresh spinach leaves (stems and coarse ribs removed)
¼ cup 1-inch capellini, vermicelli, or other very thin spaghetti pieces
2¼ to 2½ teaspoons salt
Pistou for garnish (see page 319)

Cover the beans with about 2 inches of cold water in a very large pot. Bring the water to a boil over high heat. Boil the beans, uncovered, for 3 minutes. Turn off the heat and cover the beans; let them stand for 1 hour.

Drain off and discard the liquid from the pot. Add the water and pepper. Bring the mixture to a boil over medium-high heat. Lower the heat and simmer, covered, for 1 hour and 15 minutes.

Meanwhile, combine the oil, onions, garlic, parsley, and celery in a large frying pan. Cook over high heat, stirring, for 5 to 6 minutes, or until the onions are limp; set aside.

Prepare the leek as follows: Trim off and discard the root and all except 1 inch of the leek green part. Pull off and discard the tough outer two or three leaves. Wash the leek under cool running water; then drain it. Slice the leek in quarters lengthwise. Rinse it under cool water, separating the layers to remove any grit trapped among them. Chop the leek and transfer it to a colander. Thoroughly rinse the chopped leek and let stand to drain.

When the beans have cooked for 1 hour and 10 to 15 minutes, stir the reserved sautéed vegetables into the pot. Add the leek, green beans, potatoes, and zucchini. Let the mixture return to a simmer and continue cooking, covered, for 15 minutes. Raise the heat to high and stir the spinach, pasta, and salt into the pot. Boil for 7 to 10 minutes longer, or until the vegetables are tender and the pasta is cooked through but still slightly firm. Stir about half of the pistou recipe into the soup and simmer for 1 minute longer.

To serve the soup, ladle it into large soup plates or bowls.

Serve the remainder of the pistou separately in a small bowl so diners can add more to their soup, to taste.

This soup is excellent reheated. However, it does thicken upon standing. If necessary, thin it with a bit of water and reheat over low heat, stirring occasionally, to prevent the bottom from scorching.

Makes 5 to 6 servings.

French Onion Soup

With onion soup, the secret of success is in the stock or broth used. Homemade stock yields the best results. However, it is possible to make quite a good onion soup with a high-quality commercial broth such as College Inn.

    5 tablespoons butter or margarine
    6 cups thinly sliced yellow onions
    1 large garlic clove, minced
    6 cups beef stock, brown stock, or broth
    ⅓ cup dry red wine
    5 large parsley sprigs
    1 large bay leaf
    ¼ teaspoon dried thyme leaves
    ¼ to ½ teaspoon sugar, or to taste
    ¼ teaspoon black pepper, preferably freshly ground
    ¾ teaspoon salt, or to taste
    5 to 6 ½-inch-thick French bread slices, toasted
    5 to 6 slices of Gruyère cheese, or 10 to 12 teaspoons grated
        Parmesan cheese

In a small pot, melt the butter over medium heat. Add the onions and garlic. Cook, stirring frequently, for about 10 minutes, or until the onions are very tender but not browned. Add the stock, wine, parsley, bay leaf, thyme, sugar, and pepper. Bring the mixture to a boil over medium-high heat. Cover, lower the heat, and simmer for about 45 to 50 minutes, or until the flavors are well blended. Add the salt and cook for an additional 2 minutes. With a slotted spoon, remove the parsley and bay leaf.

To serve, if Gruyère is used, ladle the soup into ovenproof serving bowls or crocks and float a piece of toasted French bread in each. Lay a slice of cheese over the top of each bowl. Set the bowls under a preheated broiler element just long enough to melt the cheese. If Parmesan is used, ovenproof crocks are not necessary. Simply sprinkle about 2 teaspoons of cheese on top of the French bread in each bowl and serve.

Makes 5 to 6 servings.

Spanish Garlic Soup

The combination of garlic, beef stock, and a smoked pork hock gives this peasant soup its distinctive flavor. Like Mexican garlic soup, it is also thickened with bread. But unlike the Mexican version, egg is not cooked in the soup. Instead a poached egg is floated in the center of each serving. (However, this can be omitted.) Although the amount of garlic may seem excessive, it doesn't overpower the soup.

2 tablespoons olive oil
6 to 7 large garlic cloves, minced
6 cups beef stock, brown stock, or broth
1 small smoked pork hock (about ½ pound)
5 or 6 large parsley sprigs
1 large celery stalk, cut in half crosswise
1 large carrot, cut in half crosswise
2 large onions, each cut into eighths
1 large bay leaf
¼ teaspoon dried thyme leaves
¼ teaspoon black pepper, preferably freshly ground
½-inch-thick untoasted French bread slices
1 poached egg per serving (optional)

In a large saucepan or small pot, combine the oil and garlic. Cook over medium-high heat, stirring frequently, for about 3 to 4 minutes, or until the garlic is tender. Add all the remaining ingredients *except* the bread and eggs. Bring the mixture to a boil over high heat. Cover, lower the heat, and simmer for about 1 hour and 30 minutes.

With a large shallow spoon, skim the fat from the top of the soup and discard it. Remove the pork hock and reserve it in a small bowl. Strain the soup through a sieve and return it to the pan in which it was cooked. Discard the solids. If desired, cut the lean meat from the pork hock into bite-sized pieces and return them to the soup. Simmer an additional 2 minutes.

To serve, place 1 or 2 ½-inch-thick French bread slices in the bottom of each soup bowl. Ladle the soup on top. Float a poached egg in the center of each serving, if desired.

Makes 4 to 6 servings.

Greek Avgolemono Soup

8 cups chicken stock or broth
Generous ½ cup long-grain white rice
4 large eggs
¼ cup fresh lemon juice
¼ teaspoon black pepper, preferably freshly ground

In a Dutch oven or large saucepan, bring the stock to a boil over high heat. Add the rice, lower the heat, and simmer for about 20 to 25 minutes, or until the rice is tender.

When the rice is cooked, beat the eggs with a wire whisk or fork in a large bowl until very frothy. Stir in the lemon juice. Remove the soup from the heat. Measure out 1 cup of the hot stock. Beat it into the egg mixture. Then, in a thin stream, add the egg-stock mixture to the soup, beating steadily. Return the soup to the heat and cook over low heat, stirring, until the soup thickens. *Do not boil.* Stir in the pepper.

Makes 6 to 8 servings.

Variations

For an interesting variation, you can make this soup with the

Greek pasta called orzo instead of rice. If orzo is used, cook it at a low boil for about 15 minutes, or until it is tender. Then proceed with the recipe as directed.

Or try this second variation. The additional ingredients go well with the rice and lemon but give the soup a whole new character. Add 2 cooked chicken breast halves, boned, skinned, and cut into small pieces; 1 8-ounce can sliced water chestnuts, drained and cut into slivers; and ¼ cup finely chopped fresh parsley leaves to the soup along with the pepper.

Matzo Ball Soup

If you've ever enjoyed this traditional Jewish dish and wanted to try it at home, you'll be glad to know that it isn't really hard to make. We've found that the secret to light, fluffy matzo balls is in mixing the ingredients very well, chilling thoroughly, and handling the uncooked mixture gently when shaping it into balls. Matzo meal is available in the specialty food section of many large grocery stores.

2 large eggs
1½ tablespoons vegetable oil
½ cup matzo meal
¼ teaspoon salt
2 tablespoons chicken stock or broth
1 medium-sized carrot, sliced (optional)
2 celery tops and leaves, chopped (optional)
5 to 8 cups chicken stock (see page 299) or broth

To prepare the matzo balls, in a small bowl lightly beat the eggs and oil together using a fork. Add the matzo meal, salt, and 2 tablespoons of chicken stock. Stir with a spoon to combine well, making sure the matzo meal is completely moistened. Cover the mixture and refrigerate for at least 1½ hours and up to 6 hours.

When the matzo ball mixture is thoroughly chilled, bring 3 quarts of water to a boil in a large pot. Add the carrot and celery (if used). To form matzo balls, scoop up a heaping table-spoonful of the matzo ball mixture and shape it into a ball with moistened fingers. Make sure the ball is fairly round and smooth, but do not press it together too tightly. Drop the matzo ball into the boiling water. Repeat with the remaining mixture, making 8 or 9 balls. Cover the pot, lower the heat, and gently boil the matzo balls for 30 to 35 minutes.

When the matzo balls are almost ready, put the chicken stock into a small Dutch oven or soup pot. Bring it to a simmer over medium-high heat. With a slotted spoon, remove the matzo balls from the water and gently place them in the chicken stock. (Discard the carrot and celery, if used.) Cover and simmer for about 5 to 8 minutes.

Makes 4 to 5 servings.

Hot and Sour Soup

4 dried Chinese black mushrooms
2 dried tree ear mushrooms
12 dried tiger lily buds
⅔ cup boiling water
4 ounces lean fresh pork
7 to 8 green onions (scallions), including green tops
2 tablespoons peanut or vegetable oil
½ cup drained and shredded bamboo shoots
6 cups chicken stock or broth
2 to 3 tablespoons red wine vinegar, or to taste
2 tablespoons soy sauce
½ to ¾ teaspoon white pepper, preferably freshly ground
1 small sliver peeled gingerroot, finely minced
½ cup cold water
3½ tablespoons cornstarch
1 cup 2-inch-long and ⅛-inch-thick strips fresh tofu
1 large egg, lightly beaten
⅛ to ¼ teaspoon salt
About 2 teaspoons finely chopped fresh coriander leaves
    for garnish (optional)

Combine the black mushrooms, tree ear mushrooms, and tiger lily buds in a small bowl. Cover them with the boiling water and let stand for 30 minutes. Drain the mushrooms and tiger lily buds; reserve the soaking water. Using a sharp knife, shred the mushrooms, discarding any tough stems. Trim off the tough ends of the tiger lily buds; then cut the buds in half crosswise and shred them. Reserve the mushrooms and tiger lily buds in a bowl.

Cut the pork into 2-inch-long shreds and add them to the bowl. Shred all except one of the green onions and add them to the bowl. (Finely chop the remaining green onion and reserve it for the garnish.)

Combine the oil and the reserved shredded mixture in a 3- to 4-quart pot. Cook over medium-high heat, stirring, for 5 to 6 minutes, or until the pork is cooked through and the green onions are limp. Stir in the reserved mushroom soaking liquid, bamboo shoots, stock, vinegar, soy sauce, pepper, and gingerroot. Bring the mixture to a boil; then lower the heat and simmer, covered, for 4 to 5 minutes.

Stir together the cold water and cornstarch in a small bowl or cup until well blended and smooth. Stir the water-cornstarch mixture into the pot. Then add the tofu. Allow the mixture to return to a simmer and cook, stirring occasionally, until it thickens slightly and becomes clear. Stir in the beaten egg and simmer for 1 minute longer. Add the salt.

Ladle the soup into individual bowls. Sprinkle each serving with some of the reserved chopped green onions and serve. The soup may also be garnished with a sprinkling of coriander, if desired.

Makes 5 to 6 servings.

3

MEAT AND POULTRY SOUPS

Many traditional meat and poultry soups can be found in this chapter. Old-Fashioned Beef and Vegetable, Favorite Oxtail, Country-Style Turkey Vegetable, Chicken Noodle, and Beefy Minestrone are just a few of the homey, family-pleasing recipes in the collection. Of course, there are also some less familiar, but equally savory recipes—Pimiento-Chicken Soup with Chives and Veal and Sweet Pepper Soup are only two of these.

Almost all of the soups presented here are hearty enough to be served as the main dish for a meal. However, you may want to add bread and a salad to complete the menu.

Keep in mind that besides the meat and poultry soups here, there are also a number of good and convenient ones in the Crock Pot chapter.

Old-Fashioned Beef and Vegetable Soup

Long, slow cooking brings out the rich flavor in this old-fashioned chunky beef and vegetable soup. For best results, use beef marrow bones and have the butcher saw them into short lengths.

3 pounds beef soup bones, preferably marrow bones sawed into 2-inch pieces
1 pound beef plate ribs or short ribs
4½ cups water, divided
2 cups beef stock, brown stock, broth, or bouillon
1¼ pounds lean stew beef, cut into ½-inch cubes
3 medium-sized celery stalks, tops and leaves chopped and stalks thinly sliced and reserved separately
3 medium-sized onions, chopped
1 medium-sized turnip, chopped (optional)
1 cup finely chopped green cabbage
3 tablespoons finely chopped fresh parsley leaves
1 bay leaf

49

¼ teaspoon dried thyme leaves

½ teaspoon black pepper, preferably freshly ground

3 medium-sized carrots, cut into ⅛-inch-thick slices

1 cup 1-inch-long fresh green bean pieces (Or substitute frozen cut green beans, if desired.)

2 tablespoons pearl barley

1 16-ounce can tomatoes, including juice, coarsely chopped

½ cup loose-pack frozen corn kernels

2 to 2¼ teaspoons salt, or to taste

Rinse the soup bones and beef plate ribs under cold water. Pat them dry with paper towels. Put the bones and plate ribs in a very large Dutch oven or roasting pan. Roast the bones in a preheated 350-degree oven 1 hour and 10 to 15 minutes; stir the bones several times to prevent them from sticking to the bottom of the pan.

Transfer the browned bones to a bowl. Drain off and discard any fat from the Dutch oven. Add 2 cups of water. Using a large wooden spoon, carefully scrape up any browned bits sticking to the bottom. (If a roasting pan was used, transfer the water and browned beef bits from it to a large soup pot at this point.) Add the remaining water, the beef stock, and the reserved bones to the Dutch oven or pot. Bring the mixture to a boil over medium-high heat. Then lower the heat and simmer, covered, 1 hour.

Transfer the soup bones to a colander. Rinse them under cool water and set them aside to drain. Strain the water-beef stock mixture through a fine sieve. Wash out the Dutch oven and return the water-beef stock mixture and the bones to it. Stir in the stew beef, celery tops and leaves, onions, turnip, cabbage, parsley, bay leaf, thyme, and pepper. Bring the mixture to a boil; then lower the heat and simmer, covered, for 1 hour.

Remove the soup bones and bay leaf from the Dutch oven and discard them. (The meat on the ribs may be cut off and reserved for another purpose, if desired, but it will not have much flavor.) Add the celery slices, carrots, green bean pieces, and barley. Cover and continue simmering for about 50 to 55 minutes longer, or until the beef cubes, barley, and carrots are tender. Stir in the tomatoes, corn, and salt and simmer for 8 to 10 minutes longer. Skim off and discard any fat floating on the surface of the soup. The soup is excellent reheated.

Makes 6 to 8 servings.

Beefy Minestrone

There are many versions of this popular Italian vegetable-pasta soup. This one is somewhat Americanized, as it substitutes beef for the more traditional salt pork. The soup tastes wonderful reheated, but should be stirred carefully to prevent burning; if it is very thick, add a bit more water.

1½ tablespoons corn oil
1½ tablespoons olive oil
2 pounds beef soup bones
1 large onion, coarsely chopped
1 large garlic clove, minced
10 cups water
½ cup dry Great Northern beans, sorted and washed
2 large celery stalks, including leaves, diced
2 medium-sized carrots, thinly sliced
2 cups coarsely shredded green cabbage
2 cups coarsely diced zucchini
1 pound lean stew beef, cut into ¾-inch cubes
½ cup finely chopped fresh parsley leaves
3 bay leaves
2 beef bouillon cubes
1½ teaspoons dried basil leaves
1½ teaspoons dried oregano leaves
½ teaspoon dried thyme leaves
½ teaspoon black pepper, preferably freshly ground
2 teaspoons salt, or to taste

1 16-ounce can tomatoes (preferably Italian-style [plum] tomatoes), including juice
1 15-ounce can tomato sauce
1 cup small elbow macaroni or other small pasta shapes
2 teaspoons sugar

In a large heavy soup pot, combine the corn oil, olive oil, and beef bones. Cook the bones for about 10 minutes, turning them with a large spoon so that the surfaces are well browned. If bits of browned meat begin to stick to the bottom of the pot or if the oil splatters, lower the heat slightly. Remove the bones from the oil with a slotted spoon and set them aside on a plate or in a medium-sized bowl.

Add the onion and garlic to the oil. Over medium-high heat, cook the vegetables in the oil until the onion is soft but not brown. Stir frequently and scrape up any bits of browned meat from the bottom of the pot. Add the water, beans, celery, carrots, cabbage, and reserved beef bones. Bring the mixture to a boil over high heat. Cover, lower the heat, and simmer for 1 hour. Add the zucchini, beef cubes, parsley, bay leaves, bouillon cubes, basil, oregano, thyme, pepper, and salt. Simmer for an additional 1 hour to 1 hour and 15 minutes, stirring occasionally, or until the beans are tender. Remove and discard the bay leaves. The soup may be refrigerated at this point, if desired, and completed later.

Skim any fat from the top of the soup and discard it. Remove the bones, cut off any meat, and return it to the pot. Add the tomatoes, breaking them up with a spoon. Add the tomato sauce, pasta, and sugar. Cover the pot and bring the soup to a boil. Cook for an additional 15 to 20 minutes, stirring frequently, or until the pasta is tender and the flavors are well blended.

Makes 9 to 11 servings.

Hunter's Beef and Mushroom Soup

This hearty soup is almost thick and chunky enough to eat like a stew.

  1 pound lean stew beef, cut into ½-inch cubes
  2 tablespoons vegetable oil
  1 large onion, chopped
  4 to 4½ cups sliced fresh mushrooms (about 1 pound)
  3 cups beef stock, brown stock, broth, or bouillon
  ½ cup water
  ¾ cup dry white wine
  ¼ teaspoon dried thyme leaves
  ¼ to ½ teaspoon black pepper, preferably freshly ground
  ¼ to ½ teaspoon salt
  2½ cups peeled and cubed potatoes
  1 cup thinly sliced carrots
  1 cup 1-inch-long fresh green bean pieces
  About ½ cup commercial sour cream for garnish

    Pat the beef cubes dry with paper towels. Heat the oil in a 3- to 4-quart Dutch oven or soup pot over high heat until very hot but not smoking. Add the beef cubes and cook, stirring, for 3 to 4 minutes, or until lightly browned. Add the onion and mushrooms and continue to cook, stirring, for about 5 minutes longer, or until the onion is limp. Stir in the beef stock, water, wine, thyme, pepper, and salt and bring the mixture to a boil. Lower the heat and simmer the mixture, covered, for 30 minutes.

    Add the potatoes, carrots, and green beans. Continue simmering, covered, for 30 to 40 minutes longer, or until the beef and vegetables are tender. With a large shallow spoon, skim the fat from the top of the soup and discard it.

    Ladle the soup into large soup plates or bowls and garnish each serving with a generous dollop of sour cream. The soup may also be made ahead and refrigerated, if desired. Garnish just before serving.

    Makes 4 to 5 servings.

√Alphabet Beef and Vegetable Soup

Kids and adults like the tangy flavor of this vegetable soup. The combination of cabbage, vinegar, and sugar helps give the recipe its zip.

2 tablespoons vegetable oil
1 large onion, finely chopped
1 large garlic clove, minced
8 cups water
1 pound lean stew beef, cut into ½-inch cubes
2 beef bouillon cubes
2 celery stalks, including leaves, thinly sliced
2 large carrots, thinly sliced
3 bay leaves
1 15-ounce can tomato sauce
1 cup grated or very finely shredded green cabbage
½ teaspoon powdered mustard
2 tablespoons apple cider vinegar
2 tablespoons sugar
1 large potato, peeled and cut into ¾-inch cubes
1 cup peeled and diced rutabaga
1½ cups loose-pack frozen corn kernels
½ teaspoon dried thyme leaves
½ teaspoon dried marjoram leaves
½ teaspoon chili powder
1 teaspoon salt, or to taste
½ teaspoon black pepper, preferably freshly ground
¾ cup alphabet pasta

In a large heavy soup pot, combine the oil, onion, and garlic. Cook, stirring frequently, over medium-high heat for about 5 to 6 minutes, or until the onion is tender. Add the water, beef, bouillon cubes, celery, carrots, bay leaves, tomato sauce, cabbage, mustard, vinegar, and sugar. Bring to a boil over high heat. Lower the heat, cover, and simmer for about 30 minutes. Add all the remaining ingredients *except* the pasta. Bring the soup to a boil again. Lower the heat, cover, and simmer for about 1 hour, or until the beef is tender and the flavors are well blended. Remove and discard the bay leaves.

Bring the soup to a boil and stir in the alphabet pasta. Gently boil the soup for an additional 8 to 10 minutes, uncovered, or until the pasta is just tender.

Makes 7 to 9 servings.

Meatball and Vegetable Soup

This is perfect as a hearty family lunch or dinner entrée.

Soup

    2 tablespoons butter or margarine
    1 medium-sized onion, finely chopped
    1 garlic clove, minced
    2 celery stalks, diced
    4 cups beef stock, brown stock, broth, or bouillon
    2 cups water
    1 16-ounce can tomatoes, puréed in a food processor or
        blender
    1 8-ounce can tomato sauce
    2 large carrots, thinly sliced
    2 cups loose-pack frozen corn kernels
    2 cups 1-inch fresh green bean pieces, *or* 2 cups loose-pack
        frozen green beans
    ¼ cup pearl barley
    2 bay leaves
    2 teaspoons sugar
    1 teaspoon dried basil leaves
    ½ teaspoon dried thyme leaves
    ½ teaspoon powdered mustard
    ½ teaspoon chili powder
    2 to 3 drops Tabasco sauce
    ¼ teaspoon black pepper, preferably freshly ground
    1 cup loose-pack frozen peas

Meatballs

    1 pound lean ground beef
    1 tablespoon instant minced onion
    1 large egg
    Scant ½ cup cracker crumbs
    ⅛ teaspoon powdered mustard
    ¼ cup ketchup
    ½ teaspoon salt
    ¼ teaspoon black pepper, preferably freshly ground

In a large soup pot, melt the butter over medium-high heat. Add the onion, garlic, and celery and cook, stirring frequently, for 4 to 5 minutes, or until the onion is tender. Add all the remaining soup ingredients *except* the peas, and stir to mix well. Cover the pot, lower the heat, and simmer for about 45 minutes.

Meanwhile, combine all the meatball ingredients in a medium-sized bowl and mix them together well. Form the meat mixture into about 30 balls, using about 1 tablespoon of the mixture for each. Place the meatballs on a rimmed baking sheet or jelly roll pan and bake in a preheated 350-degree oven for 13 to 15 minutes, or until they are nicely browned.

Discard the bay leaves from the soup. Remove the meatballs with a slotted spoon and transfer them to the soup pot. Add the peas to the soup and simmer for an additional 30 minutes.

Makes 6 to 7 servings

√ Sweet and Sour Beef and Cabbage Soup

In this recipe, preparation can be speeded up considerably if a food processor is used to shred the vegetables.

    ¾ pound lean ground beef
    3 large onions, shredded
    1 16-ounce can tomatoes, including juice

1 small head green cabbage (about 1 pound), shredded
3 cups water
2 cups beef stock, brown stock, broth, or bouillon
1 6-ounce can tomato paste
3 tablespoons packed light or dark brown sugar
2 tablespoons apple cider vinegar
1 tablespoon paprika, preferably imported sweet
½ teaspoon powdered mustard
¼ teaspoon celery seeds
¼ teaspoon black pepper, preferably freshly ground
Pinch of caraway seeds
¼ teaspoon salt, or to taste
Finely chopped fresh parsley leaves for garnish (optional)

Place the beef in a 3- to 4-quart saucepan or pot over medium-high heat. Brown the beef well, breaking it up with a spoon. Discard any excess fat from the pan. Add the onions and cook, stirring, for 5 to 6 minutes longer, or until they are limp. Add the tomatoes, breaking them up with a spoon. Add the cabbage, water, beef stock, and tomato paste and stir until well mixed. In a small cup, stir together the sugar, vinegar, paprika, and mustard until smooth and well blended. Add the mixture to the pan, along with the celery seeds, pepper, and caraway seeds.

Bring the mixture to a boil. Cover the pot, lower the heat, and simmer the soup for 25 to 30 minutes, or until the vegetables are very tender and the flavors are blended. Stir in the salt. Sprinkle the soup with chopped fresh parsley, if desired.

Makes 5 to 6 servings.

Favorite Oxtail Soup

Oxtails may seem pricey, but the incredibly rich and flavorful soup they yield definitely makes them worth it.

¼ cup vegetable oil
5 pounds oxtails, precut into 1- or 2-inch lengths
2 large onions, coarsely chopped
2 large garlic cloves, minced
2 large bay leaves
¼ cup pearl barley
10 cups water
1 pound stew beef, cut into ½-inch cubes
2 medium-sized carrots, thinly sliced
2 large celery stalks, thinly sliced
1 medium-sized leek, white part and 1 inch of green part
   only, well washed and chopped (see page 13)
2 medium-sized parsnips, peeled and diced
2 medium-sized turnips, peeled and diced
2 large boiling potatoes, peeled or unpeeled, cut into ¾-
   inch cubes
½ cup finely chopped fresh parsley leaves
1 teaspoon dried thyme leaves
1 teaspoon dried marjoram leaves
¾ teaspoon chili powder
⅛ teaspoon cayenne pepper
½ teaspoon black pepper, preferably freshly ground
2½ teaspoons salt, or to taste

    In a large pot, combine the oil and half of the oxtails. Cook the oxtails over medium-high heat, turning them so that all sides are lightly browned. With a slotted spoon, remove the oxtails and reserve them in a large bowl. Repeat the browning process with the second half. Remove the oxtails to the bowl and reserve. Scrape up any browned bits from the bottom of the pot. Add the onions and garlic to the pot and cook for 5 minutes, stirring frequently. Return the oxtails to the pot and add the bay leaves, barley, water, and meat. Bring to a boil over high heat. Lower the heat and simmer for 1 hour and 45 minutes, stirring occasionally.

Add all the remaining ingredients and simmer for an additional 50 to 60 minutes, stirring occasionally. With a large shallow spoon, skim the fat from the top of the soup and discard it. Remove and discard the bay leaves.

Remove the oxtails and reserve them. When they are cool enough to handle, cut the lean meat into bite-sized pieces and return it to the pot. Heat for an additional 2 to 3 minutes.

This soup is wonderful reheated, but it tends to thicken on standing. Reheat carefully, stirring frequently. If necessary, thin it with a bit of water.

Makes 8 to 10 servings.

Three-Meat Soup

Beef, country ham, and veal team up to give this "meal in a bowl" soup its rich, meaty flavor.

3 medium-sized leeks (about 1½ pounds total weight)
3 tablespoons olive oil
1 large onion, finely chopped
2 large garlic cloves, minced
10 cups water
1 8-ounce package country ham, trimmed of all fat and cut into bite-sized pieces
3 pounds meaty beef soup bones
¼ cup pearl barley
¼ cup dry lentils, sorted and washed
½ cup dry Great Northern beans, sorted and washed
2 large celery stalks, thinly sliced
2 large carrots, thinly sliced
½ cup finely chopped fresh parsley leaves
2 large bay leaves
1 pound veal stew meat, trimmed and cut into ½-inch cubes

2 cups shredded green cabbage (about 6 ounces)
½ teaspoon celery salt
1 teaspoon dried thyme leaves
½ teaspoon dried marjoram leaves
½ teaspoon powdered mustard
3 to 4 drops Tabasco sauce
¼ teaspoon black pepper, preferably freshly ground
1 15-ounce can tomato sauce
¼ to ½ teaspoon salt, or to taste

Trim off and discard the root end of the leeks and all but about 2 inches of the green parts. Peel off and discard one or two layers of tough outer leaves. Then, beginning at the green end, slice down about 1 inch into the leeks. Put the leeks into a colander. Wash them thoroughly under cool running water, separating the layers to remove any grit trapped between them; wash again to remove all traces of grit. Then set them aside until well drained. Chop the leeks.

In a large soup pot, combine the leeks, oil, onion, and garlic. Cook over medium-high heat, stirring frequently, for about 5 to 6 minutes, or until the onion is tender. Add the water, ham, beef bones, barley, lentils, beans, celery, carrots, parsley, and bay leaves. Bring the mixture to a boil. Cover, lower the heat, and simmer for about 1 hour and 15 minutes. Add the veal, cabbage, celery salt, thyme, marjoram, powdered mustard, Tabasco sauce, and pepper. Simmer for 1 hour and 10 minutes longer, or until the beans are tender. Remove the pot from the heat. Skim the fat from the top of the soup, using a large shallow spoon. Discard the bay leaves.

Remove the beef bones. When they are cool enough to handle, cut any lean meat from them and return it to the soup. Return the pot to the heat and bring the soup to a simmer again. Add the tomato sauce and stir to mix well. Add salt as needed. Simmer for 5 to 6 minutes before serving.

Makes 8 to 10 servings.

Veal and Sweet Pepper Soup

2 tablespoons olive oil (approximately)
1½ pounds veal stew meat, trimmed and cut into ¾-inch cubes
1 large onion, finely chopped
1 large garlic clove, minced
1 large sweet green pepper, diced
1 large sweet red pepper, diced (If unavailable, substitute 1 large sweet green pepper.)
1 large celery stalk, thinly sliced
4 cups chicken stock or broth
¼ cup dry white wine
1 14½-ounce can tomatoes (preferably Italian [plum]), including juice
½ cup finely chopped fresh parsley leaves
1 teaspoon dried basil leaves
½ teaspoon dried thyme leaves
Generous ¼ teaspoon dried oregano leaves
1 bay leaf
¼ teaspoon black pepper, preferably freshly ground
¼ to ½ teaspoon salt, or to taste
2 large boiling potatoes, peeled and cut into ½-inch cubes

In a Dutch oven or small pot, heat the oil over high heat. Add the veal and cook, stirring frequently, until lightly browned on all sides. With a slotted spoon, remove the veal from the pot and reserve it. Lower the heat to medium-high, and add the onion and garlic to the pot. Cook, stirring frequently, for about 3 to 4 minutes, or until the onion is tender. If necessary, add a bit more oil.

Add the sweet peppers, celery, stock, wine, and tomatoes, breaking up the tomatoes with a large spoon. Return the veal to the pot. Add the parsley, basil, thyme, oregano, bay leaf, black pepper, and salt. Stir to mix well. Lower the heat and simmer the soup, covered, for 45 to 50 minutes, or until the veal is almost tender. Raise the heat and bring the soup to a boil. Add the potatoes. Lower the heat once again, cover, and simmer for an additional 15 to 20 minutes, or until the potatoes and veal are tender. With a large shallow spoon, skim any fat from the surface of the soup. Discard the bay leaf.

Makes 6 to 7 servings.

√Hearty Ham Soup

This stick-to-the-ribs soup feeds a crowd, and it's a perfect way to use leftover ham. However, it can also be made with a smoked pork picnic shoulder or shank. The combination of split peas, beans, black-eyed peas, and barley complements the smoked meat perfectly.

15 cups water
1 ham bone and leftover ham, *or* 1 smoked pork shoulder or shank (about 3 pounds meat and/or bone)
2 cups (about 1 pound) dry green split peas, sorted and washed
½ cup pearl barley
½ cup dry black-eyed peas, sorted and washed
½ cup dry navy beans, sorted and washed
3 bay leaves
1 to 2 beef bouillon cubes as needed
2 large onions, coarsely chopped
2 large carrots, thinly sliced
2 large celery stalks, including leaves, thinly sliced
1 garlic clove, minced
½ teaspoon dried thyme leaves
½ teaspoon celery salt
1 teaspoon salt, or to taste
½ teaspoon black pepper, preferably freshly ground

In a large heavy soup pot, combine the water, ham bone and meat, split peas, barley, black-eyed peas, and beans. Bring to a boil over high heat. Add all the remaining ingredients. Cover and lower the heat. Simmer, stirring occasionally, until the beans are tender, about 2 to 2½ hours. As the soup thickens, stir more frequently to prevent the split peas from sticking to the bottom of the pot.

When the beans are tender, remove the meat and/or bone. While the meat is cooling slightly, skim any fat off the top of the soup with a large shallow spoon and discard it. Then cut the meat into pieces and return it to the soup. Bring the soup to a boil again. Discard the bay leaves. Stir well before serving.

This soup tastes wonderful reheated. However, it must be stirred carefully to prevent the split peas from sticking. If it thickens too much in the refrigerator, thin with a bit more water during reheating.

Makes 12 to 14 servings.

✓Country Pork Ribs and Cabbage Soup

 2 tablespoons vegetable oil
 2 pounds fresh country-style pork ribs
 2 cups coarsely chopped onion
 1 large garlic clove, minced
 4 cups chicken stock or broth
 1 8-ounce can tomato sauce
 1 large carrot, thinly sliced
 1 large celery stalk, thinly sliced
 2 tablespoons pearl barley
 ¼ cup dry black-eyed peas, sorted and washed
 1 bay leaf
 ¼ teaspoon dried thyme leaves
 ⅛ teaspoon cayenne pepper, or to taste
 ⅛ teaspoon celery salt, or to taste
 Pinch of black pepper, preferably freshly ground
 2 cups coarsely chopped green cabbage

In a large pot, combine the oil and ribs. Cook the ribs over medium-high heat, turning frequently so they brown lightly on all sides. With a slotted spoon, remove the ribs to a large bowl and reserve them.

Add the onion and garlic to the pot. Cook, stirring frequently, for 5 minutes, or until the onion is tender. Return the ribs to the pot. Add all the remaining ingredients *except* the cabbage. Bring the mixture to a boil over high heat. Cover, lower the heat, and simmer for about 1 hour, or until the meat is tender. With a large shallow spoon, skim the fat from the top of the soup and discard it. Remove the ribs and reserve them. Stir in the cabbage. Cook for an additional 20 minutes, or until the cabbage is tender.

Meanwhile, remove the lean meat from the ribs and cut it into bite-sized pieces; return them to the pot. Cook for an additional 2 to 3 minutes. Discard the bay leaf.

Makes 5 to 7 servings.

Chunky Vegetable and Sausage Soup

Savory and substantial, this is the quintessential meal-in-a-bowl soup. Don't be put off by the fact that the recipe contains collards. Although these healthful greens can sometimes taste strong, in this recipe they are quite appealing.

½ pound fresh crisp collard greens
2 tablespoons vegetable oil
2 medium-sized onions, coarsely chopped
4 cups chicken stock or broth
2½ cups water
2 medium-sized carrots, cut into ¼-inch-thick slices
1 medium-sized parsnip, peeled and cut into ¼-inch-thick slices
¼ teaspoon dried thyme leaves
¼ teaspoon black pepper, preferably freshly ground
4 cups very coarsely cubed unpeeled thin-skinned potatoes (If unavailable, substitute regular peeled boiling potatoes.)
½ pound firm smoked beef sausage, cut into ⅛-inch-thick slices

Thoroughly wash the collards under cool running water and drain them in a colander. Cut or tear the leaves from the stems and tough midribs; discard the stems and midribs. Tear the leaves into small bite-sized pieces. To remove all traces of grit, thoroughly wash the collard leaves again; then set them aside to drain.

Combine the oil and onions in a 3- to 4-quart soup pot or saucepan. Cook the onions over medium-high heat, stirring, for 5 to 6 minutes, or until they are very limp but not browned. Add the chicken stock and water and bring to a boil. Add the collards and cook, stirring, until they wilt slightly. Stir in the carrots, parsnip, thyme, and pepper and return to a boil. Cover the pot, lower the heat, and simmer the mixture for 10 minutes. Stir in the potatoes and sausage and continue cooking the soup, covered, for 25 to 30 minutes longer, or until the collards are tender. (The larger and more mature the collard leaves, the longer they will take.)

Makes 4 to 5 servings.

Chicken Noodle Soup

A favorite of kids and grown-ups, too. Prepare the soup with either commercial noodles or our Homemade Egg Noodles, page 317.

3¼ to 3½ pounds bony chicken pieces (wings, backs, etc.)
4½ cups water
2 cups chicken stock or broth
1 large whole onion
1 large carrot, halved crosswise
1 small turnip, peeled and halved
1 bay leaf
½ to ¾ teaspoon black pepper, preferably freshly ground
Generous ¼ teaspoon dried thyme leaves
3 to 4 large fresh parsley sprigs
1¼ to 1½ teaspoons salt
1 large celery stalk, cut in half crosswise
2 teaspoons lemon juice, preferably fresh

2 cups commercial egg noodles, or Homemade Egg Noodles (see page 317)

About 1 tablespoon finely chopped fresh parsley leaves for garnish (optional)

Combine all the ingredients *except* the celery, lemon juice, noodles, and parsley in a 4- to 5-quart pot over medium heat. Slowly bring the mixture to a boil, covered. Lower the heat and simmer the mixture, covered, for 45 to 50 minutes. Add the celery to the pot and continue simmering for about 30 minutes longer.

Turn out the mixture into a colander set over a large bowl; let stand until all the broth has drained into the bowl. Rinse out the soup pot previously used. Strain the reserved broth through a fine sieve into the pot previously used. Finely dice the cooked carrot and celery pieces and return them to the pot. Add the lemon juice. When the chicken is cool enough to handle, remove the meat from the bones and cut it into bite-sized pieces. Return about 1½ cups of the meat to the pot. (Reserve the remainder for another use.) Using a large shallow spoon, skim off and discard the fat on the surface of the broth. (Alternatively, at this point, cover and refrigerate the soup for later use. It can be stored for up to 48 hours. Before using, remove and discard the layer of hardened fat from the surface of the soup.)

When ready to serve the soup, bring the broth and diced vegetables to a boil over medium-high heat. Also, put the noodles in a large pot of rapidly boiling salted water and cook until almost tender, following the package directions. (Or, if our Homemade Egg Noodles are used, follow the directions provided in the recipe and boil them until cooked through but still slightly firm.) Turn the noodles out into a colander to drain. Then add them to the soup and simmer for 1 minute longer. Sprinkle the soup with parsley, if desired.

Makes 5 to 6 servings.

Chicken Rice Soup

Tarragon, along with shredded turnip and parsnip, helps give this soup its rich flavor. Interestingly, the shredded white vegetables masquerade as additional rice.

1 large onion, finely chopped
1 large garlic clove, minced
2 tablespoons vegetable oil
1 medium-sized parsnip, peeled, trimmed, and grated or shredded
1 medium-sized turnip, peeled, trimmed, and grated or shredded
2 medium-sized carrots, thinly sliced
2 celery stalks, thinly sliced
8 cups water
2 bay leaves
1 chicken bouillon cube
¾ teaspoon dried thyme leaves
½ teaspoon dried tarragon leaves
¼ teaspoon celery salt
½ to ¾ teaspoon salt, or to taste
Generous ¼ teaspoon black pepper, preferably freshly ground
2½ to 3 pounds meaty chicken pieces
½ cup long-grain white rice

In a large Dutch oven or soup pot, combine the onion, garlic, and oil. Cook over medium-high heat, stirring frequently, for about 4 to 5 minutes, or until the onion is tender. Add all the remaining ingredients *except* the chicken and rice. Bring the soup to a boil. Cover, lower the heat, and simmer for about 20 minutes. Add the chicken and simmer for an additional 45 to 50 minutes, or until the chicken is very tender and the flavors are well blended. Remove the soup from the heat. With a large shallow spoon, skim the fat from the top and discard it. Remove the chicken pieces and set them aside. Remove the bay leaves and discard them.

Return the soup to the heat. Add the rice. Bring the soup to a boil. Cover, lower the heat, and simmer for 20 to 25 minutes, or until the rice is tender.

Meanwhile, remove the chicken meat from the bones and cut it into bite-sized pieces. When the rice is tender, return the chicken meat to the pot. Heat for an additional 2 minutes.

Makes 7 to 8 servings.

Chunky Chicken and Vegetable Soup with Little Dumplings

A homey, heartwarming soup like Grandma used to make.

8 to 10 medium-sized green onions (scallions)
2½ tablespoons butter or margarine
⅓ cup chopped fresh parsley leaves
1 large celery stalk, finely chopped
1 medium-sized parsnip, peeled and finely chopped
1 cup shredded green cabbage
6½ cups water
3 to 3¼ pounds bony chicken parts (wings, backs, etc.)
3 medium-sized carrots, cut into ⅛-inch-thick slices
1 large celery stalk, cut into ⅛-inch-thick slices
1 small rutabaga, peeled and cut into ¼-inch cubes
2 cups coarsely chopped small cauliflower flowerets
1¼ teaspoons salt, or to taste
Generous ¼ teaspoon black pepper, preferably freshly
    ground

Dumplings

⅓ cup whole or lowfat milk
1 tablespoon butter or margarine
Scant ½ teaspoon salt
½ cup all-purpose white flour
1 large egg yolk

Trim the roots from the green onions and discard them. Trim off the green tops and coarsely chop them. Cut the white portions crosswise into ½-inch lengths and set them aside.

Melt the butter in a 4- to 5-quart soup pot over medium-high heat. Stir in the green onion tops, parsley, and chopped celery and cook for 4 to 5 minutes, or until the vegetables are limp. Add the parsnip, cabbage, water, and chicken and bring to a boil. Lower the heat and simmer the mixture, covered, for 1 hour and 15 minutes. Remove the chicken pieces from the pot and set them aside to cool. Add the reserved green onion white parts, carrots, sliced celery, rutabaga, cauliflower, salt, and pepper. Cover the pot and simmer for 45 minutes, stirring occasionally.

Meanwhile, when the chicken is cool enough to handle, remove the meat from the bones and cut it into bite-sized chunks. Set them aside.

Prepare the dumpling dough as follows: In a small saucepan over medium-high heat, combine the milk, butter, and salt. Heat, stirring occasionally, until the mixture comes to a boil. Remove the pan from the heat and, using a wooden spoon, vigorously stir in the flour until it is thoroughly incorporated and the mixture is smooth. Set the mixture aside for about 10 minutes, or until it cools to lukewarm. Vigorously stir in the egg yolk until the dough is smooth and well-blended.

With lightly greased fingers, pull off marble-sized bits of dough and roll them between the palms of your hands to form smooth round dumplings. Set the dumplings aside on a sheet of wax paper until all are formed. Then transfer them to the soup pot. Cover the pot and simmer for 6 to 7 minutes, or until the dumplings are cooked through. Add the chicken meat to the pot. Gently stir the chicken and dumplings into the soup and continue simmering for 3 to 4 minutes, or until the chicken is heated through.

Makes 6 to 8 servings.

Pimiento-Chicken Soup with Chives

Pimientos and chives make this soup very colorful. A savory broth and sour cream make it very tasty as well. Although the recipe is festive and rather elegant, it is also economical to prepare.

2 to 2¼ pounds bony chicken pieces (wings, backs, etc.)
3½ cups chicken stock or broth
1 cup dry white wine
1 large onion, cut into eighths
1 large carrot, coarsely sliced
1 large celery stalk, coarsely sliced
¼ cup coarsely chopped fresh parsley leaves
¼ cup coarsely chopped sweet green pepper
1 bay leaf
1 teaspoon whole black peppercorns
¼ teaspoon dried thyme leaves
2 tablespoons butter or margarine
3½ tablespoons all-purpose white flour
½ cup commercial sour cream
1 6-ounce jar whole pimientos, drained
¼ teaspoon white pepper, preferably freshly ground
1 tablespoon chopped fresh chives, or 1¼ teaspoons dried
   chopped chives
⅛ to ¼ teaspoon salt

Combine the chicken, stock, wine, onion, carrot, celery, parsley, green pepper, bay leaf, peppercorns, and thyme in a 3- to 4-quart pot over medium heat. Slowly bring the mixture to a boil, covered. Lower the heat and simmer the mixture, covered, for 1 hour. Skim off and discard any fat on the broth surface, using a large shallow spoon.

Turn out the broth into a colander set over a large bowl; let stand until all the broth drains into the bowl.

Rinse out and dry the pot previously used. Add the butter to the pot and melt it over medium-high heat. Using a wooden spoon, stir in the flour until well blended and smooth. Cook, stirring, for 2 minutes. Strain the reserved broth through a fine sieve into the pot. Bring the mixture to a boil, stirring until well blended and smooth. Lower the heat and simmer, covered, for about 5 minutes.

Meanwhile, put the sour cream in a blender. Discard any seeds clinging to the pimientos. Add *all but one* of the pimientos and the white pepper to the blender. Blend until completely puréed and smooth. Set the mixture aside. Cut the remaining pimiento into very thin, 1-inch-long strips and reserve them.

When the chicken is cool enough to handle, remove the meat from the bones and cut it into bite-sized pieces. Return the meat to the pot, along with the sour cream-pimiento purée, reserved pimiento strips, chives, and salt. Continue heating until the soup is piping hot, *but do not* allow it to boil.

Makes 4 to 5 servings.

Home-Style Chicken and Vegetable Chowder

A homey, comforting recipe featuring potatoes, corn, and carrots, along with savory chunks of chicken meat. It's a favorite with families.

2 tablespoons butter or margarine
2 medium-sized onions, chopped
1 medium-sized celery stalk, diced
¼ cup diced turnip (optional)
3⅓ cups water
1 chicken bouillon cube
1 large (bone-in) chicken breast half, skin removed
1 medium-sized carrot
¾ to 1 teaspoon salt
⅛ to ¼ teaspoon white or black pepper, preferably freshly ground
2 medium-sized potatoes, peeled and diced
1½ cups loose-pack frozen corn kernels, thawed under cool running water and drained

    1 tablespoon all-purpose white flour
    1 cup whole milk (or a little more, if desired)

Melt the butter in a 3- to 4-quart saucepan or pot over medium-high heat. Add the onions, celery, and turnip (if used) and cook, stirring, for 4 to 5 minutes, or until the onions are limp. Add the water, bouillon cube, chicken breast, carrot, salt, and pepper. Bring the mixture to a boil. Cover the pan, lower the heat, and simmer for 16 to 20 minutes, or until the chicken and carrot are tender when pierced with a fork.

Remove the chicken breast and carrot and set them aside until cool enough to handle. Add the potatoes to the pan and simmer, covered, for 8 to 9 minutes longer. Stir in the corn. Scoop 2 cups of the vegetables from the pan and transfer them to a blender or a food processor fitted with a steel blade. Add the flour to the blender or processor. Blend or process the mixture until completely puréed and smooth. (If the mixture is too thick to purée easily in the blender, thin it with some of the liquid from the pan.) Return the puréed mixture to the pan and add 1 cup of milk; if the chowder seems too thick, add a bit more milk until the desired consistency is obtained. Bring the chowder to a simmer and cook, covered, for 5 to 8 minutes longer, or until the potatoes are tender but not mushy. Meanwhile, cube the carrot and cut the meat from the chicken breast into small bite-sized pieces. Add the carrot and chicken pieces to the chowder and cook for 3 to 4 minutes longer, or until the mixture is heated through.

Makes 4 to 5 servings.

Alphabet Chicken Soup

Kids like the alphabet letters in this traditional chicken soup. Canned chicken broth makes the preparation easy.

    1 tablespoon vegetable oil
    1 medium-sized onion, finely chopped
    1 large garlic clove, minced

5½ cups canned chicken broth
1½ cups water
2 large (bone-in) chicken breast halves, skins removed
2 large carrots, thinly sliced
2 large celery stalks, thinly sliced
2 tablespoons finely chopped fresh parsley leaves
1 large bay leaf
Scant ½ teaspoon dried thyme leaves
¼ teaspoon celery salt
¼ teaspoon salt
¼ teaspoon black pepper, preferably freshly ground
¾ cup alphabet pasta

In a Dutch oven or small soup pot, combine the vegetable oil, onion, and garlic. Cook over medium-high heat, stirring frequently, until the onion is tender. Add all the remaining ingredients *except* the alphabet pasta. Bring the soup to a boil over high heat. Lower the heat, cover, and cook the mixture for about 45 minutes, or until the chicken is tender. Remove the pot from the heat. With a large spoon, skim off and discard any fat from the top of the soup. Remove the chicken from the soup and reserve it in a medium-sized bowl.

Return the soup to the heat and bring to a boil over high heat. Add the alphabet pasta. Lower the heat and gently boil for 8 to 10 minutes, uncovered, or until the pasta is tender.

Meanwhile, when the chicken is cool enough to handle, remove the meat from the bones and cut it into small pieces. When the pasta is just cooked through, return the chicken to the soup. Heat for an additional 2 to 3 minutes. Discard the bay leaf.

Makes 6 to 8 servings.

Chicken and Curly Endive Soup

Curly endive tends to be a little bitter when it is eaten fresh, but the flavor mellows considerably during cooking. In this unusual chicken-vegetable-noodle soup, it adds a distinctive and appealing taste, as well as attractive bits of green color.

3¼ to 3½ pounds bony chicken pieces (wings, backs, etc.)
1 pound (bone-in) chicken breast halves (about 2 medium sized)
8 cups water
3½ cups chicken stock or broth
½ cup dry white wine
2 large onions, finely chopped
2 large carrots, finely chopped
2 large celery stalks, finely chopped
1 large bay leaf
1 teaspoon dried marjoram leaves
½ teaspoon dried basil leaves
½ teaspoon dried thyme leaves
1 teaspoon black pepper, preferably freshly ground
1 large boiling potato, peeled and finely diced
Generous ¾ pound curly endive or chicory (1 very large head), washed and drained
1½ cups canned imported Italian (plum) tomatoes, including juice, chopped
2½ to 2¾ teaspoons salt
2 cups fettuccine noodles, cooked *al dente,* following the package directions and then drained
About ¼ cup grated Romano or Parmesan cheese for garnish

Combine the chicken pieces, chicken breast halves, water, stock, wine, onions, carrots, celery, bay leaf, marjoram, basil, thyme, and pepper in a very large pot. Bring the mixture to a boil over medium-high heat. Lower the heat and simmer, covered, for 1 hour. Remove the chicken breast halves and set them aside to cool. Add the potato. Continue simmering the mixture, covered, for 30 minutes longer.

Meanwhile, trim off and discard the tough stems and any tough outer leaves from the endive. Finely chop the endive; there should be enough to measure about 8 to 8½ lightly packed cups. Put the chopped endive in a colander and rinse it thoroughly under cool running water. Set it aside to drain.

Skim off and discard any fat on the surface of the broth, using a large shallow spoon. Remove the bony chicken pieces and the bay leaf from the pot, using a slotted spoon; discard them.

Stir the endive, tomatoes, and salt into the pot. Bring the mixture to a boil, stirring. Lower the heat and simmer, covered, for about 12 to 15 minutes, or until the endive is almost tender.

Remove the chicken breast meat from the bones and cut it into bite-sized pieces. Stir the chicken meat and the cooked fettuccine into the soup. Continue cooking, covered, for 2 to 3 minutes longer, or until the chicken and noodles are heated through. Pass the grated cheese in a small bowl at the table so diners can sprinkle some over their soup.

Makes 8 to 10 servings.

Spicy North African–Style Chicken Soup

The tangy flavors and hearty textures of North African cuisine combine in this satisfying chicken soup with a difference. The dish makes a nice introduction to bulgur wheat, which can be purchased in the specialty food section of many large grocery stores. However, if you prefer, brown rice or even white rice could be substituted. If white rice is used, reduce the cooking time for the grain to about 20 minutes.

2 tablespoons olive oil
3 cups coarsely chopped red onion (If unavailable, substitute yellow onion.)
2 large garlic cloves, minced
4½ cups chicken stock or broth
1 cup water
4 (bone-in) chicken breast halves, skins removed (about 2 pounds total weight)
2 large celery stalks, thinly sliced

½ cup finely chopped fresh parsley leaves
1 14½- to 16-ounce can tomatoes, including juice
1 3-inch-long cinnamon stick
⅛ teaspoon ground cloves
2 large bay leaves
¾ teaspoon dried marjoram leaves
½ teaspoon dried thyme leaves
⅛ teaspoon cayenne pepper
¼ teaspoon black pepper, preferably freshly ground
½ teaspoon salt, or to taste
Scant ½ cup dry bulgur wheat

In a large pot, combine the olive oil, onion, and garlic. Cook over medium-high heat, stirring frequently, for about 4 to 5 minutes, or until the onion is tender. Add the stock, water, chicken, celery, and parsley; then add the tomatoes, breaking them up with a large spoon. Add the cinnamon stick, cloves, bay leaves, marjoram, thyme, cayenne pepper, black pepper, and salt. Stir to mix well. Bring the mixture to a boil. Then lower the heat, cover, and simmer for 45 to 50 minutes, or until the chicken is tender. With a slotted spoon, remove the chicken and reserve it in a medium-sized bowl. Remove the cinnamon and bay leaves and discard them. With a large shallow spoon, skim any fat from the top of the soup and discard it.

Bring the soup to a boil. Stir in the bulgur. Lower the heat and simmer for an additional 40 to 45 minutes, or until the bulgur is tender.

Meanwhile, remove the chicken meat from the bones and cut it into bite-sized pieces. When the bulgur is tender, return the chicken to the pot and simmer for an additional 2 to 3 minutes.

Makes 6 to 8 servings.

Country-Style Turkey Vegetable Soup

A homey, stick-to-the-ribs soup that's very popular with families. The recipe is designed to yield a lot of soup as it disappears fast and is great reheated. It can also be frozen.

4¼ to 4½ pounds turkey wings (about 4 medium-sized wings)
10 cups water
1 chicken bouillon cube
⅓ cup dry Great Northern beans, sorted and washed
3 large onions, coarsely chopped
1 cup peeled and diced rutabaga, turnip, or parsnip
1 cup chopped celery
1 cup finely chopped green cabbage
¼ cup chopped fresh parsley leaves
3 tablespoons pearl barley
4 to 5 carrots, cut crosswise into ⅛-inch-thick slices
2 celery stalks, cut crosswise into ⅛-inch-thick slices
⅓ cup medium-sized elbow macaroni
¼ teaspoon dried marjoram leaves
⅛ teaspoon dried thyme leaves
2½ teaspoons salt, or more to taste
½ to ¾ teaspoon black pepper, preferably freshly ground
1½ cups loose-pack frozen corn kernels
1 16-ounce can tomatoes, including juice, broken up with a spoon

Combine the turkey wings, water, bouillon cube, beans, onions, rutabaga, chopped celery, cabbage, parsley, and barley in a 5- to 6-quart soup pot and bring to a boil over high heat. Lower the heat, cover, and simmer the mixture for 1 hour and 20 to 30 minutes, or until the turkey wings are tender.

Remove the turkey wings and set them aside. When they are cool enough to handle, remove the meat and cut it into bite-sized pieces.

Add the carrots, sliced celery, macaroni, marjoram, thyme, salt, and pepper to the pot. Bring the mixture to a simmer and continue cooking, covered, for 30 minutes. Stir in the corn, tomatoes, and reserved turkey meat, and simmer for 5 to 10 minutes longer, or until the carrots are tender and the corn is cooked through. The soup may be refrigerated or frozen for later use.

Makes 9 to 11 servings.

4
FISH AND SHELLFISH SOUPS

The gifts of the sea are celebrated in this chapter. Recipes here range from simple and homey to rather elaborate. They spotlight all manner of fish and shellfish, singly and in delicious combinations. For example, we've included a number of classic and regional favorites, such as Bouillabaisse, Shrimp Bisque, Cioppino, and Oyster, Sausage, and Ham Gumbo. There is also a collection of white and red chowder recipes— Snow Crab and Shrimp, Manhatten-Style Clam, creamy Scallop, and spicy Bermuda Fish Chowder—to name just a few. (Not surprisingly, many of these specialties originated in coastal regions where good seafood is abundant.) And we've provided some of our own creations, such as fragrant Mussel Soup with Saffron and delicate Cream of Crab.

The secret to any good fish or shellfish soup is the quality of the seafood used. When fresh seafood is called for it must be exactly that—*supremely* fresh. With fish, appearance provides one indication of condition; the scales should be shiny, the gills bright, and the eyes clear. However, the best indicator—and often the only one for mollusks and some crustaceans—is the smell. Fresh seafood has the clean, slightly salty, almost refreshing scent of ocean air, not a strong or unpleasant "fishy odor." If it isn't possible to sniff before buying, the only insurance is to stick with suppliers you know and trust.

Don't be tempted to make do and prepare a recipe with less than very fresh seafood. At best, the end product will be tasteless; at worst, it will be downright unappealing to the palate and nose. In fact, if the choice is between a "fresh" offering of uncertain age and good-quality frozen, we recommend the latter. In particular, frozen fish fillets are very satisfactory for soupmaking. Not only are they convenient and fairly economical, but freezing normally has only a minimal effect on their texture and flavor. Indeed, because commercial packers often process incoming catches immediately upon arrival, frozen fish may actually taste fresher than so-called "fresh" that has been trucked great distances or handled and displayed too long.

Bouillabaisse

There are purists who claim you can't make a real bouillabaisse without the same varieties of fish that are used in Marseilles. If you feel that way, too, then just think of this as a very good Mediterranean-style fish soup!

Note: For a simpler, easier, and more economical dish, the mussels, clams, and shrimp can all be omitted from this recipe. In this case, add another ½ to ¾ pound of any of the fish called for. The recipe will yield about 5 servings.

> 18 to 24 fresh mussels
> 12 small fresh clams
> 3 tablespoons olive oil
> 1½ cups cleaned and coarsely chopped leek green parts (see page 13), *or* ¾ cup coarsely chopped green onions (scallions) and ¾ cup coarsely chopped onion
> 1 small celery stalk, including leaves, coarsely chopped
> 3 large garlic cloves
> 8 cups fish stock (see page 301)
> 2 cups bottled clam juice
> 1½ cups drained and chopped canned imported Italian (plum) tomatoes
> ¼ cup coarsely chopped fresh parsley leaves
> 1 large bay leaf
> ½ teaspoon coarsely chopped fresh orange rind (orange part only)
> ½ teaspoon dried thyme leaves
> ¼ teaspoon paprika
> Generous ¼ teaspoon very finely crumbled saffron threads
> ⅛ teaspoon fennel seeds
> ⅛ teaspoon dried crushed red (hot) pepper
> Pinch of coriander seeds
> 12 to 18 large fresh shrimp
> ¾ pound fresh or frozen (thawed) boneless and skinless haddock fillets
> ¾ pound fresh or frozen (thawed) boneless and skinless flounder or sole fillets

½ pound fresh or frozen (thawed) boneless and skinless monkfish or red snapper fillets

¾ to 1 teaspoon salt, or to taste

About 2 tablespoons finely chopped fresh parsley leaves for garnish

Croûtes *or* croutons for garnish (see pages 316 and 315)

To clean the mussels and clams, first rinse and drain them. Wash them in several changes of cool water, scrubbing the shells with a vegetable brush. Debeard the mussels (trim off any dark, root-like debris) using kitchen shears or a sharp knife. Continue changing the water until it is clear and no traces of sand remain. Then soak the mussels and clams in cool water to just cover for at least 1 hour and up to 3 or 4 hours to allow them to disgorge any sand.

Prepare the bouillabaisse broth as follows: Combine the oil, leek green parts, celery, and garlic in a very large soup pot. Cook over medium heat, stirring, for 6 to 7 minutes, or until the leeks are almost tender. Stir in the fish stock, clam juice, tomatoes, parsley, bay leaf, orange rind, thyme, paprika, saffron, fennel, dried red pepper, and coriander seeds. Bring the mixture to a boil over medium-high heat. Then lower the heat and gently simmer, uncovered, for 50 to 60 minutes.

Meanwhile, ready the shrimp by peeling the shells from the bodies; leave the tail portions of the shell intact. Devein the shrimp, if desired. Cut the fish into 1¼-inch chunks. Return the shrimp and fish to the refrigerator until needed.

When the broth has simmered for at least 50 minutes, strain it through a fine sieve into a large bowl, pressing down hard on the solids to force through as much liquid as possible. Discard the solids. Add the salt to the broth. Rinse out the pot previously used and return the broth to it. (Alternatively, at this point the broth may be covered and refrigerated for later use.)

About 20 minutes before serving time, rinse the mussels and clams well under cool running water and set them aside to drain in a colander. Discard any "gapers" that have not closed up during the soaking period.

Bring the broth to a boil over high heat. Add the clams to the broth; lower the heat to medium-high and simmer, covered, for 5 minutes. Add the fish and continue simmering, covered, for 3 minutes. Then add the mussels and shrimp. Continue simmering for 7 to 9 minutes longer, or until the fish is tender but holds its shape, the mollusks have opened, and the shrimp are pink and curled. Discard any mussels or clams that failed to open. Sprinkle the bouillabaisse with the parsley.

If croûtes are used for garnish, lay one in each soup plate. Ladle the soup over the croûtes and serve immediately. If garlic croutons are used for garnish, pass a bowl of them separately, so diners can sprinkle some over their soup. Also, furnish some extra soup plates at the table so diners can discard the empty shells as they eat.

Makes 6 servings.

Cioppino

24 to 28 fresh mussels, preferably cultured
3 tablespoons olive oil
2 medium-sized onions, finely chopped
1 small celery stalk, finely chopped
½ cup diced sweet green pepper
¼ cup finely chopped fresh parsley leaves
1 large garlic clove, minced
1 35-ounce can imported Italian (plum) tomatoes, including juice, puréed in a blender or food processor
1 cup fish stock (see page 301) or bottled clam juice
½ cup dry red wine
1 teaspoon sugar
1 small bay leaf
½ teaspoon dried oregano leaves
½ teaspoon dried basil leaves
¼ teaspoon black pepper, preferably freshly ground
Generous pinch of dried crushed red (hot) pepper
¾ to 1 teaspoon salt
1½ pounds fresh or frozen (thawed) skinless cod, haddock, or similar lean white fish fillets

1½ pounds fresh cooked or frozen (thawed) Dungeness
crab legs, *or* 1½ pounds frozen (thawed) Alaskan snow
crab or king crab legs
1½ pounds fresh or frozen peeled medium-sized or large
shrimp
About 1 tablespoon finely chopped fresh chives or parsley
leaves for garnish

To clean the mussels, rinse and drain them. Wash them
in several changes of cool water, scrubbing the shells with a
vegetable brush. Debeard the mussels (trim off any dark, root-
like debris) using kitchen shears or a sharp knife. Continue
changing the water until it is clear and no traces of sand remain. Set the mussels aside to soak in cool water to just cover
for at least 1 hour (and up to 2 or 3 hours, if more convenient).

When ready to complete preparation of the soup, combine
the oil, onions, celery, green pepper, parsley, and garlic in a
very large pot. Cook over medium-high heat, stirring, for 5 to
6 minutes, or until the onions are limp. Stir in the tomatoes,
stock, wine, sugar, bay leaf, oregano, basil, black pepper, and
dried red pepper, and bring the mixture to a boil. Lower the
heat and simmer, covered, for 30 to 35 minutes, or until the
flavors have mingled and the mixture has thickened slightly.
Stir in the salt.

Cut the fish fillets into 2-inch chunks. Crack the crab legs and
break them into 4- to 5-inch lengths. Turn out the mussels into
a colander. Rinse them well under cool running water and set
them aside to drain.

Discard the bay leaf. Add the mussels and fish to the pot and
simmer for 4 minutes. Stir in the crab legs and then the shrimp
and continue simmering, covered, for about 5 to 6 minutes, or
until the mussels open, the fish pieces are cooked through but
hold their shape, and the shrimp turn pink and curl. Discard
any mussels that have not opened.

Ladle the soup into soup plates or large bowls. Garnish the
servings with a sprinkling of chopped fresh chives. Furnish
some additional soup plates or bowls so diners can discard the
empty shells from their soup as they eat.

Makes 6 servings.

Portuguese-Style Fisherman's Pot

We prefer to use cultured mussels for soupmaking because they are usually cleaner and less likely to contain grit. However, uncultured mussels can certainly be substituted. Just be sure to wash them especially well.

This is a robust, attractive, well-seasoned soup. It makes a great meal-in-a-bowl.

    20 to 24 fresh mussels, preferably cultured
    1½ tablespoons butter or margarine
    1½ tablespoons olive oil
    2 large onions, finely chopped
    1 large carrot, finely chopped
    1 small celery stalk, finely chopped
    ¼ cup diced sweet red pepper (If unavailable, substitute
        sweet green pepper.)
    ¼ cup finely chopped fresh parsley leaves
    1 large garlic clove, minced
    1½ cups chicken stock or broth
    2 to 3 medium-sized boiling potatoes, peeled and cut into
        ½-inch cubes
    1 35-ounce can imported Italian (plum) tomatoes, includ-
        ing juice
    ¾ cup dry white wine
    1 teaspoon sugar
    1 large bay leaf
    1 teaspoon paprika, preferably imported sweet paprika
    1 teaspoon chili powder
    ¼ teaspoon celery seeds
    ¼ teaspoon black pepper, preferably freshly ground
    ⅛ teaspoon dried thyme leaves
    Pinch of saffron threads, very finely crumbled (optional)
    Generous pinch of dried crushed red (hot) pepper
    ¾ to 1 teaspoon salt, or to taste
    1½ pounds fresh or frozen (thawed) skinless cod, haddock,
        or similar lean white fish fillets

½ pound fresh or frozen (thawed) peeled medium-sized shrimp

About 1 tablespoon finely chopped fresh parsley leaves for garnish

Clean the mussels as follows: First, rinse and drain them. Wash them in several changes of cool water, scrubbing the shells with a vegetable brush. Debeard the mussels (trim off any dark, root-like debris) using kitchen shears or a sharp knife. Continue changing the water until it is clear and no traces of sand remain. Then soak the mussels in cool water to just cover for at least 2 or 3 hours to allow them to disgorge any more sand.

When ready to complete preparations for the soup, combine the butter and oil in a 5- to 6-quart pot. Heat over medium-high heat until the butter melts. Add the onions, carrot, celery, sweet pepper, parsley, and garlic, and cook stirring, for 4 to 5 minutes, or until the onions are limp. Stir in the chicken stock and potatoes and bring the mixture to a boil. Lower the heat and simmer, covered, for 12 to 13 minutes, or until the potatoes are just cooked through; stir occasionally to prevent the potatoes from sticking to the bottom of the pot. Add the tomatoes, breaking them up with a spoon. Stir in the wine, sugar, bay leaf, paprika, chili powder, celery seeds, black pepper, thyme, saffron (if used), and dried red pepper. Cover the pot and simmer, covered, for 20 to 25 minutes, or until the mixture is slightly thickened and the flavors have mingled.

Meanwhile, turn out the mussels into a colander. Rinse them well under cool running water. Discard any mussels that are not tightly closed at this point. Set the rest aside to drain. Cut any large fish fillets into quarters; cut the small fillets in half. Set the fish aside.

Stir the salt into the pot. Add the mussels and fish to the pot and simmer for 4 minutes. Stir in the shrimp and continue simmering, covered, until the mussels open, the fish pieces are cooked through but hold their shape, and the shrimp turn pink and curl, about 4 to 6 minutes longer. Discard the bay leaf and any mussels that have not opened.

Ladle the soup into soup plates or large bowls. Garnish each serving with a sprinkling of chopped parsley. Furnish diners with some extra bowls so they can discard the mussel shells from their soup as they eat.

Makes 4 to 6 servings.

Bermuda Fish Chowder

Like Manhattan-style chowders, Bermuda chowders typically contain tomatoes. However, they have a wonderful flavor and robustness all their own. The following recipe makes a very savory, not to mention economical, meal-in-a-bowl. It is excellent reheated.

The chowder may be prepared either with the simple fish stock included in the recipe or with 1 quart of fresh or frozen (thawed) fish stock (see page 301) if you happen to have it on hand. If preparing the stock given here, be sure to use the frames and heads of only very fresh and clean, non-oily, white-fleshed fish. And do not make the broth or the chowder in an aluminum pot, as it may lend a metallic taste or dark color.

Simple Stock

2¼ to 2½ pounds frames and heads from flounder, sole, haddock, etc.
4¼ cups water
¼ cup dry white wine
1 small onion, coarsely chopped
1 small bay leaf
¾ teaspoon salt

Chowder

2 ¼-inch-thick strips slab bacon (rind removed), finely diced
3 tablespoons butter or margarine
2 large onions, finely chopped
4 medium-sized celery stalks, including leaves, chopped

4 medium-sized carrots, chopped

½ medium-sized sweet green pepper, chopped

2½ teaspoons Worcestershire sauce

2 large bay leaves

½ teaspoon dried thyme leaves

¼ teaspoon black pepper, preferably freshly ground

Generous ⅛ teaspoon curry powder

3 cups ½-inch peeled boiling potato cubes

1½ cups chopped Italian-style (plum) tomatoes, including juice

¼ cup ketchup

3 tablespoons dark rum

1 to 1¼ teaspoons salt, or to taste

1 to 1½ pounds fresh or frozen lean skinless white fish fillets (flounder, haddock, cod, etc.), cut into 1-inch chunks

Bermuda sherry peppers for garnish, optional (Or substitute Tabasco sauce and a teaspoon or two of dry sherry.)

To prepare the stock, thoroughly rinse the fish frames and drain them. Rinse the heads, being careful to wash out any blood. (If they seem bloody, soak them in cold water for a few minutes and rinse them again.) Combine the frames and heads in a medium-sized pot with all the remaining stock ingredients. Bring the mixture to a boil over medium heat. Cover the pot, lower the heat, and simmer for 20 to 25 minutes. Strain the stock through a fine sieve, discarding the bones and seasoning ingredients.

To prepare the chowder: Cook the bacon in a large pot over medium-high heat, stirring, until well browned and almost crisp. Push the bacon to one side and add the butter. When it melts, stir in the onions and celery. Continue to cook, stirring, for 5 to 6 minutes, or until the onions are limp. Stir in the carrots and green pepper, and cook, stirring, for 2 minutes longer. Stir in the simple stock (or previously prepared fish stock), Worcestershire sauce, bay leaves, thyme, black pepper, and curry powder. Add the potatoes, and bring the mixture to a boil over medium-high heat. Lower the heat and simmer, covered, for 20 minutes. Stir in the tomatoes, ketchup, and rum; cover the pot and simmer for 1 hour and 30 minutes longer. Stir in the salt and fish and continue simmering, covered, for about 30 minutes longer. Discard the bay leaves.

Traditionally in Bermuda, a bottle of sherry peppers is passed at the table and diners sprinkle some over their chowder. (Sherry peppers are very small hot peppers steeped in dry sherry until their flavor and fire permeate the liquid. Only the liquid is actually used to garnish the chowder.) Alternatively, each serving may be garnished with a light sprinkling of dry sherry, and a bottle of Tabasco sauce may be passed at the table. Or, simply omit the garnishes; the chowder is delicious as is!

Bermuda Fish Chowder is good reheated. Reheat over medium-high heat until piping hot. Thin the chowder with a little water, if desired.

Makes 5 to 7 servings.

Scandinavian-Style Fish Chowder with Dill

Dillweed and seafood are often teamed up in Scandinavian cooking. In this hearty chowder, fresh dill not only complements the mild flavor of the fish, but adds an attractive touch of green as well. A garnish of capers gives the soup an appealing zip.

2 tablespoons butter or margarine
1 large onion, chopped
3 tablespoons all-purpose white flour
½ teaspoon powdered mustard
2 cups whole milk
1 cup fish stock (see page 301) *or* chicken stock or broth
3 cups peeled and diced boiling potatoes
¼ to ½ teaspoon black pepper, preferably freshly ground
1 pound fresh or frozen (thawed) skinless haddock fillets (or a similar mild, white firm-fleshed fish)
½ cup light cream or half-and-half

2 tablespoons finely chopped fresh dillweed, coarse stems
    removed
1½ teaspoons finely chopped fresh chives
½ to ¾ teaspoon salt
2 to 3 tablespoons drained capers for garnish

Combine the butter and onion in a 3- to 4-quart pot or saucepan. Cook over medium-high heat, stirring, 4 to 5 minutes, or until the onion is limp. Using a wooden spoon, stir in the flour and mustard until well blended and smooth. Cook, stirring, for 1 minute. Stir in the milk and stock until thoroughly incorporated and smooth. Add the potatoes and pepper. Bring the mixture to a boil; then lower the heat and cover the pot. Simmer for about 10 minutes, stirring occasionally to prevent the potato from sticking to the bottom of the pot. Meanwhile, cut the haddock into 1½-inch chunks.

Stir the haddock, cream, dillweed, chives, and salt into the pot and allow the soup to return to a simmer. Simmer, covered, for 3 to 5 minutes longer, or until the fish pieces are cooked through but still hold some shape.

Serve the soup in large soup plates or bowls. Garnish individual servings with a teaspoon or two of capers.

The soup may also be served reheated. Rewarm it over medium heat, stirring occasionally to prevent the potatoes from sticking. *Do not* allow the soup to come to a boil.

Makes 4 to 5 servings.

√Manhattan-Style Fish Chowder with Vegetables

1 large onion, finely chopped
2 celery stalks, including leaves, coarsely chopped
3 tablespoons butter or margarine
1 1-quart, 14-ounce can tomato juice
1 large carrot, very thinly sliced
1½ cups 1-inch-long fresh green bean pieces
1 cup loose-pack frozen corn kernels

1 large potato, peeled and diced
1 bay leaf
1 teaspoon sugar, or to taste
Scant ½ teaspoon dried thyme leaves
½ teaspoon dried marjoram leaves
¼ teaspoon powdered mustard
3 to 4 drops Tabasco sauce
½ to ¾ teaspoon salt
Generous ¼ teaspoon black pepper, preferably freshly
   ground
1 pound fresh or frozen (thawed) skinless flounder or hal-
   ibut fillets, cut into ¾-inch pieces

In a large heavy saucepan or small Dutch oven, combine the onion, celery, and butter. Cook over medium-high heat, stirring frequently, for about 5 to 6 minutes, or until the onion is tender. Add all the remaining ingredients *except* the fish. Bring the soup to a boil. Cover, lower the heat, and simmer for 25 to 30 minutes, or until the vegetables are tender. Stir in the fish. Cook for an additional 3 or 4 minutes, or until the fish flakes easily when tested with the tines of a fork. Discard the bay leaf before serving.

Makes 5 to 6 servings.

New England–Style Clam Chowder

A perennial favorite, this is both easy and good.

3 tablespoons butter or margarine
1 large onion, coarsely chopped
1 cup bottled clam juice
2 10½-ounce cans minced clams, including juice
4 cups peeled and diced boiling potatoes
1 2-inch piece salt pork or slab bacon (rind removed)
Scant ½ teaspoon white pepper, preferably freshly ground
Scant ⅛ teaspoon ground nutmeg

Scant ⅛ teaspoon ground thyme
3 cups whole milk
1 cup light cream or half-and-half
Salt to taste
Small pats of butter for garnish (optional)

Melt the butter in a medium-sized soup pot or 3- to 4-quart saucepan over medium-high heat. Add the onion and cook, stirring, for 5 to 6 minutes, or until it is soft. Stir in the clam juice, clams and their juice, potatoes, salt pork, pepper, nutmeg, and thyme and bring the mixture to a boil over medium-high heat. Lower the heat and gently simmer, uncovered, for about 15 minutes, or until the potatoes are tender and much of the liquid has evaporated from the pan; stir occasionally to prevent the potatoes from sticking to the bottom of the pan.

Stir in the milk and cream, and heat to piping hot *but not* boiling, about 5 minutes longer. Discard the salt pork. Add salt to taste. Garnish each serving with a small pat of butter, if desired.

Makes 6 to 8 servings.

Manhattan-Style Clam Chowder

2 bacon strips, cut in half crosswise
1 tablespoon butter or margarine
1 large onion, finely chopped
2 large celery stalks, including leaves, diced
½ large sweet green pepper, diced
2 6½-ounce cans chopped clams, including juice
Water
1 large potato, peeled and diced
1 16-ounce can tomatoes, including juice
2 cups tomato juice
3 drops Tabasco sauce
1 bay leaf
Scant ½ teaspoon dried thyme leaves

½ teaspoon salt
⅛ teaspoon black pepper, preferably freshly ground

In a large heavy saucepan or Dutch oven, cook the bacon over medium to medium-high heat, turning it once or twice with a large fork. If necessary, lower the heat slightly. When the bacon is crisp, remove it and set it aside to drain on a double thickness of paper towels. Do not drain the bacon fat from the saucepan. When the bacon is cool enough to handle, finely crumble and reserve it.

Add the butter, onion, celery, and green pepper to the pan used for the bacon. Cook the vegetables over medium heat, stirring frequently, for about 4 to 5 minutes, or until the onion is tender.

Drain the liquid from the clams into a measuring cup and add enough water to make 1¾ cups of liquid. Add the liquid to the pan, along with the potato and crumbled bacon. Bring to a boil. Cover, lower the heat, and simmer for 10 minutes, stirring occasionally, or until the potato is tender. Remove and discard the bay leaf and add all the remaining ingredients, breaking up the tomatoes with a spoon. Cover and simmer for about 5 minutes longer, or until the flavors are well blended.

Makes 5 to 6 servings.

Cream of Crab Soup

5 tablespoons butter or margarine
⅓ cup finely chopped onion
⅓ cup all-purpose white flour
¼ teaspoon powdered mustard
3 cups chicken stock or broth
2¼ cups whole milk, divided
¼ to ½ teaspoon salt
Generous ¼ teaspoon white pepper, preferably freshly ground
1½ cups light cream or half-and-half
1½ teaspoons lemon juice, preferably fresh
½ teaspoon soy sauce

¾ pound fresh backfin crabmeat, carefully picked over to remove any bits of cartilage or shell

Buttered Crumbs

3 tablespoons butter
1 cup fine fresh white bread crumbs

Melt the 5 tablespoons of butter in a 3-quart saucepan over medium-high heat. Add the onion and cook, stirring, for 3 to 4 minutes, or until the onion is limp. Lower the heat and continue cooking the onion, stirring, for 3 to 4 minutes longer, or until it is tender and translucent *but not* brown. Using a wooden spoon, stir in the flour and mustard until completely incorporated. Continue to cook, stirring, for 1 minute. Stir in the chicken stock until well blended and smooth. Then stir in milk, salt, and pepper. Bring the mixture to a boil; lower the heat and simmer, uncovered, for 5 minutes. Stir in the cream, lemon juice, and soy sauce. Very gently stir in the crabmeat, being careful not to break up the lumps. Heat the mixture, uncovered, over medium heat until piping hot *but not* boiling.

Meanwhile, prepare the buttered crumbs as follows: Melt the butter in a medium-sized frying pan over medium-high heat. Stir in the crumbs and cook, stirring constantly, for 2 minutes. Lower the heat to medium and continue cooking for 2 to 3 minutes longer, or until the crumbs are crisp and golden brown. Remove the pan from the heat and continue to stir for 30 seconds. Set the crumbs aside.

When the soup is heated through, ladle it into bowls or cups and garnish each serving with a sprinkling of buttered crumbs. Serve immediately.

Makes 5 to 6 servings.

Maryland Crab Soup

Except in Creole and Cajun cookery and in the San Francisco dish Cioppino, crab is not often featured in spicy soups in the United States. This deliciously peppery Maryland specialty is an obvious exception. Numerous versions of the dish can be found throughout the Chesapeake Bay area, particularly in seafood restaurants.

Like the gumbos typical in Deep South cookery, this soup derives its rich, distinctive character from the melding of a varied assortment of ingredients—smoked pork, beef stock, vegetables, a unique blend of herbs and spices, and, of course, the shellfish. And, as in the case of gumbos, the resulting dish is robust, earthy, and very satisfying.

The soup is normally quite piquant, if not downright hot. If you prefer a milder, less zippy version, try adding only half the red pepper called for in the recipe.

5 ¼-inch-thick slices slab bacon (rind removed), finely diced
1½ tablespoons butter or margarine
2 large onions, finely chopped
2 large carrots, finely chopped
2 large celery stalks, finely chopped
½ cup finely chopped fresh parsley leaves
6 cups beef stock, brown stock, or beef broth
2½ cups simple crab stock (see Note), fish stock (see page 301), or bottled clam juice
4 large bay leaves
1 teaspoon powdered mustard
½ teaspoon celery salt
½ teaspoon paprika
Generous ½ teaspoon celery seeds
Generous ¼ teaspoon black pepper, preferably freshly ground
¼ teaspoon crushed dried red (hot) pepper, or to taste
Scant ⅛ teaspoon ground cloves
Generous pinch of ground mace
Generous pinch of ground ginger
3 cups peeled and finely diced boiling potatoes
2½ cups canned Italian-style (plum) tomatoes, including juice
12 to 16 ounces fresh backfin crabmeat, carefully picked over to remove any cartilage or shell
Salt to taste

In a 3- to 4-quart pot, fry the bacon over medium-high heat until cooked through and almost crisp. Add the butter, onions, carrots, celery, and parsley and cook, stirring, for 4 to 5 minutes, or until the onions are limp. Add the beef stock, crab stock, bay leaves, mustard, celery salt, paprika, celery seeds, black pepper, dried red pepper, cloves, mace, and ginger. Bring the mixture to a boil; then lower the heat and simmer, covered, for 10 minutes. Stir the potatoes into the pot and continue simmering, covered, for 20 to 25 minutes longer, or until they are very tender.

Add the tomatoes, breaking them up with a spoon. Gently stir in the crabmeat, being careful not to break up the lumps. Gently heat the soup over medium heat, covered, for about 10 minutes longer, or until it is piping hot. Add salt to taste. Discard the bay leaves before serving.

Makes 6 to 8 servings.

Note: In Maryland, Crab Soup is often enriched with a stock made using the shells left over from a meal of steamed blue crabs. If you are preparing this soup with crabmeat picked right from the shells, or happen to have steamed crab shells on hand, prepare a simple crab stock by rinsing the shells thoroughly, then combining them with 3½ to 4 cups of water (or enough to almost cover them) and simmering, uncovered, for 30 to 40 minutes, or until the liquid is reduced to about 2½ cups. Strain the liquid through a *very fine sieve,* or a fairly fine sieve lined with a lightly dampened triple thickness of cheesecloth. The simple crab stock can be used immediately or frozen for later use.

Snow Crab and Shrimp Chowder

2½ tablespoons butter or margarine
¾ cup finely chopped onion
⅓ cup finely sliced green onions (scallions), including
    green tops
2 tablespoons finely chopped celery, including leaves
3 tablespoons all-purpose white flour

¼ teaspoon powdered mustard
1 cup chicken stock or broth
2½ cups whole milk, scalded
4 cups peeled and finely diced potatoes
¼ teaspoon black pepper, preferably freshly ground
3 slices slab bacon (rind removed), finely diced
6 ounces fresh or frozen (thawed) snow crabmeat
8 ounces fresh or frozen (thawed) medium-sized shelled
    shrimp
½ cup light cream or half-and-half
½ to ¾ teaspoon salt
Finely chopped fresh parsley leaves for garnish (optional)

Combine the butter, onions, green onions, and celery in a 3- to 4-quart soup pot. Cook over medium-high heat, stirring, for 4 to 5 minutes, or until the onions are limp. Using a wooden spoon, stir in the flour and mustard until well blended and smooth. Cook, stirring, for 1 minute longer. Add the stock and milk and stir until thoroughly incorporated. Add the potatoes and pepper, and bring the mixture to a simmer. Lower the heat and simmer, covered, for 13 to 15 minutes, or until the potatoes are tender.

Meanwhile, place the bacon in a small frying pan and fry over medium-high heat until cooked through and almost crisp. Transfer the bacon pieces to paper towels to drain briefly; then add them to the pot.

When the potatoes are tender, add the crab, shrimp, cream, and salt and continue cooking for 5 to 6 minutes, or until the shrimp are pink and curled and the chowder is piping hot *but not* boiling. Garnish each serving with a light sprinkling of finely chopped parsley, if desired.

Makes 4 to 6 servings.

Shrimp Bisque

Because the shrimp and their shells are the essential flavor elements in this classic bisque, use only the freshest, cleanest-smelling shrimp available. (Any size will do.) You will need the shells from the entire 1½ pounds, but only 1 cup of the shrimp themselves. Plan to use the rest in another recipe.

> 1½ pounds very fresh unpeeled shrimp (If unavailable, substitute top-quality unpeeled frozen shrimp, thawed.)
> 3 tablespoons olive oil
> 2½ tablespoons butter, divided
> 1 medium-sized onion, chopped
> 1 medium-sized carrot, chopped
> 1 small celery stalk, chopped
> 2 tablespoons brandy
> 3½ tablespoons all-purpose white flour
> 2½ cups beef stock or broth
> 2 cups bottled clam juice
> ½ cup canned tomatoes, including juice, chopped
> ¼ cup dry white wine
> ¼ teaspoon ground thyme
> ¼ teaspoon black pepper, preferably freshly ground
> Generous pinch of ground allspice
> Generous pinch of cayenne pepper
> 1 small bay leaf
> 1 cup light cream
> ⅛ to ¼ teaspoon salt (optional)

Peel the shrimp, reserving the shells in one bowl and 1 cup of the shrimp in another. (The remaining shrimp are not needed for the recipe and can be reserved for another use.) Dice the 1 cup of shrimp; then cover and refrigerate them.

Combine the olive oil and 1 tablespoon of the butter in a large frying pan. Heat over high heat until the butter melts and the mixture is very hot but not smoking. Add the shrimp shells and cook, stirring, until they are heated through and turn red, about 3 to 4 minutes; do not allow the shells to burn. Stir in the onion, carrot, and celery and lower the heat slightly. Continue cooking, stirring, for 4 to 5 minutes, or until the onion is limp. Pour the brandy over the mixture and ignite it. Stir until the flames die out. Using a wooden spoon, stir in the flour until well blended and smooth. Cook, stirring, for 1½ minutes longer. Remove the pan from the heat.

In a large saucepan, combine the stock, clam juice, tomatoes, wine, thyme, black pepper, allspice, cayenne pepper, and the mixture from the frying pan. Stir well and lay the bay leaf on the surface. Bring the mixture to a boil over medium-high heat; then lower the heat and simmer, covered, for 30 minutes. Discard the bay leaf. Strain most of the liquid through a fine sieve into a bowl and reserve it. Put the shells, vegetables, and a small amount of the liquid in a blender. Blend the mixture until completely puréed. Put the purée in a fine sieve over the bowl containing the sieved liquid and press down with a spoon to force through as much of the purée as possible.

In another large saucepan, melt the remaining 1½ tablespoons of butter over medium-high heat. Add the reserved diced shrimp and cook, stirring, for 1 to 2 minutes, or until the pieces turn pink and curl. Strain the reserved sieved purée and liquid through a *very fine sieve* (or a fairly fine sieve lined with a triple thickness of lightly dampened cheesecloth) into the saucepan. Stir in the cream. Add salt, if necessary. Heat the mixture to piping hot *but not* boiling. Garnish the bisque with a sprinkling of chopped fresh chives, if desired.

Makes 4 to 5 servings.

Shrimp and Chicken Gumbo

A bit of work, but worth it. This is good!

Roux

> 3½ tablespoons peanut or vegetable oil
> ⅓ cup all-purpose white flour

Soup

> 2 tablespoons peanut or vegetable oil
> 12 to 13 medium-sized green onions (scallions), including green tops, chopped
> 2 large garlic cloves, minced
> ½ cup coarsely chopped sweet red pepper (If unavailable, substitute sweet green pepper.)
> ½ cup coarsely chopped fresh parsley leaves
> 4½ cups water
> 3 cups chicken stock or broth
> 2 small smoked pork hocks (about 1 pound total weight)
> 3 (bone-in) medium-sized chicken breast halves, skins removed
> 3 large bay leaves
> 2 teaspoons dried thyme leaves
> ¼ teaspoon ground allspice
> ¾ teaspoon Tabasco sauce
> Scant ½ teaspoon black pepper, preferably freshly ground
> Scant ⅛ teaspoon cayenne pepper, or more to taste
> 1½ cups fresh or frozen (thawed) sliced okra (¼-inch-thick pieces)
> ¾ cup ⅛-inch-thick celery slices
> 1½ cups chopped canned Italian-style (plum) tomatoes, including juice
> 1½ cups loose-pack frozen corn kernels
> ¾ pound fresh or frozen medium-sized peeled shrimp
> ½ teaspoon salt, or to taste

To Serve

> 3 to 4 cups hot cooked long-grain white rice

To prepare the roux, combine the 3½ tablespoons oil and the flour in a heavy 1- to 2-quart saucepan over medium heat. Stir the mixture until well blended and smooth. Heat the mixture, stirring, until it begins to bubble. Lower the heat to very low and cook, stirring occasionally, for 25 to 30 minutes, or until the roux is a rich nut-brown color; be careful not to burn it. (The cooking time can be reduced by cooking over slightly higher heat. In this case, stir the roux almost constantly and watch carefully to prevent burning.) The roux can be prepared at the same time as the soup or, if desired, made ahead and stored in the refrigerator for up to 3 or 4 days. (It does not have to be reheated before it is used.)

In a 3- to 4-quart pot or saucepan, combine the 2 tablespoons of oil, the green onions, garlic, sweet pepper, and parsley over medium-high heat. Cook the vegetables, stirring, for 4 to 5 minutes, or until the green onions are limp. Add the water, stock, pork hocks, chicken, and bay leaves. Bring the mixture to a boil; then lower the heat and simmer, covered, for 18 minutes.

Remove the chicken with a slotted spoon and set it aside; when the meat is cool enough to handle, remove it from the bones and cut it into bite-sized pieces.

Stir the thyme, allspice, Tabasco sauce, black pepper, and cayenne pepper into the pot and continue simmering, covered, for 15 minutes longer. Stir in the okra, celery, and roux and simmer, covered, for 20 minutes.

Add the tomatoes and corn and simmer for 7 to 8 minutes longer, or until the corn is cooked through. Stir in the chicken pieces, shrimp, and salt and continue cooking just until the shrimp turn pink and curl slightly. Discard the bay leaves and pork hocks and serve immediately.

To serve, place a spoonful or two of rice in each soup plate. Ladle the gumbo over the rice. The gumbo is also good reheated. However, to prevent the shrimp from overcooking and becoming tough, heat only until piping hot.

Makes 7 to 8 servings.

Scallop Chowder

A delicately flavored, thoroughly comforting white chowder that lets the nutty-sweet taste of the scallops come through.

¾ pound fresh bay scallops, *or* ¾ pound fresh sea scallops, quartered
3½ tablespoons butter or margarine
1 small onion, coarsely chopped
1 cup fish stock (see page 301) or bottled clam juice
1 small boiling potato, peeled and finely chopped
3 cups whole milk, scalded
4 medium-sized boiling potatoes, peeled and cut into ¼-inch cubes
¾ to 1 teaspoon salt, or to taste
Scant ½ teaspoon white pepper, preferably freshly ground
Pinch of ground nutmeg
1½ cups light cream or half-and-half
Small pats of butter for garnish

Rinse and thoroughly drain the scallops. Melt the butter in a 3- to 4-quart saucepan over medium-high heat. Add the scallops and cook, stirring, for about 1½ minutes, or until they become opaque and are just cooked through. Using a slotted spoon, immediately transfer the scallops to a bowl; set them aside. Add the onion to the saucepan and cook, stirring, for 3 to 4 minutes, or until it is limp. Stir in the stock and the finely chopped potato and bring the mixture to a boil over medium-high heat. Lower the heat and simmer, uncovered, for 10 to 12 minutes, or until the potato is tender and some of the stock has evaporated from the pan; stir occasionally to prevent the potato from sticking to the bottom of the pan. Transfer the mixture to a food processor or blender. Process or blend until completely puréed and smooth.

Return the purée to the saucepan, along with the scalded milk, cubed potatoes, salt, pepper, and nutmeg. Bring the mixture to a simmer over medium-high heat. Lower the heat and cook the potatoes, uncovered, stirring occasionally, for 12 to 15 minutes, or until they are tender but still hold their shape. Stir the cream into the chowder. Also stir in the reserved scallops and any juice they have exuded. Heat the chowder, uncovered, over medium heat until it is piping hot *but not* boiling.

Ladle the soup into bowls. Garnish each serving with a small pat of butter.

Makes 5 to 6 servings.

Mussel Soup with Saffron

Brightly colored bits of vegetables and a buttery, golden broth bring out the flavor of the mussels in this delicious, eye-catching soup. It should be served immediately, as the colors and flavors begin to fade if the soup is allowed to stand.

Note that "cultured" mussels are recommended in the recipe. These are commercially raised in off-bottom beds, which means they tend to be less sandy and, thus, easier to clean than uncultured mussels. However, uncultured mussels can certainly be used, and some people even prefer them, feeling they are more flavorful. We ourselves haven't noticed much difference.

Also note that if mussels are purchased in plastic bags they may tend to "gape" from being out of water. "Gapers" should close up during the cleaning and soaking process. Discard any that don't.

2¼ to 2½ pounds fresh mussels, preferably cultured
1¼ cups bottled clam juice
¾ cup water
⅔ cup dry white wine
2½ tablespoons butter or margarine
⅓ cup 1½-inch-long julienne (matchstick strips) carrot
⅓ cup 1½-inch-long julienne (matchstick strips) celery
1 large garlic clove, minced
4 green onions (scallions), including green tops, cut into matchstick strips

1 large bay leaf
Pinch of saffron threads, very finely crumbled
Generous pinch of cayenne pepper
2 tablespoons peeled, seeded, and finely chopped fresh
    tomato *or* chopped canned tomato
About 2 teaspoons finely chopped fresh chives for garnish
About 2 teaspoons finely chopped fresh parsley leaves for
    garnish

To clean the mussels, first rinse and drain them. Discard any shells that are extremely lightweight (or empty!). Wash the mussels in several changes of cool water, scrubbing the shells with a vegetable brush. Continue changing the water until it is clear and no traces of sand remain. Debeard the mussels (trim off any dark, root-like debris) using kitchen shears or a sharp knife. Soak the mussels in cool water to just cover for at least 2 or 3 hours or overnight to allow them to disgorge any sand. Turn out the mussels into a colander. Discard any "gapers" that have not closed up. Rinse the mussels well under cool running water and set them aside to drain.

Combine the clam juice, water, and wine in a large pot. Cover and bring the mixture to a boil over high heat. Add the mussels and cover the pot. Steam the mussels, shaking the pot several times to redistribute them, for 4 to 5 minutes, or until the shells open. Remove the pot from the heat and let stand for a few minutes. Carefully drain off and reserve the mussel cooking liquid. Discard any mussels that remain unopened.

In a 2- to 3-quart saucepan, melt the butter over medium-high heat. Stir in the carrot, celery, and garlic and cook, stirring, for 5 minutes. Add the green onions and cook, stirring, for 2 minutes longer. Using a slotted spoon, transfer the vegetables from the saucepan and reserve them in a small bowl. Using a fine sieve lined with several thicknesses of dampened cheesecloth, strain the mussel cooking liquid into the saucepan previously used. Add the bay leaf, saffron, and cayenne pepper. Bring the mixture to a boil over medium-high heat. Then lower the heat and simmer, covered, for 10 minutes.

Meanwhile, remove the mussels from their shells and reserve them in a bowl.

Return the reserved vegetables to the pan and continue simmering for 2 to 3 minutes, or until the carrots are just cooked through. Stir in the tomatoes and reserved mussels and simmer for 2 minutes longer. Discard the bay leaf.

Divide the mussels among 4 or 5 soup plates or shallow bowls. (White bowls show off the contrasting colors of the soup ingredients and broth particularly nicely.) Sprinkle each bowl with some chives and parsley and serve immediately.

Makes 4 to 5 servings.

Oyster, Sausage, and Ham Gumbo

An old Cajun cook once told us a good gumbo *had* to have bay leaf, garlic, and thyme. We think she's right.

The smoky-rich flavors of sausage, ham, and oysters meld with the herbs to yield wonderful results in this distinctive, earthy soup.

Roux

¼ cup peanut or vegetable oil
⅓ cup all-purpose white flour

Soup

2 tablespoons peanut or vegetable oil
½ pound spicy Creole smoked sausages or Polish kielbasa, split lengthwise and cut into thin half-slices
2½ cups finely chopped onions
2 garlic cloves, minced
1 small celery stalk, including leaves, finely chopped
⅓ cup chopped fresh parsley leaves
2 tablespoons diced sweet red pepper
4¼ cups water
2 cups chicken stock or broth
2 small smoked pork hocks (about 1¼ pounds total weight)
2 large bay leaves
1 teaspoon dried thyme leaves

Scant ⅛ teaspoon ground cloves
½ teaspoon black pepper, preferably freshly ground
½ teaspoon white pepper, preferably freshly ground
Scant ⅛ teaspoon cayenne pepper, or more to taste
¾ cup fresh or frozen (thawed) sliced okra (¼-inch-thick pieces)
¾ cup finely diced lean country ham
2 to 3 green onions (scallions), including green tops, thinly sliced
12 to 16 ounces shucked fresh oysters, including their liquor (about 1½ to 2 cups)
Salt to taste

To Serve

2 to 3 cups hot cooked long-grain white rice

To prepare the roux, combine the ¼ cup oil and the flour in a heavy 1- to 2-quart saucepan over medium heat. Stir the mixture until well blended and smooth and cook, stirring, until it begins to bubble. Lower the heat to very low and cook the mixture, stirring occasionally, for 25 to 30 minutes, or until the roux is a rich nut-brown color; be careful it does not burn. (The cooking time can be reduced by cooking the mixture over slightly higher heat. In this case, stir the roux constantly and watch carefully to prevent burning.) The roux can be prepared at the same time as the soup or, if desired, made ahead and stored in the refrigerator for up to 3 or 4 days.

In a 3- to 4-quart saucepan or pot over high heat, heat the 2 tablespoons of oil until hot but not smoking. Add the sausage pieces and cook, stirring constantly, for 7 to 9 minutes, or until they are nicely browned; if necessary, lower the heat to prevent the sausage from burning. Using a slotted spoon, remove the sausage from the pot and reserve in a small bowl. Lower the heat to medium-high and add the onions, garlic, celery, parsley, and sweet pepper to the pot. Cook the vegetables, stirring, for 4 to 5 minutes, or until the onions are limp. Add the water, stock, pork hocks, bay leaves, thyme, cloves, black pepper, white pepper, and cayenne pepper and bring the mixture to a boil. Then lower the heat and simmer, covered, for 1 hour and 5 to 10 minutes longer. Stir in the okra, ham, reserved sausage pieces, and roux and simmer, covered, for 20 minutes longer. Skim off and discard any fat on the surface of the soup, using a large shallow spoon. Add the sliced green onions and simmer for 5 minutes more. Stir in the oysters and their liquor and continue to simmer for 3 to 4 minutes, or until the oysters begin to shrink slightly and curl at the edges. Taste the gumbo and add a little salt, if necessary. (Often, the pork hocks and ham add enough salt so that no extra is required.) Discard the bay leaves and pork hocks and serve the gumbo.

To serve, place a spoonful or two of rice in each soup plate or bowl. Ladle the gumbo over the rice.

The gumbo may also be made ahead and reheated. Rewarm it over medium-high heat until piping hot; do not cook the gumbo further or the oysters may toughen.

Makes 5 to 6 servings.

5

VEGETABLE SOUPS

The vegetables available in American markets are among the cook's greatest resources when it comes to soupmaking. Singly and in nearly endless combinations, these gifts of the earth lend delightful flavor, texture, and color to soup. As an added bonus, they are rich in many of the vitamins and other nutrients vital for good health. Moreover, depending on their individual character and use in a recipe, they can introduce a variety of appealing notes into menus.

For example, our Tyrolean Cabbage Soup and Cream of Potato-Bacon Soup offer gratifying robustness. The Carrot-Orange Soup with Ginger and Tomato Bisque with Thyme and Bacon provide zip and zing. And the creamy Cauliflower-Leek Potage and Potato and Parsley Soup add wonderful subtlety and richness.

This chapter showcases recipes based primarily on vegetables. However, since vegetables are so useful in soupmaking, they are also featured in numerous other recipes in this book. In particular, check out the Cold Soups, Vegetarian Soups, Quick Soups, and Elegant Soups chapters for possibilities.

Cream of Asparagus Soup

1 pound fresh asparagus
3 cups chicken stock or broth
1 tablespoon butter or margarine
1 small onion, finely chopped
1 small garlic clove, minced
⅛ teaspoon white pepper, preferably freshly ground
2 tablespoons cornstarch
¼ cup cold water
1 cup light cream or half-and-half
¼ teaspoon salt (optional)

Wash the asparagus well. Break off and discard the woody ends. In a medium-sized saucepan, combine the asparagus spears and stock. Bring the mixture to a boil over high heat. Cover and simmer for 4 to 5 minutes, or until the asparagus tips are tender. With a slotted spoon, remove the spears from the stock. Cut the tips from the spears and reserve them in a small bowl. Cut the spears crosswise into 1-inch pieces and reserve them separately.

In another medium-sized saucepan, melt the butter over medium heat. Add the onion and garlic and cook, stirring frequently, for about 4 minutes, or until the onion is tender. Add the asparagus stem pieces to the pan with the onion and butter, along with the reserved stock and the pepper. Simmer, covered, for about 7 to 9 minutes, or until the asparagus is very tender.

Cool the mixture slightly. In batches, blend in a blender on low speed for 10 seconds. Then raise the speed to high, and purée until completely smooth. Transfer the purée to the pan in which the whole asparagus was cooked and bring it to a simmer.

In a small bowl, stir together the cornstarch and water until well blended. Add the cornstarch-water mixture to the purée and cook, stirring, until the mixture thickens, about 1 or 2 minutes. Lower the heat, stir in the cream, and mix well. Then add the salt and asparagus tips. Cook the soup for an additional 2 to 3 minutes, stirring frequently, *but do not boil.*

Makes about 4 servings.

Cream of Broccoli-Potato Soup

Broccoli-Potato Soup can also be served cold as a Broccoli Vichyssoise. To serve cold, stir in 1 tablespoon of lemon juice, increase the salt slightly to taste, cover, and chill for about 5 hours. Garnish individual servings with lemon slices.

4 medium-sized leeks (about 1¾ pounds total weight)
2 tablespoons butter or margarine
3½ cups chicken stock or broth
1½ pounds boiling potatoes, peeled and diced (3½ cups diced potatoes)
4 cups broccoli flowerets
¾ teaspoon salt, or to taste
¼ teaspoon white pepper, preferably freshly ground

1¼ cups light cream or half-and-half
1 to 2 teaspoons finely chopped fresh chives for garnish (optional)

Trim off and discard the root end of the leeks and all but about 1 inch of the green parts. Peel off and discard one or two layers of tough outer leaves. Then, beginning at the green end, slice down about 1 inch into the leeks. Put the leeks into a colander. Wash them thoroughly under cool running water, separating the leaves to remove any grit trapped among them. Wash again to remove all traces of grit. Then set them aside until well drained. Cut the leeks crosswise into ½-inch pieces.

In a Dutch oven or very large saucepan, melt the butter over medium heat. Add the leeks and cook, stirring frequently, for about 10 minutes, or until the leeks are tender but not browned. If they begin to brown, lower the heat slightly. Add the stock, potatoes, broccoli, salt, and pepper. Bring to a boil over high heat. Lower the heat, cover, and simmer for about 11 to 14 minutes, or until the potatoes and broccoli are tender. Remove the pot from the heat and let cool slightly. In batches, purée the mixture in a blender on low speed for 10 seconds. Then raise the speed to high and purée until completely smooth. Return the purée to the pot in which it was cooked. Add the cream and stir to mix well. Cook for an additional 4 to 5 minutes, *but do not boil*.

Serve in medium-sized bowls. Garnish individual servings with a sprinkling of chopped chives, if desired.

Makes 6 to 8 servings.

Stonebridge House Herbed Cabbage Soup

The idea of featuring cabbage in a creamy soup may seem unusual, but, as this recipe proves, the results can be quite good. This is surprisingly delicate, yet delightful tasting; the chives and tarragon complement the cabbage well.

¼ cup butter or margarine

¼ cup finely chopped fresh chives (If unavailable, substitute finely chopped green onions [scallions], including tops.)

1 large onion, finely chopped

3½ tablespoons all-purpose white flour

3¾ cups chicken stock or broth

6 cups finely shredded green cabbage (about ¾ pound)

1 small boiling potato, peeled and finely chopped

1 tablespoon finely chopped fresh tarragon, *or* ¾ teaspoon dried tarragon leaves

¼ teaspoon white pepper, preferably freshly ground

1 cup whole milk

¾ cup light cream or half-and-half

½ to 1 teaspoon salt

About 1 teaspoon finely chopped fresh chives for garnish (optional)

Melt the butter in a large saucepan over medium heat. Add the ¼ cup of chives and the onion and cook, stirring, for 8 to 9 minutes, or until the onion is tender and golden, but not browned. (Lower the heat, if necessary, to prevent the onion from browning.) Using a wooden spoon, stir in the flour until thoroughly incorporated and smooth. Cook, stirring, for 1 minute longer. Stir in the stock until well blended and smooth. Add the cabbage, potato, tarragon, and pepper. Bring the mixture to a boil. Then lower the heat and simmer, covered, for about 18 to 20 minutes, or until the potato and cabbage are tender; stir occasionally to prevent the potato from sticking to the bottom of the pan.

Let the mixture cool slightly. Scoop about 2 cups of the cabbage mixture and transfer it to a blender. Blend on low speed for 10 seconds. Then raise the speed to high and blend until completely puréed. Return the purée to the pan and add the milk, cream, and salt. Heat the soup over medium-high heat, stirring occasionally, until piping hot *but not* boiling. Garnish each serving with a pinch or two of finely chopped fresh chives, if desired.

Makes 4 to 5 servings.

Tyrolean Cabbage Soup

This is a thick, hearty, meal-in-a-bowl peasant soup with a rich and savory flavor.

3½ tablespoons butter or margarine
2 medium-sized onions, finely chopped
2 large celery stalks, finely chopped
1 cup peeled and chopped rutabaga
1 medium-sized carrot, finely diced
1 large tart apple, peeled and chopped
¼ cup finely chopped fresh parsley leaves
¼ cup all-purpose white flour
5 cups beef stock, brown stock, or broth
7 cups very coarsely shredded green cabbage (about ¾
   pound), divided
1 small smoked pork hock (about ½ pound)
3 tablespoons pearl barley
1 large bay leaf
1½ teaspoons paprika, preferably imported sweet paprika
½ teaspoon dried thyme leaves
3 tablespoons tomato paste
¾ cup water
¼ teaspoon caraway seeds
¼ teaspoon black pepper, preferably freshly ground
About 1 tablespoon finely chopped fresh chives or parsley
   leaves for garnish

Melt the butter in a very large soup pot over medium-high heat. Add the onions, celery, rutabaga, carrot, apple, and parsley and cook, stirring, for 6 to 7 minutes, or until the onions are limp. Using a wooden spoon, stir in the flour until well blended and smooth. Cook, stirring, for 1 minute. Stir in the stock until it is thoroughly incorporated and the mixture is smooth. Add 3 cups of the cabbage, the pork hock, barley, bay leaf, paprika, and thyme to the pot. Bring the mixture to a boil; then lower the heat and simmer, covered, for 1 hour.

Stir together the tomato paste and water in a cup and add

the mixture to the soup, along with the remaining 4 cups of cabbage, the caraway seeds, and pepper. Continue simmering, covered, for 15 to 20 minutes longer, or until the cabbage is cooked through but is still slightly crisp. Discard the bay leaf and pork hock. Sprinkle the soup with finely chopped fresh chives and serve.

Makes 5 to 7 servings.

Hearty Cabbage Soup Mediterranean Style

A robust and homey cabbage soup in which herbs, savory vegetables, and a bit of smoked pork bring out the fine flavor. This is perfect warmer-upper on a chilly day!

3 thick slices slab bacon (rind removed), finely diced
3 medium-sized onions, finely chopped
1 large carrot, finely chopped
1 large celery stalk, finely chopped
1 large garlic clove, minced
5 cups chicken stock or broth
1 cup water
1 small smoked pork hock (about ¾ pound)
1 large bay leaf
¼ cup dry lentils, sorted and washed
2 teaspoons dried basil leaves
Generous ½ teaspoon dried thyme leaves
Generous ½ teaspoon dried oregano leaves
¼ teaspoon black pepper, preferably freshly ground
Pinch of dried crushed red (hot) pepper
6 cups very coarsely shredded green cabbage (about ¾ pound)
1 16-ounce can tomatoes, including juice
⅛ to ¼ teaspoon salt (optional)

In a 3- to 4-quart pot, fry the bacon over medium-high

heat until well browned and crisp. Using a slotted spoon, re-move the bacon from the pot and reserve it in a small bowl. Add the onions, carrot, celery, and garlic to the bacon fat and cook the vegetables, stirring, for 5 to 6 minutes, or until the onions are limp. Add the stock, water, pork hock, and bay leaf to the pot. Bring the mixture to a boil; then lower the heat and simmer, covered, for 30 minutes. Stir in the lentils, basil, thyme, oregano, black pepper, and dried red pepper and con-tinue simmering, covered, for 40 to 45 minutes longer. Stir in the cabbage and reserved diced bacon and simmer, covered, for 15 minutes more. Stir in the tomatoes, breaking them up with a spoon. Gently simmer the soup for about 5 minutes longer, or until the cabbage is cooked through but not limp. Discard the bay leaf and pork hock. Add the salt, if needed.

Makes 7 to 8 servings.

Cream of Carrot Soup

3 tablespoons butter or margarine
1 large onion, chopped
1 small celery stalk, finely chopped
1 pound carrots, chopped (about 8 medium sized)
2½ cups beef stock or broth
2 tablespoons long-grain white rice
1 tablespoon tomato paste
1 teaspoon lemon juice, preferably fresh
¼ teaspoon white pepper, preferably freshly ground
Scant ⅛ teaspoon ground allspice
1¼ cups whole milk
1 cup light cream or half-and-half
½ to ¾ teaspoon salt, or to taste
Finely chopped fresh chives for garnish (optional)

Melt the butter in a large saucepan over medium-high heat. Add the onion and celery and cook, stirring, for 4 to 5 minutes, or until the onion is limp. Stir in the carrots and cook, stirring, for about 2 minutes longer. Stir in the stock, rice, tomato paste, lemon juice, pepper, and allspice. Bring the mixture to a boil. Then lower the heat and simmer, covered, for about 20 minutes, or until the carrots and rice are tender; stir occasionally to prevent the rice from sticking to the bottom of the pan. Remove the pan from the heat and cool slightly.

In batches, transfer the mixture to a blender. Blend on low speed for 10 seconds. Raise the speed to high and blend until completely puréed and smooth. Wash out the saucepan previously used and return the purée to it. Stir in the milk, cream, and salt. Heat the soup over medium-high heat, stirring occasionally, until piping hot *but not* boiling. Garnish each serving with a pinch of finely chopped fresh chives, if desired.

Makes 4 to 6 servings.

Carrot-Orange Soup with Ginger

3 tablespoons butter or margarine
1 large onion, coarsely chopped
¾ pound fresh carrots, peeled and coarsely chopped (about 5 large)
1½ tablespoons all-purpose white flour
2¼ cups chicken stock or broth
1 cup orange juice
1 tablespoon packed light or dark brown sugar
1 3-inch-long cinnamon stick
Scant ¾ teaspoon peeled and minced gingerroot
⅛ teaspoon white pepper, preferably freshly ground
¾ cup light cream or half-and-half
½ teaspoon salt, or more to taste
Finely chopped fresh chives for garnish (optional)

Melt the butter in a large saucepan over medium-high heat. Add the onion and carrots and cook, stirring, for 4 to 5 minutes, or until the onion is limp. Using a wooden spoon, stir in the flour until thoroughly incorporated and smooth. Cook, stirring, for 1½ minutes longer. Stir in the stock until well blended and smooth. Add the orange juice, brown sugar, cinnamon stick, gingerroot, and pepper. Bring the mixture to a boil. Then lower the heat and simmer, covered, for about 15 minutes, or until the carrots are tender. Discard the cinnamon stick. Set the pot aside to cool slightly.

In batches, transfer the mixture to a blender. Blend on low speed for 10 seconds. Raise the speed to high and blend until completely puréed. Rinse out the pan previously used and return the purée to it. Add the cream and salt. Heat the soup over medium-high heat, stirring occasionally, until piping hot *but not* boiling. Garnish each serving with a pinch of finely chopped fresh chives, if desired.

Makes 4 to 6 servings.

Cauliflower-Leek Potage

The subtle flavors of leeks and cauliflower complement one another nicely in this smooth and savory soup.

    3 to 4 medium-sized leeks, white parts only
    2 tablespoons butter or margarine
    1 small garlic clove, minced
    3½ cups chicken stock or broth, divided
    4¼ to 4½ cups sliced cauliflower flowerets
    ¾ cup peeled and diced boiling potato
    ½ teaspoon salt, or more to taste
    ⅛ teaspoon white pepper, preferably freshly ground
    ½ cup commercial sour cream
    Paprika for garnish

Thoroughly rinse the leek white parts under cool running water. Slice them in half lengthwise. Wash them under cool running water, separating the layers to remove all traces of grit trapped among them. Coarsely chop the leeks. Transfer them to a colander. Rinse well and set them aside until well drained.

Melt the butter in a 2- to 3-quart saucepan over medium-high heat. Add the garlic and leeks and cook, stirring, for 4 to

5 minutes, or until the leeks are limp. Stir in 1¼ cups of the stock, the cauliflower, potato, salt, and pepper. Bring the mixture to a boil; then lower the heat and cover the pan. Simmer, stirring occasionally, for 10 to 12 minutes, or until the potato is just cooked through. Remove the pan from the heat and cool slightly.

Transfer the mixture to a blender or food processor and purée until completely smooth. (Add a little of the reserved stock if the mixture is too thick to purée easily in the blender.) Rinse out the saucepan previously used and return the purée to it.

Combine the sour cream and an additional ½ cup of the stock in the processor or blender and process or blend until smooth. Add the sour cream mixture and the remaining 1¾ cups of stock to the pan. Reheat the soup over medium heat, stirring frequently, until it is piping hot *but not* boiling. Garnish individual servings with a light sprinkling of paprika.

The soup may be served reheated, if desired. Carefully rewarm it over medium heat, stirring occasionally; *do not* allow it to come to a boil, or it will curdle.

Makes 5 to 6 servings.

Creamy Celery-Leek Soup

The rich flavor and texture of this soup is achieved without using cream.

    2 pounds small tender leeks (about 6 or 7)
    2 tablespoons butter or margarine
    4 large celery stalks, including leaves
    1 medium-sized garlic clove
    1¾ cups chicken broth or stock
    ¼ cup dry white wine
    1 large potato, peeled and cut into ¾-inch cubes
    ¼ teaspoon white pepper, preferably freshly ground
    ¼ teaspoon dried thyme leaves

½ teaspoon powdered mustard
2½ cups whole milk
¼ teaspoon celery salt
¼ teaspoon dried dillweed
¼ teaspoon salt

Trim off and discard the root end of the leeks and all but about 1 inch of the green parts. Peel off one or two layers of tough outer leaves and discard them. Then, beginning at the green end, slice down about 1 inch into the leeks. Put the leeks into a colander. Wash them thoroughly under cool running water, separating the leaves to remove any grit among them. Wash again to remove all traces of grit. Then set them aside until well drained. Cut the leeks crosswise into ½-inch pieces.

In a large saucepan or Dutch oven, melt the butter over medium-high heat. Add the leeks, celery, and garlic. Cook, stirring often, for about 10 minutes, or until the leeks are very tender but not browned. Add the broth, wine, potato, pepper, and thyme. Bring to a boil. Cover, lower the heat, and simmer for about 25 minutes, or until the vegetables are very tender. Remove the pan from the heat. Stir in the mustard. Set the mixture aside to cool slightly.

In batches, transfer the mixture to a blender. Blend on low speed for 10 seconds. Then raise the speed to high and blend for 2 to 3 minutes, or until completely puréed. If the purée is not completely smooth, strain it through a fine sieve.

Return the purée to the pan. Add the milk, celery salt, dill, and salt and stir well to combine. Cook, *without boiling*, for an additional 10 minutes. Stir frequently.

Makes 4 to 6 servings.

Corn and Potato Chowder

3 tablespoons butter or margarine
2 medium-sized onions, finely chopped
1 large garlic clove, minced
1 large celery stalk, diced

3 cups chicken stock or broth

3 cups whole milk, divided

5½ to 6 cups ¾-inch peeled boiling potato cubes (about 4 medium-sized potatoes)

5 cups loose-pack frozen corn kernels (1 24-ounce package)

1½ teaspoons dried basil leaves

¾ teaspoon powdered mustard

½ teaspoon dried marjoram leaves

¼ teaspoon celery salt

Generous ¼ teaspoon black pepper, or to taste, preferably freshly ground

¾ teaspoon salt

½ cup instant nonfat dry milk powder

In a large heavy pot over medium-high heat, melt the butter. Add the onions, garlic, and celery. Cook, stirring frequently, for about 5 minutes, or until the onions are soft. Add the stock, 2 cups of the whole milk, potatoes, corn, basil, mustard, marjoram, celery salt, pepper, and salt. Bring to a boil. Lower the heat, cover, and simmer for about 15 to 17 minutes, or until the potatoes are tender. Remove about 2 cups of the mixture from the pot and transfer it to a blender or food processor. Add the remaining 1 cup milk and the dry milk powder. Blend or process until the vegetables are puréed—about 20 to 30 seconds. Return the purée to the pot and stir to blend.

Bring the soup to a boil over medium-high heat, stirring frequently. Then lower the heat and simmer for 5 to 8 minutes, stirring occasionally, or until the flavors are well blended.

Makes 7 to 9 servings.

√ Cucumber and Potato Soup

2 tablespoons butter or margarine

1 medium-sized onion, finely chopped

1 medium-sized garlic clove, minced

3 cups chicken stock or broth
½ teaspoon dried dillweed
¼ teaspoon white pepper, preferably freshly ground
3 cups peeled and diced boiling potatoes (about 1 pound)
2 large cucumbers, peeled, seeded, and finely diced
2 teaspoons minced fresh chives, *or* 1 teaspoon dried chives
¼ teaspoon salt, or to taste
¾ cup light cream or half-and-half

In a medium-sized saucepan, melt the butter over medium heat. Add the onion and garlic and cook, stirring frequently, for about 4 to 5 minutes, or until the onion is tender. Add the stock, dillweed, pepper, and potatoes; bring the mixture to a boil over medium-high heat. Cover, lower the heat, and simmer for about 10 to 12 minutes, or until the potatoes are tender.

Cool the mixture slightly. In batches, blend in a blender on low speed for 10 seconds. Then raise the speed to high and purée until completely smooth. Return the purée to the pan. Stir in the cucumbers, chives, and salt. Simmer for an additional 10 to 15 minutes, stirring frequently. Add the cream and heat to piping hot *but do not boil.*

Makes 4 to 5 servings.

Cream of Green Bean Soup

2½ tablespoons butter or margarine
7 to 8 medium-sized green onions (scallions), including
    green tops, coarsely chopped
2 tablespoons all-purpose white flour
2½ cups chicken stock or broth
½ pound green beans, cut into 1-inch lengths
2 tablespoons chopped fresh chives, *or* 1 tablespoon dried
    chopped chives
⅛ teaspoon dried tarragon leaves
Pinch of ground savory
1½ teaspoons soy sauce

1 medium-sized boiling potato, peeled and coarsely chopped
⅛ teaspoon white pepper, preferably freshly ground
½ to ¾ cup light cream or half-and-half (approximately)
Finely chopped fresh chives for garnish (optional)

Melt the butter in a large saucepan over medium-high heat. Add the green onions and cook, stirring, for 4 to 5 minutes, or until they are limp. Using a wooden spoon, stir in the flour until thoroughly incorporated and smooth. Cook, stirring, for 1 minute longer. Stir in the stock until well blended and smooth. Add the green beans, chives, tarragon, savory, soy sauce, potato, and pepper. Bring the mixture to a boil. Then lower the heat and simmer, covered, for about 20 to 25 minutes, or until the potato and beans are very tender; stir occasionally to prevent the potato from sticking to the bottom of the pan. Cool the mixture slightly.

In batches, transfer the mixture to a blender and blend on low speed for 10 seconds. Raise the speed to high and blend until completely puréed and smooth. Return the purée to the pan and add ½ cup of the cream. Add a bit more cream if a thinner soup is desired. Heat the soup over medium-high heat, stirring occasionally, until piping hot *but not* boiling. Garnish each serving with a pinch of finely chopped fresh chives, if desired.

Makes 4 to 5 servings.

Cream of Leek Soup

Although Cream of Leek Soup is simple to make and looks quite unpretentious, the flavor is wonderfully rich and satisfying.

2½ pounds leeks (about 6 or 7 medium sized)
5 cups chicken stock or broth
1 large carrot, coarsely sliced
1 large celery stalk, coarsely sliced
1 small turnip, peeled and coarsely chopped (optional)

1 small bay leaf
1 teaspoon whole black peppercorns, coarsely crushed
⅛ teaspoon dried thyme leaves
3½ tablespoons butter or margarine
⅓ cup all-purpose white flour
1 cup light cream or half-and-half
⅛ to ¼ teaspoon salt (optional)
Paprika for garnish (optional)

Trim off and discard the root and the top 3 inches of the leeks. Pull off and discard the tough outer two or three leaves. Wash the leeks under cool running water; then drain them. Cut off the leek green parts and coarsely chop them. (Reserve the leek white parts separately.) Transfer the chopped green parts to a colander. Very thoroughly rinse them under cool running water to remove all traces of grit. Drain well.

Combine the chopped leek green parts, stock, carrot, celery, turnip (if used), bay leaf, peppercorns, and thyme in a large saucepan or small soup pot. Bring the mixture to a boil over medium-high heat. Lower the heat and simmer, covered, for 30 minutes.

Meanwhile, working from the top end, slice the leek white parts lengthwise into quarters. Rinse them well under cool running water, separating the layers to remove any grit trapped among them. Then cut the lengths crosswise into ½-inch pieces. Transfer the pieces to a colander and thoroughly rinse them under cool running water to remove any remaining traces of grit. Set them aside to drain.

When the leek greens have cooked for 30 minutes, strain the stock through a fine sieve and reserve it in a bowl; discard the leek green parts and vegetables. Rinse out and dry the saucepan. Add the butter to the pan and melt it over medium-high heat. Add the leek white parts and cook, stirring, for 8 to 9 minutes, or until they are tender but not browned. If necessary, lower the heat slightly to prevent them from browning. Using a wooden spoon, stir in the flour until thoroughly incorporated. Cook, stirring constantly, for 1 minute longer. Return the reserved stock to the pan, stirring until the mixture is well blended and smooth. Bring the mixture to a boil; then lower the heat and continue simmering, covered, for 12 to 15 minutes, or until the leeks are tender but not mushy. Stir in the cream and heat the soup for about 5 minutes, or until piping hot; *do not* allow it to boil. Stir in the salt, if needed. Garnish the soup with a light sprinkling of paprika, if desired.

Makes 4 to 5 servings.

Hearty Mushroom and Wild Rice Soup

This rustic, full-bodied soup goes well in a menu featuring game.

2½ tablespoons butter or margarine
1¾ cups chopped onions
2 tablespoons chopped fresh parsley leaves
6 cups chicken stock or broth
3 tablespoons wild rice
3¼ cups coarsely sliced fresh mushrooms (about ⅔ pound)
2 tablespoons long-grain white rice
¼ teaspoon dried thyme leaves
¼ teaspoon dried marjoram leaves
Generous ¼ teaspoon black pepper, preferably freshly ground
1½ tablespoons tomato paste
¼ cup water
1 to 2 teaspoons finely chopped fresh chives for garnish (optional)

Combine the butter, onions, and parsley in a 3- to 4-quart pot. Cook over medium-high heat, stirring, for 7 to 9 minutes, or until the onions are tender and golden but not browned; if necessary, lower the heat to prevent the onions from browning. Stir in the stock and wild rice and bring the mixture to a boil. Lower the heat and gently simmer the mixture, covered, for about 30 minutes.

Stir in the mushrooms, white rice, thyme, marjoram, and pepper. Continue simmering the mixture, covered, for 15 to 20 minutes longer, or until the wild rice is cooked through but still slightly chewy.

In a small bowl, stir together the tomato paste and water until well blended; then add the mixture to the soup. Continue simmering for about 10 minutes longer. Sprinkle the soup with chopped chives, if desired.

Makes 5 to 7 servings.

Red Onion and Apple Soup with Curry

An unusual, mild, and fragrant onion soup enlivened with curry and bits of sweet-tart apple. It's perfect for a first course or light lunch, particularly on an autumn day.

1¼ pounds sweet red onions (about 3 to 4 medium sized)
¼ cup butter or margarine
6½ cups chicken stock or broth
2 cups coarsely grated or shredded peeled tart cooking apples, divided
¼ cup coarsely grated or shredded carrot
¼ cup coarsely grated or shredded peeled rutabaga or turnip
2 tablespoons finely chopped celery
1 large bay leaf
½ teaspoon mild curry powder
¼ teaspoon black pepper, preferably freshly ground
⅛ teaspoon dried thyme leaves
⅛ teaspoon ground cinnamon
Generous pinch of ground allspice
¼ teaspoon salt, or to taste
Chutney for garnish (optional)

Trim and peel the onions. Halve them lengthwise; then cut them crosswise into thin half-slices. Separate the half-slices into half-rings. Melt the butter in a large soup pot over medium-high heat. Add all *except* 1 cup of the onion half-rings and lower the heat to medium. Cook, stirring, for 8 to 9 minutes, or until the onions are limp and translucent but not browned. Stir in the stock, 1 cup of the apples, the carrot, rutabaga, celery, bay leaf, curry powder, pepper, thyme, cinnamon, allspice, and salt. Bring the mixture to a boil; then lower the heat and cover the pot. Simmer the mixture for 20 minutes. Stir in the reserved 1 cup of onion and continue simmering, covered, for 5 minutes. Stir in the reserved 1 cup of apple and simmer for 5 minutes longer. Discard the bay leaf. If desired, garnish individual bowls with a teaspoon of chutney.

Makes 5 to 6 servings.

Creamy Parsnip and Carrot Soup

Parsnips and carrots have a natural affinity for one another, and this recipe takes advantage of that fact. This is a very smooth and gratifying soup.

1½ teaspoons sugar
2 tablespoons water
1¾ cups beef stock or broth
½ pound parsnips, peeled and cut into ¼-inch-thick slices (2 to 3 medium sized)
½ pound carrots, peeled and cut into ⅛-inch-thick slices (4 to 5 medium sized)
1 small onion, coarsely chopped
1 1-inch-square piece salt pork or slab bacon (rind removed)
¼ teaspoon white pepper, preferably freshly ground
Generous pinch of ground nutmeg
Generous pinch of ground ginger
1½ tablespoons butter or margarine
1½ tablespoons all-purpose white flour
1¾ cups whole milk
½ cup light cream or half-and-half

¼ teaspoon salt, or to taste
About 1 teaspoon finely chopped fresh parsley leaves for
  garnish (optional)

Combine the sugar and water in a heavy 2½- to 3-quart saucepan over high heat. Heat the mixture, stirring, until it comes to a boil. Lower the heat slightly and continue boiling for about 2 minutes, or until most of the liquid evaporates and the mixture bubbles and turns amber-colored (caramelizes); watch carefully so it doesn't burn. Immediately remove the pan from the heat and stir the stock into it. Stir the caramel-stock mixture until the caramel dissolves and is thoroughly incorporated.

Add the parsnips, carrots, onion, salt pork, pepper, nutmeg, and ginger to the pan and return it to the heat. Bring the mixture to a boil; then lower the heat and simmer, covered, for 10 to 12 minutes, or until the carrots are tender. Discard the piece of salt pork. Cool the mixture slightly.

Transfer the mixture to a blender. Blend on low speed for 10 seconds. Then raise the speed to high and blend until completely puréed and smooth. Rinse out and dry the saucepan previously used. Add the butter and melt it over medium-high heat. Using a wooden spoon, stir in the flour until completely blended and smooth. Cook, stirring, for 1½ minutes. Stirring vigorously, add the milk until well mixed and smooth. Stir in the purée. Bring the soup to a boil over medium-high heat. Lower the heat and gently simmer for 2 to 3 minutes. Stir in the cream and salt. Reheat the soup, stirring occasionally, until piping hot *but not* boiling.

Ladle the soup into individual bowls. Garnish each serving with a pinch or two of finely chopped fresh parsley, if desired.

Makes 5 to 6 servings.

Roasted Sweet Red Pepper Soup

4 medium-sized sweet red peppers
3 tablespoons butter or margarine
2 medium-sized onions, coarsely chopped

1 large garlic clove, minced
1¾ cups canned Italian-style (plum) tomatoes
1 cup beef stock, brown stock, or broth
¼ cup dry red wine
½ teaspoon salt, or more to taste
⅛ teaspoon white pepper, preferably freshly ground
Pinch of cayenne pepper
¼ cup light cream or half-and-half, scalded
1 tablespoon finely chopped fresh chives for garnish (optional)

Roast the peppers in a preheated broiler, about 5 to 6 inches from the heating element. Turn the peppers frequently so they will cook evenly and continue roasting until they are charred on the outside but not burned through, about 15 to 20 minutes. Transfer the peppers to a plastic bag and close it tightly. Set aside for about 10 to 12 minutes, or until the peppers are cool enough to handle and their skins peel off easily.

Meanwhile, melt the butter in a large saucepan over medium-high heat. Add the onions and garlic and cook, stirring, for 6 to 7 minutes, or until the onions are soft. Transfer the onion-garlic mixture to a blender. Add the tomatoes to the blender. Rinse out and dry the saucepan previously used.

When the peppers are cool enough to handle, trim off the stems. Peel off and discard their skins. Remove and discard the seeds and any coarse interior ribs. Cut enough pepper into 1-inch-long julienne (matchstick strips) to equal about ¾ cup. Set 1 tablespoon of the strips aside for the soup garnish. Put the remainder in the saucepan previously used. Very coarsely chop the remainder of the red peppers and add them to the blender. Blend on low speed for 10 seconds. Then raise the speed to high and blend until the mixture is thoroughly puréed and smooth.

Return the purée to the saucepan with the pepper strips. Stir in the stock, wine, salt, white pepper, and cayenne pepper. Bring the mixture to a boil over medium-high heat. Cover the pan, lower the heat, and simmer, covered, for 12 to 15 minutes, or until the pepper strips are tender but not mushy. Stir in the cream and heat for about 2 minutes longer, or until piping hot *but not* boiling.

Garnish each serving of the soup with a light sprinkling of chopped fresh chives, if desired. Lay two reserved strips of red pepper across one another on each serving.

Makes 4 to 5 servings.

Cream of Potato-Bacon Soup

Ham stock and bacon flavor this peasant-style soup.

> 6 cups ham stock (see page 300)
> 3 pounds boiling potatoes, peeled and cut into ¾-inch cubes (about 6¾ cups)
> ¼ teaspoon dried thyme leaves
> ⅛ teaspoon black pepper, preferably freshly ground
> 1 cup light cream or half-and-half
> ¼ to ½ teaspoon salt, or to taste
> 6 bacon strips, fried crisp, drained on paper towels, and finely crumbled
> 1 to 2 teaspoons chopped fresh parsley leaves for garnish (optional)

In a Dutch oven or large saucepan, combine the ham stock, potatoes, thyme, and pepper. Cover and bring to a boil over high heat. Lower the heat and simmer, covered, stirring occasionally, for about 15 minutes, or until the potatoes are very tender. Remove the pan from the heat and let cool slightly.

In batches, if necessary, purée about half of the potato-stock mixture in a blender or food processor until completely smooth. Return the purée to the pot. Stir in the cream. Taste the soup and add salt as needed. Reheat the soup over medium heat, stirring. *Do not boil.* Stir in the crumbled bacon and cook for 2 minutes longer.

Ladle the soup into bowls and sprinkle the individual servings with chopped parsley, if desired.

Makes 5 to 6 servings.

Potato-Kale Soup

Fresh kale adds a subtle and pleasing flavor to this creamy soup.

    3 tablespoons butter or margarine
    1 very large garlic clove, minced
    2 medium-sized onions, finely chopped
    3 pounds boiling potatoes, peeled and cut into ¾-inch
       cubes (about 6¾ cups)
    3 cups beef bouillon, reconstituted from beef bouillon
       cubes
    4½ cups whole milk
    6 cups tender kale leaves, midribs removed, and coarsely
       chopped
    ¾ teaspoon salt, or to taste
    Generous ¼ teaspoon black pepper, preferably freshly
       ground

In a Dutch oven or soup pot, combine the butter, garlic, and onions. Cook, stirring frequently, over medium-high heat for 5 to 6 minutes, or until the onions are tender. Add the potatoes, bouillon, and milk. Bring to a boil. Cover, lower the heat, and simmer for about 15 minutes, or until the potatoes are very tender. Remove the pot from the heat and cool slightly.

In a food processor or blender, in batches, if necessary, purée about half of the milk-potato mixture and return it to the pot. Return the pot to the heat. Add the kale, salt, and pepper. Bring the soup to a boil and lower the heat. Simmer for an additional 12 to 15 minutes, or until the kale is just tender.

Makes 6 to 7 servings.

Potato and Parsley Soup

4 medium-sized leeks (about 1 pound total weight)
2 tablespoons butter or margarine
1 large garlic clove, minced
1½ pounds boiling potatoes, peeled and cut into ¾-inch
   cubes (about 3½ cups)
3 cups chicken stock or broth
½ teaspoon dried basil leaves
½ teaspoon salt
¼ teaspoon white pepper, preferably freshly ground
2 cups whole milk
1 cup finely chopped fresh parsley leaves
1 cup light cream
4 to 5 small parsley sprigs for garnish (optional)

Trim off and discard the root end of the leeks and all but about 1 inch of the green parts. Peel off and discard one or two layers of tough outer leaves. Then, beginning at the green end, slice down about 1 inch into the leeks. Put the leeks into a colander. Wash them thoroughly under cool running water, separating the layers to remove any grit trapped among them; wash again to remove all traces of grit. Then set them aside until well drained. Cut the leeks into ½-inch pieces.

In a small Dutch oven or large saucepan over medium-high heat, melt the butter. Add the leeks and garlic and cook, stirring, for about 5 minutes. Add the potatoes, stock, basil, salt, and pepper. Bring the mixture to a boil; then lower the heat and simmer, stirring occasionally, for about 20 minutes or until the potatoes are very tender. Remove the pot from the heat. Let cool slightly.

In batches, if necessary, transfer half of the mixture to a blender. Blend on low speed for 10 seconds. Then raise the speed to high and blend until the mixture is thoroughly puréed and smooth.

Return the mixture to the pan, and add the milk and parsley. Simmer, stirring occasionally, for an additional 20 minutes, or until the parsley is tender. Stir in the cream. Heat for an additional 1 to 2 minutes *but do not* allow the soup to boil. Garnish individual servings with parsley sprigs, if desired.

Makes 4 to 5 servings.

Spiced Pumpkin Soup

1½ tablespoons butter or margarine
1 medium-sized onion, coarsely chopped
1 tablespoon all-purpose white flour
2¾ cups chicken stock or broth, divided
Generous ½ teaspoon peeled and finely minced gingerroot
⅛ teaspoon ground mace
Pinch of ground allspice
1 1-pound can solid-pack pumpkin (not pumpkin pie filling)
¼ to ½ teaspoon salt, or to taste
⅔ cup light cream or half-and-half
Small pats of butter for garnish (optional)

Melt the butter in a large saucepan over medium-high heat. Add the onion and cook, stirring, for 6 to 7 minutes, or until the onion is very tender but not browned. Stir in the flour until thoroughly incorporated, using a large wooden spoon. Cook, stirring, for 1½ minutes longer. Gradually add 1 cup of the stock, stirring vigorously until the mixture is well blended and smooth. Add the gingerroot, mace, and allspice. Cover and continue cooking, stirring occasionally, for 5 minutes. Cool the mixture slightly.

Transfer the mixture to a blender or food processor and purée until completely smooth. Return the purée to the saucepan. Stir in the remaining stock, the pumpkin, salt, and cream until well blended and smooth. Heat the soup, covered, for 4 to 5 minutes longer, or until it is piping hot *but not* boiling; stir occasionally.

Ladle the soup into small warm bowls. Float a small pat of butter in the center of each serving, if desired.

Makes 4 to 5 servings.

Butternut Harvest Bisque

A smooth and mellow soup featuring a subtle blending of the fruits of autumn and winter squash. If Winesap apples are unavailable, substitute Rome Beauty or another tart, flavorful variety.

1 large butternut squash (about 3 pounds)
2½ tablespoons butter or margarine
1 large onion, coarsely chopped
2 large Winesap apples, peeled, cored, and cut into eighths
1 large, ripe Bartlett pear, peeled, cored, and cut into large chunks
3½ cups chicken stock or broth
¼ teaspoon dried thyme leaves
⅛ teaspoon dried crumbled sage leaves
½ teaspoon whole black peppercorns
1 large bay leaf
⅛ teaspoon ground nutmeg
½ cup light cream (or a little more)
3 tablespoons cream sherry (optional)
½ to 1 teaspoon salt, or to taste
⅛ teaspoon white pepper, preferably freshly ground
About 2 tablespoons very finely chopped walnuts for garnish (optional)

Using a sharp knife, cut the squash in half lengthwise. Scoop out the seeds and stringy pulp from the seed cavity and discard them. Remove the rind with a vegetable peeler. Cut the squash flesh into 1½-inch chunks.

Melt the butter in a 4-quart or larger pot over medium-high heat. Add the onion and cook, stirring, for 3 to 4 minutes, or until it is limp. Stir in the squash, apples, pear, and stock. Combine the thyme, sage, peppercorns, and bay leaf in a small muslin or cheesecloth bag (or a metal tea ball). Tie the bag closed with string. Add it to the pot along with the nutmeg. Bring the mixture to a boil over medium-high heat. Lower the heat and simmer the mixture, covered, for about 20 minutes, or until the squash is tender when pierced with a fork. Remove the spice bag from the pot. Set the pot aside to cool slightly.

In three or four batches, transfer the mixture to a blender. Blend on low speed for 10 seconds. Then raise the speed to medium and blend until completely puréed and smooth. Rinse out the pot and return the purée to it. Stir in the ½ cup cream and the sherry (if used). (The soup should be fairly thin, but still have some body. If necessary, thin it slightly with a bit more cream.) Add the salt and pepper. Reheat the bisque to piping hot *but not* boiling. Sprinkle each serving with about a teaspoon of chopped walnuts, if desired.

Makes 7 to 8 servings.

Spinach-Garlic Soup

2 tablespoons butter or margarine
1 medium-sized onion, finely chopped
1 large celery stalk, including leaves, diced
2 very large garlic cloves, minced
3 cups peeled, coarsely diced boiling potatoes (about 1¼ pounds)
3½ cups chicken stock or broth
3 cups whole milk
1½ teaspoons dried basil leaves
2 to 3 drops Tabasco sauce
1 tablespoon cornstarch
¼ cup cold water
¼ teaspoon celery salt
⅛ teaspoon ground nutmeg
¼ teaspoon salt
¼ teaspoon black pepper, preferably freshly ground
10 to 11 cups well-washed fresh spinach leaves, coarse stems removed, torn into 1-inch pieces (about 1¼ to 1⅓ pounds)

In a large saucepan over medium-high heat, combine

the butter, onion, celery, and garlic. Cook, stirring frequently, for about 5 to 6 minutes, or until the onion is tender. Add the potatoes, stock, milk, basil, and Tabasco sauce. Bring to a boil. Cover, lower the heat, and cook for about 15 minutes, stirring occasionally, until the potatoes are very tender.

Remove the pot from the heat and let cool slightly. In a food processor or a blender, in batches, if necessary, purée the milk-potato mixture and return it to the pot.

Meanwhile, stir together the cornstarch and water. Return the pot to the heat. Add the cornstarch-water mixture to the soup and stir to mix well. Stir in the celery salt, nutmeg, salt, and pepper. Then stir in the spinach. At first the spinach leaves will overflow the pot, but they will reduce in volume quickly. Bring the soup to a boil over medium-high heat, stirring frequently. Lower the heat and simmer the soup, uncovered, for an additional 4 to 5 minutes, or until the spinach is just tender.

Makes 5 to 6 servings.

Swiss Chard Soup

It's a shame Swiss chard isn't more readily available, since it has a delicious flavor and isn't difficult to prepare. In this recipe, the mild, leafy vegetable is teamed up with potatoes and a bit of Monterey Jack cheese.

Either regular green-leafed chard or red Swiss chard can be used in the following recipe. Although each of the varieties yields a different look, they taste about the same. In case you're wondering, red chard does not bleed much or turn the soup red!

    1 pound Swiss chard, including stalks
    2 tablespoons butter or margarine
    1 large onion, finely chopped
    1 garlic clove, minced
    5 tablespoons all-purpose white flour, divided
    4 cups chicken stock or broth
    2 cups peeled and diced boiling potatoes

¼ to ½ teaspoon salt

Generous ¼ teaspoon white pepper, preferably freshly
    ground

Pinch of ground nutmeg

2 cups whole or lowfat milk

½ cup grated or shredded Monterey Jack cheese (about 2
    ounces)

Wash and thoroughly drain the Swiss chard. With a
sharp knife, cut the green part of the leaves away from the
stalks. Cut the stalks crosswise into ¼-inch lengths; set them
aside. Cut or tear the leafy portions into bite-sized pieces and
set them aside separately.

Melt the butter in a 4- to 5-quart pot over medium-high heat.
Add the onion, garlic, and chard stalk pieces and cook, stirring,
for 4 to 5 minutes, or until the onion is limp. Using a wooden
spoon, stir 3½ tablespoons of the flour into the vegetable mixture until well blended and smooth. Cook, stirring, for 1½
minutes. Stir in the stock until thoroughly incorporated and
smooth. Bring the mixture to a boil, stirring occasionally. Add
the potatoes, salt, pepper, and nutmeg and let the mixture
return to a boil. Lower the heat and simmer the mixture, covered, for 10 minutes.

Stir in the chard leafy pieces, and continue cooking, covered,
for 10 minutes longer, or until the potatoes are tender but not
soft. Stir in the milk.

Toss the cheese with the remaining 1½ tablespoons of flour
until the cheese is evenly coated. Stir the coated cheese into the
pot. Heat the mixture, stirring occasionally, for 6 to 8 minutes
longer, or until the cheese melts and the soup is piping hot *but
not boiling*.

The soup may be served reheated, if desired. Reheat over
low heat and do not allow the mixture to come to a boil.

Makes 5 to 6 servings.

Cream of Tomato Soup

A classic tomato soup with rich, mellow taste and pleasant smoothness.

4 large, fully ripe, vine-ripened tomatoes (about 2 pounds total weight)
3 tablespoons butter or margarine
1 large onion, coarsely chopped
1 medium-sized celery stalk, finely chopped
2 tablespoons finely chopped carrot
2½ tablespoons all-purpose white flour
1 cup chicken stock or broth
1 6-ounce can tomato paste
1½ teaspoons sugar
½ teaspoon celery salt
¼ to ½ teaspoon white pepper, preferably freshly ground
½ teaspoon dried basil leaves
Generous ¼ teaspoon ground thyme
Scant ⅛ teaspoon ground cinnamon
1½ cups whole milk, scalded
1 cup light cream or half-and-half, scalded
½ to ¾ teaspoon salt, or to taste
Croutons for garnish, optional (see page 315)

Core the tomatoes. Plunge them into boiling water for 10 seconds; then immediately transfer them to a colander to drain and cool. When they are cool enough to handle, slip off and discard their skins. Quarter the tomatoes and gently squeeze them to expel their seeds. Using a small spoon, scrape away any other seeds clinging to the tomato cavities. Chop the tomatoes and set them aside.

Combine the butter, onion, celery, and carrot in a 2- to 3-quart saucepan. Cook over medium-high heat, stirring, for 4 to 5 minutes, or until the onion is limp. Using a large wooden spoon, stir in the flour until well blended and smooth. Cook, stirring, for 1 minute. Vigorously stir in the stock until well blended and smooth. Then stir in the tomato paste, chopped tomatoes, sugar, celery salt, pepper, basil, thyme, and cinnamon. Bring the mixture to a boil, stirring. Then lower the heat and gently simmer, covered, for 18 to 20 minutes, or until the celery and carrots are soft; stir occasionally to prevent the mixture from sticking to the bottom of the pan.

Remove the pan from the heat and let the mixture cool slightly. Then, in batches, if necessary, transfer it to a blender or food processor and blend or process until completely puréed and smooth. (If a food processor is used, process for 2½ to 3 minutes to be sure the mixture is thoroughly puréed and smooth.) Return the purée to the pan and add the milk and cream. Add the salt. Heat the soup over medium-high heat, stirring occasionally, until piping hot *but not* boiling. Garnish the soup with croutons, if desired.

Makes 4 to 5 servings.

Tomato Bisque with Thyme and Bacon

A rich, full-bodied tomato bisque that always wins compliments. If a food processor is available for chopping the vegetables, the bisque is also rather easy to prepare.

2 bacon strips
2 tablespoons butter or margarine
1 large onion, finely chopped
2 medium-sized celery stalks, finely chopped
¼ cup finely chopped carrot
2 large garlic cloves, minced
3 tablespoons all-purpose white flour
1 35-ounce can imported Italian (plum) tomatoes, including juice, coarsely puréed in a blender or food processor
1½ cups beef stock, brown stock, or broth
1 6-ounce can tomato paste
1 large bay leaf
¾ teaspoon ground thyme

¼ teaspoon black pepper, preferably freshly ground
⅛ teaspoon ground allspice
Pinch of ground mace
Pinch of celery seeds
2 to 3 drops Tabasco sauce
1¾ cups whole or lowfat milk
2 cups light cream or half-and-half
1 to 1¼ teaspoons salt
About 1 tablespoon finely chopped fresh chives for garnish
Garlic croutons for garnish, optional (see page 315)

In a large saucepan over medium-high heat, fry the bacon until cooked through and almost crisp. Remove the bacon strips from the pan and drain them on a double thickness of paper towels. Add the butter, onion, celery, carrot, and garlic to the pan. Cook, stirring, for 5 to 6 minutes, or until the onion is limp. Add the flour to the pan, stirring until well blended. Continue cooking, stirring constantly, for 2 minutes longer. Stir in the puréed tomatoes, stock, tomato paste, bay leaf, thyme, pepper, allspice, mace, celery seeds, Tabasco, and milk until well blended. Bring the mixture to a boil, stirring occasionally. Lower the heat and simmer, covered, for 30 minutes, stirring occasionally to prevent the mixture from sticking to the bottom of the pan.

Very finely crumble the reserved bacon strips and add them to the pan. Continue simmering, covered, for 5 to 10 minutes more, or until the vegetables are very tender. Discard the bay leaf. Stir in the cream and the salt. Heat the bisque over medium-high heat, stirring occasionally, or until it is piping hot. *Do not* allow it to come to a full boil or it may curdle. Garnish the soup with chopped fresh chives. Individual servings may also be garnished with a tablespoon or two of garlic croutons, if desired.

The bisque is excellent reheated. Bring it to a gentle simmer over medium-high heat, stirring occasionally. Add the garnishes at serving time.

Makes 7 to 8 servings.

√ Creamy Turnip Soup

This mild and creamy soup will appeal to any turnip lover and may even win over some folks who think they don't care for this economical root vegetable.

For best results, use only small firm turnips in the recipe; the large and mature or flabby ones sometimes taste a bit strong and are often too tough and fibrous to yield the velvety texture desired.

> 3 tablespoons butter or margarine
> 1 large onion, coarsely chopped
> 1½ tablespoons chopped celery
> 4½ cups chicken stock or broth
> 1½ pounds peeled small, tender turnips (about 7 to 8 2¼-inch-diameter or less)
> 2 medium-sized boiling potatoes, peeled and coarsely chopped
> ¼ teaspoon white pepper, preferably freshly ground
> Generous pinch of ground nutmeg
> 1 cup light cream or half-and-half
> ¼ to ½ teaspoon salt, or to taste
> About 1 teaspoon finely chopped fresh parsley leaves (optional)

Combine the butter, onion, and celery in a large saucepan. Cook over medium-high heat, stirring, for 4 to 5 minutes, or until the onion is limp. Stir in the stock, turnips, potatoes, pepper, and nutmeg. Bring the mixture to a boil; then lower the heat and simmer, covered, for about 25 minutes, or until the turnips are very tender. Remove the pan from the heat and let it cool slightly.

In batches, transfer the mixture to a blender. Blend on low speed for 10 seconds. Then raise the speed to high and blend for 2 to 3 minutes, or until completely puréed. If the purée looks and tastes very smooth at this point, return it to the saucepan previously used. If small bits of turnip remain, strain the mixture through a fine sieve into the saucepan. Add the cream and salt and heat the soup over medium-high heat, stirring occasionally, until it is piping hot *but not* boiling. Garnish each serving with a pinch of chopped parsley, if desired.

Makes 5 to 7 servings.

Garden Gold Bisque

Sweet potatoes and tomatoes may seem an unlikely combination, but their marriage yields very pleasing results. The bisque is a rich, golden-orange color.

¼ cup butter or margarine
2 medium-sized onions, coarsely chopped
3 medium-sized sweet potatoes (about 2¼ pounds total weight), peeled and cut into ¾-inch chunks
6 cups beef stock, brown stock, or broth
2 medium-sized fully ripe, vine-ripened tomatoes, peeled, seeded, and coarsely chopped
Scant ¼ teaspoon white pepper, preferably freshly ground
¼ cup orange juice
¼ to ½ teaspoon salt, or to taste
1 to 1⅓ cups water, approximately
Small pats of butter for garnish (optional)

Melt the butter in a large saucepan over medium-high heat. Add the onions and cook, stirring, for 4 to 5 minutes, or until they are limp. Add the sweet potatoes and stock and bring the mixture to a boil. Lower the heat and simmer, covered, for 25 to 30 minutes, or until the sweet potatoes are very tender. Stir in the tomatoes and pepper. Set the mixture aside to cool slightly.

In batches, transfer the mixture to a blender. Blend on low speed for 10 seconds. Then raise the speed to high and blend until completely puréed and smooth. Rinse out the pan previously used and return the purée to it. Stir in the orange juice, salt, and 1 cup water. If the soup seems too thick, thin it with more water until the desired consistency is obtained. Heat the soup over medium-high heat, stirring occasionally, until piping hot. If desired, garnish the servings by floating a small pat of butter in the center of each.

Makes 5 to 7 servings.

Italian Garden Soup

A light and colorful soup showcasing an appealing blend of "Italian" vegetables and herbs.

2 tablespoons olive oil
2 tablespoons butter or margarine
1 medium-sized onion, finely chopped
2 large celery stalks, cut into 1-inch-long julienne (matchstick strips)
2 garlic cloves, minced
5 cups chicken stock or broth
1 cup water
1 cup canned white cannellini or Great Northern beans, well drained
3 medium-sized carrots, cut into 1-inch-long julienne (matchstick strips)
1 small bay leaf
¾ teaspoon dried basil leaves
Generous ¼ teaspoon dried marjoram leaves
Generous ⅛ teaspoon dried oregano leaves
Pinch of dried thyme leaves
¼ teaspoon white pepper, preferably freshly ground
½ cup 1-inch-long julienne strips zucchini
½ cup 1-inch-long julienne strips yellow squash
2 medium-sized fresh plum tomatoes, peeled, seeded, and cut into 1¼-inch-long julienne (If unavailable, substitute 2 small regular tomatoes.)
2 tablespoons coarsely chopped fresh chives (If unavailable, substitute finely chopped fresh parsley leaves.)
Grated Parmesan cheese for garnish

Combine the oil and butter in a very large saucepan or small soup pot over medium-high heat. Heat until the butter melts. Add the onion, celery, and garlic to the pan and cook, stirring, for 3 to 4 minutes, or until the onion is limp. Add the stock, water, beans, carrots, bay leaf, basil, marjoram, oregano, thyme, and pepper. Bring the mixture to a boil; then lower the heat and simmer, covered, for 15 minutes.

Add the zucchini and yellow squash, and simmer for 6 to 8 minutes longer, or until all the vegetables are tender. Stir in the tomatoes and chives and heat the soup for 3 to 4 minutes longer. Discard the bay leaf.

Pass a small bowl of grated Parmesan at the table so diners can sprinkle some over their soup.

Makes 5 to 6 servings.

Creamy Country Garden Soup

A savory bouquet of garden vegetables gives this creamy soup its appealing taste.

3 tablespoons butter or margarine
1 large onion, finely chopped
2 tablespoons finely chopped celery
1 large garlic clove, minced
2 medium-sized carrots, finely diced
1 cup coarsely chopped cauliflower flowerets
¾ cup coarsely chopped broccoli flowerets
½ cup fresh ¾-inch green bean pieces
4½ cups chicken stock or broth
1½ cups peeled and finely diced potato cubes
Scant ¼ teaspoon white pepper, preferably freshly ground
Generous pinch of dried thyme leaves
1 cup light cream or half-and-half
1 cup packed fresh spinach leaves, well washed and stems
  removed

1 large peeled and finely chopped fresh tomato, *or* 2 drained and finely chopped canned tomatoes

⅛ to ¼ teaspoon salt, or to taste

Melt the butter in a large saucepan or small pot over medium heat. Add the onion, celery, garlic, and carrots and cook, stirring, for 8 to 9 minutes, or until the onion is tender and golden, but not browned. Stir in the cauliflower, broccoli, and green bean pieces and cook, stirring, for 4 minutes longer. Stir in the stock, potato, pepper, and thyme. Bring the mixture to a boil. Then lower the heat and simmer, covered, for about 15 to 18 minutes, or until the potato, green beans, and carrots are tender; stir occasionally to prevent the potato from sticking to the bottom of the pan. Set the pan aside to cool slightly.

Scoop up about 2 cups of the vegetables and a little broth and transfer them to a blender. Blend on low speed for 10 seconds. Then raise the speed to high and blend until completely puréed. Return the purée to the pan.

Combine the cream and the spinach in the blender. Blend for 5 to 8 seconds, or until the spinach is just chopped, but small flecks remain. Add the cream-spinach mixture to the pan. Stir in the chopped tomato and the salt. Heat the soup over medium-high heat for 4 to 5 minutes, or until piping hot *but not* boiling.

Makes 5 to 6 servings.

6

BEAN AND
GRAIN SOUPS

M any of the heartiest and most satisfying soups we know are rich with the tastes and textures of grains, beans, and other legumes. Some of these, like Split Pea and Ham Soup, are old favorites we enjoyed as youngsters. Others, like Savory Brown Rice and Lentil Soup, and Lima Bean and Barley Soup, are products of our own creative cookery.

These full-bodied dishes are easy on the budget because only small amounts of meat are used for flavoring. And don't worry about their calorie content. Beans and grains are high in complex carbohydrates and low in fat. That means they fill you up without filling you out.

Incidentally, while we usually recommend that beans be covered with water, brought to a boil, and soaked for an hour before cooking, this procedure isn't absolutely necessary. Soaking makes beans more digestible and helps them cook more evenly, but if you're in a hurry, you can omit the step. Depending on the variety, the beans will need to simmer 15 to 30 minutes longer than if they had been soaked. And they should be stirred several times to help ensure even cooking.

Eastern European–Style Beef and Bean Soup

> 4 to 4½ pounds beef soup bones, preferably marrow bones, sawed into 2-inch lengths
> 8 cups water
> 1¼ pounds stew beef, trimmed of all fat and cut into ½-inch cubes
> 2 bay leaves
> 2 large celery stalks, including leaves, thinly sliced
> 1 large carrot, thinly sliced
> 1 large onion, thinly sliced
> 2 large garlic cloves, minced
> 1 cup dry Great Northern beans, sorted and washed
> 1 16-ounce can tomatoes, including juice
> 1 8-ounce can tomato sauce
> 1 tablespoon sugar
> 1 teaspoon Dijon-style mustard

½ teaspoon dried basil leaves
½ teaspoon chili powder
½ teaspoon dried thyme leaves
½ teaspoon paprika
2 to 3 drops Tabasco sauce
¾ teaspoon salt, or to taste
¼ teaspoon black pepper, preferably freshly ground

In a colander, rinse the bones under running water and pat them dry with paper towels. In a roasting pan, roast the bones in a 350-degree oven for 1 hour to 1 hour and 15 minutes; stir occasionally. They should be well browned but not sticking to the bottom of the pan.

With a slotted spoon, transfer the browned bones to a large heavy soup pot, discarding the fat in the bottom of the roasting pan. Add 1 cup of the water to the roasting pan. Scrape up any browned bits from the bottom. Transfer the water and bits to the soup pot. Add the stew beef, remaining 7 cups of water, bay leaves, celery, carrot, onion, and garlic. Bring to a boil. Then cover, lower the heat, and simmer, stirring occasionally, for about 1 hour and 30 minutes.

While the bones and vegetables are cooking, put the beans in a medium-sized saucepan and cover them with about 2 inches of cold water. Bring to a boil over high heat and boil, covered, for 2 minutes. Remove the beans from the heat and let them stand for 1 hour, covered. Then drain them well in a colander and discard the soaking water.

Add the beans to the pot. Bring the mixture to a boil over high heat, stirring frequently. Lower the heat and simmer for an additional 1 hour and 20 minutes to 1 hour and 30 minutes, or until the beans are tender. With a slotted spoon, remove the bones and bay leaves from the pot and discard them. The soup may be refrigerated at this point and completed later.

With a large shallow spoon, skim the fat from the top of the soup and discard it. Add the tomatoes, breaking them up very well with a large spoon. Add all the remaining ingredients. Bring the soup to a boil over medium-high heat, stirring frequently. Cover, lower the heat, and cook for 30 minutes, or until the flavors are well blended.

Makes 7 to 8 servings.

Lamb and White Bean Soup

This hearty soup can be made with either lamb shanks or riblets. If shanks are used, for best flavor, the bones should be cracked before cooking. When you buy the shanks, ask the butcher to do this. Lamb riblets give the soup a rich flavor, but they are also quite fatty. If riblets are used, refrigerate the soup overnight so that the fat can be removed easily.

1½ cups dry Great Northern or navy beans, sorted and washed
4 lamb shanks (about 3¾ pounds total weight), or 4 pounds lamb riblets
2 tablespoons vegetable oil
8 cups water
1 large carrot, grated or shredded
2 celery stalks, grated or shredded
1 large onion, very finely chopped
2 large garlic cloves, minced
3 bay leaves
2 beef bouillon cubes
1 medium-sized rutabaga, peeled and cut into ¾-inch cubes (optional)
1 teaspoon dried thyme leaves
1 teaspoon celery salt
1 teaspoon powdered mustard
1 teaspoon dried marjoram leaves
3 to 4 drops Tabasco sauce
¼ teaspoon salt
¼ teaspoon black pepper, preferably freshly ground

Put the beans in a large saucepan and cover with about 2 inches of cold water. Bring to a boil over high heat. Cover, lower the heat, and simmer for 2 minutes. Remove the pot from the heat and let it stand at room temperature for 1 hour. Drain the beans in a colander and discard the soaking water.

In a large heavy soup pot, brown the lamb shanks in the oil over medium to medium-high heat. Turn the shanks with a large fork so that all sides are browned. If necessary, lower the heat to prevent the shanks from burning. Add the water, carrot, celery, onion, garlic, and bay leaves to the pot. Bring to a boil. Cover, lower the heat, and simmer for 30 minutes. Add all the remaining ingredients. Simmer for an additional 1 hour and 30 minutes, or until the beans are very tender and the soup has thickened slightly.

With a large shallow spoon, skim the fat from the top of the soup and discard it. Discard the bay leaves.

With a slotted spoon, remove the bones and meat to a large bowl. Cut the meat into bite-sized pieces and return them to the pot. Cook for an additional 4 to 5 minutes to reheat the meat.

Makes 7 to 8 servings.

Tuscan White Bean Soup

An acquaintance from Tuscany told one of us that the Northern Italians love beans. She said she could eat them every day! This hearty, spicy soup is one of the reasons why. It is very good served with hot, crusty loaves of Italian bread.

2 cups dry cannellini or Great Northern beans, sorted and washed
¼ cup olive oil, divided
2 large onions, chopped
3 garlic cloves, minced
½ cup chopped fresh parsley leaves
1 small celery stalk, finely chopped
6 cups water
2 bay leaves
1 teaspoon dried rosemary leaves, finely crumbled
½ teaspoon dried marjoram leaves
¼ teaspoon dried thyme leaves
¼ teaspoon dried crushed red (hot) pepper, or to taste
½ to ¾ teaspoon salt
½ teaspoon black pepper, preferably freshly ground
1½ cups finely diced lean country ham

2 large carrots, finely diced
1 large celery stalk, finely diced
1½ cups chopped canned Italian-style (plum) tomatoes, including juice
Parmesan cheese for garnish

Cover the beans with about 2 inches of cold water in a 3- to 4-quart pot. Bring the water to a boil over high heat. Boil the beans, uncovered, for 2 minutes. Turn off the heat and cover the beans; let them stand for 1 hour.

Meanwhile, combine 2 tablespoons of the oil with the onions, garlic, parsley, and celery in a large frying pan. Cook the vegetables over medium-high heat, stirring, for 4 to 5 minutes, or until the onions are limp. Set the vegetable mixture aside.

When the beans have soaked for an hour, drain them well and discard the soaking water. In the pot used to soak the beans, combine the water, reserved vegetable mixture, bay leaves, rosemary, marjoram, thyme, dried red pepper, salt, and black pepper. Bring to a boil over medium-high heat. Lower the heat and simmer, covered, for 50 to 55 minutes.

Meanwhile, combine the remaining 2 tablespoons of olive oil, ham, carrots, and celery in the frying pan already used. Cook the mixture over medium-high heat, stirring, for 4 to 5 minutes. Set it aside.

Stir the reserved ham-vegetable mixture into the pot. Continue simmering, covered, for 25 to 30 minutes, or until the vegetables and beans are tender. Remove and discard the bay leaves. Scoop about 2 cups of the beans and liquid from the pot and transfer to a food processor or blender. Process or blend until puréed; return the purée to the pot. Stir in the tomatoes and continue simmering for about 5 minutes longer.

Ladle into large soup plates or bowls. Pass a small bowl of grated Parmesan cheese so diners can garnish their soup with a teaspoon or two of it.

The soup is excellent reheated. However, it does thicken upon standing. If necessary, thin it with a bit of water and reheat over low heat, stirring occasionally to prevent the bottom from scorching.

Makes 5 to 6 servings.

Black Bean Soup

1 pound (2⅓ cups) dry black beans, sorted and washed
1 smoked pork shoulder butt or shoulder roll, quartered
   (about 1¾ pounds)
8 cups water
1 large garlic clove, minced
1 large onion, finely chopped
1 large carrot, thinly sliced
2 large bay leaves
¼ teaspoon dried thyme leaves
¼ teaspoon black pepper, preferably freshly ground
½ to 1 teaspoon salt, or to taste
Chopped hard-boiled egg for garnish (optional)

Put the beans in a Dutch oven or large pot. Cover them with 2 inches of cold water and bring to a boil over high heat. Lower the heat and boil for 2 minutes. Remove the pot from the heat, cover, and let the beans stand for 1 hour.

Drain the beans in a colander and discard the soaking water. Return them to the pot in which they were soaked. Add the pork shoulder butt and water. Cover the mixture and bring it to a boil over high heat. Lower the heat and simmer for 2 hours. Add the garlic, onion, carrot, bay leaves, thyme, pepper, and salt. Simmer for an additional 1 hour, or until the beans have softened and thickened the soup. With a large shallow spoon, skim the fat from the top of the soup and discard it.

Remove the pork from the pot and set it aside until cool enough to handle. Cut the lean portion into bite-sized pieces. Return the lean meat to the pot and cook for an additional 3 to 4 minutes. Discard the bay leaves. Garnish individual servings with chopped hard-boiled egg, if desired.

Makes 7 to 9 servings.

✓Red Bean and Sausage Soup

Smoked beef sausage gives this easy but satisfying soup its zip.

> 8 ounces smoked, firm beef sausage, cut into ¼-inch-thick
>   slices
> 1 large onion, finely chopped
> 1 large garlic clove, minced
> 1 tablespoon vegetable oil
> 3½ cups chicken broth
> 1 15-ounce can tomato sauce
> 2 15-ounce cans red kidney beans, drained
> 1 large celery stalk, diced
> ¼ teaspoon dried thyme leaves
> ¼ teaspoon black pepper, preferably freshly ground

In a Dutch oven or small soup pot, combine the sausage, onion, garlic, and vegetable oil. Cook over medium-high heat, stirring frequently, until the onion begins to brown. Drain off and discard any fat in the bottom of the pot. Add all the remaining ingredients. Bring the soup to a boil over high heat. Lower the heat, cover, and simmer, stirring occasionally, for about 45 minutes, or until the flavors are well blended and the soup has thickened slightly.

Makes 5 to 7 servings.

Split Pea and Ham Soup

A smoked pork picnic shank or butt flavors this traditional soup and provides satisfying chunks of meat as well. A meaty ham bone can be substituted, but a beef bouillon cube may be needed to enhance the flavor. If you prefer the soup without meat, you can use 3 pounds of smoked pork hocks in place of the picnic shank or butt. Discard the pork hocks when the soup has finished cooking.

2 tablespoons vegetable oil
2 large garlic cloves, minced
2 large onions, finely chopped
9 cups water
1 smoked pork picnic shank or butt (about 3½ pounds meat and/or bone)
2 cups (about 1 pound) dry green split peas, sorted and washed
2 bay leaves
2 large carrots, thinly sliced
¼ cup finely chopped fresh parsley leaves
2 large celery stalks, including leaves, thinly sliced
½ teaspoon dried thyme leaves
½ teaspoon dried marjoram leaves
½ teaspoon celery salt
½ teaspoon black pepper, preferably freshly ground
¾ to 2 teaspoons salt, or to taste

In a large soup pot, combine the oil, garlic, and onions. Cook over medium-high heat, stirring frequently, for about 4 to 5 minutes, or until the onions are tender. Add all the remaining ingredients *except* the salt. Bring to a boil over high heat. Cover and lower the heat. Simmer, stirring occasionally, until the split peas have cooked completely and thickened the soup, about 1 hour and 30 minutes to 1 hour and 45 minutes. As the soup thickens, stir more frequently to prevent the split peas from sticking to the bottom of the pot.

Remove the meat and/or bone. While the meat is cooling slightly, skim any fat off the top of the soup with a large shallow spoon and discard it. Then cut the meat into bite-sized pieces and return it to the soup. Add ¾ teaspoon of salt and taste. Add additional salt as needed. Discard the bay leaves. Bring the soup to a boil again. Stir well before serving.

This soup tastes wonderful reheated. However, it must be stirred carefully to prevent the split peas from sticking. If it thickens too much in the refrigerator, thin it with a bit more water during reheating.

Makes 7 to 9 servings.

Bean with Bacon Soup

2 cups dry pinto beans, sorted and washed
8 bacon strips
1 large onion, finely chopped
2 large garlic cloves, minced
7 cups water
1 large carrot, grated or shredded
1 small turnip, peeled and grated or shredded
2 large celery stalks, including leaves, finely chopped
2 large bay leaves
3 beef bouillon cubes
2 teaspoons light molasses
1 teaspoon Dijon-style mustard
½ teaspoon dried thyme leaves
¼ teaspoon celery salt
¼ teaspoon chili powder
¼ teaspoon black pepper, preferably freshly ground
1 8-ounce can tomato sauce

Put the beans in a Dutch oven or soup pot and cover them with about 2 inches of cold water. Bring to a boil over high heat. Cover, lower the heat, and simmer for 2 minutes. Remove the pot from the heat and let it stand at room temperature for 1 hour. Drain the beans and discard the soaking water.

In a large heavy frying pan, cook the bacon over medium-high heat, turning it several times with a large fork. Lower the heat, if necessary, to prevent the bacon from burning or sticking to the bottom of the pan. When the bacon is crisp, remove it from the pan and let it drain on a double thickness of paper towels. (Reserve 2 tablespoons of the fat.) When the bacon is cool enough to handle, finely crumble it. Cover and refrigerate the bacon until needed.

Transfer the reserved bacon fat to the pot in which the beans were soaked. Add the onion and garlic and cook over medium heat, stirring frequently. When the onion is tender, add the water, carrot, turnip, celery, bay leaves, bouillon cubes, molasses, and beans to the pot. Bring the mixture to a boil. Cover, lower the heat, and simmer for 30 minutes, stirring occasionally. Add the mustard, thyme, celery salt, chili powder, and pepper to the pot. Stir to mix well. Continue simmering, stirring occasionally, for 1 hour to 1 hour and 15 minutes, or until the liquid has thickened slightly and the beans are tender. With a large shallow spoon, skim off and discard any fat from the surface of the soup. Add the tomato sauce and the crumbled bacon and simmer for an additional 10 minutes. Discard the bay leaves.

Makes 6 to 7 servings.

Lentil-Barley Soup with Beef

Very hearty and satisfying, yet economical, too.

> 3 tablespoons vegetable oil
> 3 pounds beef neck bones (Choose the meatiest ones available.)
> 3 medium-sized onions, finely chopped
> 3 large celery stalks, finely chopped
> ⅓ cup chopped fresh parsley leaves
> 1 large garlic clove, minced
> 5½ cups beef stock, brown stock, or broth
> 2 cups water
> ¼ cup dry lentils, sorted and washed
> 3½ tablespoons pearl barley
> 3 tablespoons brown rice, washed and drained
> ¾ teaspoon dried thyme leaves
> Pinch of ground allspice
> Generous ¼ teaspoon black pepper, preferably freshly ground
> 2 medium-sized carrots, diced
> 1 large parsnip, peeled and diced
> 1 cup loose-pack frozen corn kernels
> ½ teaspoon salt, or more to taste
> About 1 tablespoon finely chopped fresh parsley leaves for garnish

Heat the oil to hot but not smoking in a large pot over medium-high heat. Add the beef bones and cook, turning frequently, until they are well browned on all sides. Remove the bones from the pot and set them aside. Lower the heat to medium. Add the onions, celery, parsley, and garlic, and cook, stirring, for 4 to 5 minutes, or until the onions are limp. Add the stock and water to the pot. Return the beef bones to the pot. Bring the mixture to a boil over medium-high heat. Lower the heat and simmer, covered, for 40 to 45 minutes.

Add the lentils, barley, rice, thyme, allspice, pepper, carrots, and parsnip and continue simmering, covered, for 1 hour longer. Remove the bones from the pot and set them aside to cool. Stir the corn into the soup and simmer for about 10 minutes longer.

When the meat is cool enough to handle, remove it from the bones and return it to the pot, along with the salt. Heat the soup for about 2 minutes longer. Add the parsley and serve.

The soup is also good reheated, although it tends to thicken a bit on standing. Thin it with a little beef stock or water during reheating, if necessary.

Makes 5 to 7 servings.

Red Lentil-Tomato Soup

Red lentils can often be found in ethnic Middle Eastern food shops and in health food stores. These small, flat legumes add interesting color, as well as the pleasing nutty taste characteristic of all lentils. Regular lentils may be substituted in this recipe if red ones can't be obtained.

3 bacon strips
1 large onion, finely chopped
2 large carrots, finely chopped
1 large celery stalk, finely chopped
1 large turnip, peeled and finely chopped
¼ cup finely chopped fresh parsley leaves

3½ cups beef stock, brown stock, or broth
1 cup water
⅓ cup dry red lentils, sorted and washed (If unavailable, substitute regular lentils.)
1 large bay leaf
Generous ¾ teaspoon dried thyme leaves
Scant ½ teaspoon black pepper, preferably freshly ground
⅛ teaspoon celery seeds
⅛ teaspoon ground allspice
Pinch of ground cinnamon
Pinch of cayenne pepper
1 to 2 drops Tabasco sauce
1 cup finely shredded green cabbage
1 35-ounce can imported Italian (plum) tomatoes, including juice, coarsely puréed in a food processor or blender
½ teaspoon salt, or more to taste

Cook the bacon in a large pot over medium-high heat until crisp. Transfer the bacon to a double thickness of paper towels to drain. Add the onion, carrots, celery, turnip, and parsley to the pot. Cook in the bacon fat, stirring, for 5 to 6 minutes, or until the onion is limp. Add the stock, water, lentils, bay leaf, thyme, pepper, celery seeds, allspice, cinnamon, cayenne pepper, and Tabasco sauce. Bring the mixture to a boil; then lower the heat and simmer, covered, for about 40 minutes. (If regular lentils are used, cook for about 50 minutes.)

Stir the cabbage and tomatoes into the pot. Also, crumble the bacon slices and add them to the pot. Continue simmering the soup, covered, for about 15 to 20 minutes longer, or until the lentils are tender. Discard the bay leaf. Stir in the salt.

Makes 5 to 6 servings.

Savory Brown Rice and Lentil Soup

A simple, homey, economical soup with wonderful flavor, this is one of our favorites. Brown rice adds nutritional enrichment, but not a "health foody" taste.

2½ tablespoons butter or margarine
2 medium-sized onions, finely chopped
1 large garlic clove, minced
½ cup diced sweet green pepper
3 cups chicken stock or broth
1 large (bone-in) chicken breast half, skin removed
3 cups water
2 large carrots, cut into ⅛-inch-thick slices
2 large celery stalks, cut into ¼-inch-thick slices
¼ cup brown rice, washed and drained
3 tablespoons dry lentils, sorted and washed
2 large bay leaves
Generous ½ teaspoon dried thyme leaves
⅛ teaspoon ground cloves
Scant ¼ teaspoon black pepper, preferably freshly ground
¼ to ½ teaspoon salt, or more to taste

Melt the butter in a large pot over medium-high heat. Add the onions, garlic, and green pepper and cook, stirring, for 5 to 6 minutes, or until the onions are limp. Add the stock, chicken breast, water, carrots, celery, rice, lentils, bay leaves, thyme, cloves, and pepper. Bring the mixture to a boil; then lower the heat and simmer, covered, for 30 minutes. Remove the chicken from the pot and set it aside to cool. Continue simmering the soup, covered, for 30 minutes longer.

Remove the chicken meat from the bone and cut into bite-sized pieces. When the soup has simmered for 30 minutes, return the meat to the pot and simmer for about 5 minutes longer, or until the chicken is heated through and the brown rice and lentils are tender. Discard the bay leaves. Add the salt.

Makes 5 to 6 servings.

Beef and Barley Soup

Rich and thick, this soup makes a great meal in a bowl.

> 4 pounds beef soup bones, preferably marrow bones, sawed into 2-inch lengths
> 10 cups water
> 2 celery stalks, including leaves, thinly sliced
> 2 medium-sized carrots, thinly sliced
> 1 large Spanish onion, finely chopped
> 1½ pounds stew beef, well trimmed and cut into ¾-inch cubes
> ½ cup pearl barley
> 3 bay leaves
> 1 garlic clove, minced
> 1 15-ounce can tomato sauce
> ½ cup finely chopped fresh parsley leaves
> 3 medium-sized potatoes, peeled and cut into ¾-inch cubes
> 1 teaspoon dried thyme leaves
> ½ teaspoon dried marjoram leaves
> ½ teaspoon chili powder
> ½ teaspoon celery salt
> 1 teaspoon salt, or to taste
> ½ teaspoon black pepper, preferably freshly ground

Rinse the bones in a colander under cold running water. Pat them dry with paper towels. In a roasting pan, cook the bones in a 350-degree oven for 1 hour to 1 hour and 15 minutes; stir occasionally. They should be well browned but not sticking to the bottom of the pan. With a slotted spoon, transfer the bones to a large heavy soup pot, discarding the fat in the bottom of the roasting pan. Add 1 cup of the water to the roasting pan. Scrape up any browned bits from the bottom. Transfer the water and bits to the soup pot.

Add the remaining 9 cups of water, celery, carrots, onion, stew beef, barley, bay leaves, and garlic, and bring the mixture to a boil over high heat. Cover, lower the heat, and simmer, stirring occasionally, for about 2 hours. With a slotted spoon, remove the bones from the pot and discard them. The soup may be refrigerated at this point and completed later.

With a large shallow spoon, remove the fat from the top of the soup and discard it. Discard the bay leaves.

Bring the soup to boiling again over medium-high heat and add all the remaining ingredients. Cover, lower the heat, and simmer the soup for an additional 30 to 40 minutes, or until the potatoes are tender.

Makes 7 to 8 servings.

✓ Lima Bean and Barley Soup

2 tablespoons vegetable oil
1 large onion, finely chopped
1 large celery stalk, thinly sliced
6 cups ham stock (see page 300)
1 16-ounce can tomatoes, including juice
1 large carrot, thinly sliced
1 cup loose-pack frozen baby lima beans
½ cup finely chopped fresh parsley leaves
¼ cup pearl barley
½ cup peeled and diced turnip
1 small bay leaf
1 to 2 teaspoons sugar, or to taste
¼ teaspoon dried marjoram leaves
¼ teaspoon celery salt
¼ teaspoon dried thyme leaves
Pinch of cayenne pepper
¼ to ½ teaspoon salt, or to taste
⅛ teaspoon black pepper, preferably freshly ground

In a Dutch oven or very large saucepan, combine the oil with the onion and celery. Cook over medium-high heat, stirring frequently, for about 5 to 6 minutes, or until the onion is tender. Add the stock and tomatoes, breaking up the tomatoes with a large spoon. Add all the remaining ingredients and stir to blend well. Bring the soup to a boil. Cover, lower the heat, and simmer the soup for about 1 hour and 30 minutes, or until the flavors are well blended and the barley has thickened the liquid. Discard the bay leaf.

Makes 5 to 6 servings.

Spicy Celery-Rice Soup

1 tablespoon olive oil
1 tablespoon butter or margarine
1 large onion, finely chopped
1 small sweet green pepper, diced
2 large garlic cloves, minced
7 cups beef stock, brown stock, or broth
1½ tablespoons dry lentils, sorted and washed
1 bay leaf
Generous ½ teaspoon dried thyme leaves
Scant ½ teaspoon fennel seeds, crushed
Scant ½ teaspoon black pepper, preferably freshly ground
Generous pinch of cayenne pepper
4½ cups thinly sliced celery (about 1 medium-sized bunch)
½ cup long-grain white rice, rinsed and drained
¾ cup chopped canned tomatoes, including juice
⅛ to ¼ teaspoon salt, or to taste

In a large soup pot, combine the oil and butter. Heat over medium-high heat until the butter melts. Add the onion, green pepper, and garlic and cook, stirring, for 4 to 5 minutes, or until the onion is limp. Stir in the stock, lentils, bay leaf, thyme, fennel seeds, black pepper, and cayenne pepper. Bring the mixture to a boil; then lower the heat and simmer, covered, for 25 minutes.

Stir in the celery and rice and continue simmering, covered, for about 20 to 25 minutes longer, or until the lentils and rice are tender. Stir in the tomatoes and salt. Simmer for 3 to 4 minutes longer. Discard the bay leaf.

Makes 5 to 7 servings.

Peanut Soup Gold Coast Style

Though we Americans think of peanuts as nuts, they are, in fact, part of the legume, or dried bean, family. Hence, this recipe is not really out of place in this chapter.

The following is a very nourishing and tasty peanut and chicken dish from the West African country of Ghana. The soup is slightly zesty and exotic in flavor, but still very agreeable to the American palate. It makes a filling one-dish meal.

2½ tablespoons peanut or vegetable oil
1 2- to 2¼-pound frying chicken, cut up
2 medium-sized onions, finely chopped
1 large garlic clove, minced
3 cups chicken stock or broth
1¾ cups water, divided
Generous ¼ teaspoon ground ginger, *or* ¼ teaspoon finely
    minced gingerroot
Generous ¼ teaspoon dried crushed red (hot) pepper
1½ cups canned tomatoes, including juice
1 cup unsalted peanuts, preferably dry roasted
½ to ¾ teaspoon salt, or more to taste
About 1 tablespoon chopped unsalted peanuts for garnish
    (optional)

Heat the oil to hot but not smoking in a large pot over medium-high heat. Add the chicken pieces and cook, turning frequently, until they are well browned on all sides. Remove the chicken from the pot and set it aside. Add the onions and garlic and cook, stirring, for 4 to 5 minutes, or until the onions are limp. Add the stock and 1 cup of the water to the pot. Stir in the ginger and dried red pepper. Return the chicken to the pot. Bring the mixture to a boil over medium-high heat. Lower the heat and simmer, covered, for 1 hour and 5 to 10 minutes, or until the chicken is very tender. Remove the chicken from the pot and set it aside to cool.

Meanwhile, combine the tomatoes and 1 cup peanuts in a blender. Blend on low speed for about 30 seconds, or until the peanuts are coarsely puréed and the mixture begins to thicken. Add the remaining ¾ cup water and blend on high speed for about 2 to 2½ minutes, or until the mixture is *completely blended* and smooth; set it aside.

Using a large shallow spoon, skim off and discard any fat floating on the surface of the broth. Stir the tomato-peanut purée into the broth.

When the chicken is cool enough to handle, remove the meat from the bones, cut it into bite-sized pieces, and return it to the pot, along with the salt. Simmer the soup for about 10 minutes longer to allow the flavors to blend. If desired, serve the soup garnished with a sprinkling of chopped peanuts.

Makes 5 to 6 servings.

7
VEGETARIAN SOUPS

Vegetarian chowders, bisques, and potages have pleasing tastes and textures all their own; yet they can be as robust and satisfying as soups containing meat. In fact, meatless or not, a number of the recipes in this chapter are among our favorites.

Most feature garden-fresh vegetables or hearty beans and grains. Many are relatively quick and easy to prepare—as well as quite inexpensive. Some, like East Indian Lentil Soup, Santa Fe Potato-Corn Chowder, and Cuban Black Bean Soup, are substantial enough to serve as a supper entrée. Others, like Beet and Cabbage Borscht and Savory Vegetarian Mushroom Soup, are excellent for lunch served with a salad and bread or crackers.

Hearty Barley Soup

A satisfying barley soup enlivened with a flavorful blend of herbs and spices.

    3 tablespoons vegetable oil
    2 large onions, finely chopped
    1 large garlic clove, minced
    ¼ pound fresh mushrooms, sliced (about 8 medium sized)
    8 cups of water and 4 vegetarian bouillon packets or cubes,
        or 8 cups vegetable stock (see page 302)
    1 large carrot, thinly sliced
    2 large celery stalks, thinly sliced
    3 tablespoons tomato paste
    ½ cup peeled and diced turnip
    ¼ cup pearl barley
    ¼ cup chopped fresh parsley leaves
    2 large bay leaves
    1 teaspoon dried marjoram leaves
    ½ teaspoon dried thyme leaves
    ½ teaspoon powdered mustard
    ¼ teaspoon celery salt
    2 drops Tabasco sauce

¼ teaspoon salt, or to taste
¼ teaspoon black pepper, preferably freshly ground, or to
   taste

In a very large saucepan or small soup pot, combine the oil, onions, garlic, and mushrooms. Cook over medium-high heat, stirring frequently, for about 5 minutes, or until the onions are tender. Add all the remaining ingredients, stirring well to thoroughly incorporate the tomato paste. Bring the mixture to a boil. Cover, lower the heat, and simmer for about 1 hour and 30 minutes, or until the barley is tender and has thickened the soup. With a large shallow spoon, skim any oil from the surface of the soup and discard it. Discard the bay leaves.

Makes 6 to 7 servings.

Cuban Black Bean Soup

Although a number of steps are required to make this soup, the rich, spicy flavor is ample reward.

2 cups (about 1 pound) dry black beans, sorted and washed
8 cups water
3 large onions, finely chopped
3 large garlic cloves, minced
2 teaspoons salt, or to taste
½ teaspoon black pepper, preferably freshly ground
⅛ teaspoon cayenne pepper

Rice

1 cup long-grain white rice
1 tablespoon chopped onion
3 cups water
2 tablespoons olive oil
1½ tablespoons apple cider vinegar

Green Pepper and Spices

    2 large sweet green peppers, finely chopped
    2 tablespoons olive oil
    1½ teaspoons ground cumin
    1½ teaspoons dried oregano leaves

Put the beans in a Dutch oven or small soup pot and cover them with about 2 inches of cold water. Bring them to a boil over high heat and boil for 2 minutes. Remove the pot from the heat and soak the beans for 1 hour, covered. Drain the beans in a colander and discard the soaking water.

In the pot in which the beans were soaked, combine them with the water, onions, garlic, salt, black pepper, and cayenne pepper. Bring to a boil over medium-high heat. Cover, lower the heat, and simmer for about 3 hours, or until the beans have softened, cooked down somewhat, and thickened the cooking water.

About an hour before the beans have finished cooking, combine the rice, 1 tablespoon onion, and 3 cups water in a medium-sized saucepan. Cover and bring to a boil over high heat. Lower the heat and simmer the rice for about 20 minutes, or until it is tender. When the rice is done, stir in the olive oil and vinegar. Cover and set the mixture aside to marinate.

About 15 minutes before the beans have finished cooking, combine the green peppers and olive oil in a medium-sized frying pan. Cook the peppers, stirring frequently, over medium-high heat, until they are very tender, about 10 minutes. Stir in the cumin and oregano. Cook, stirring, for an additional 2 minutes. Add this mixture to the soup and stir to blend well. Simmer the soup for about 15 minutes to allow the flavors to blend.

To serve the soup, spoon approximately 2 tablespoons of the rice mixture on top of each serving.

Makes 8 to 10 servings.

Tangy Three-Bean Soup

The spicy barbecue flavor of this dish is a nice change of pace from the usual "tamer" bean soup.

½ cup dry black-eyed peas, sorted and washed
½ cup dry pinto beans, sorted and washed
½ cup dry Great Northern beans, sorted and washed
6½ cups water
1 large garlic clove, minced
1 large onion, finely chopped
1 large carrot, thinly sliced
1 large celery stalk, thinly sliced
⅛ teaspoon ground cloves
1 large bay leaf
1 15-ounce can tomato sauce
2 tablespoons packed dark or light brown sugar
1 tablespoon apple cider vinegar
1 tablespoon light molasses
½ teaspoon powdered mustard
½ teaspoon chili powder
½ teaspoon celery salt
¼ teaspoon dried thyme leaves
¼ teaspoon paprika
3 to 5 drops Tabasco sauce, or to taste
¼ teaspoon black pepper, preferably freshly ground
½ teaspoon salt, or to taste

Put the beans in a large saucepan or small pot. Cover them with 2 inches of cold water. Bring to a boil over high heat, and boil for 2 minutes. Remove the pan from the heat and let the beans stand, covered, for 1 hour. Drain the beans in a colander and discard the soaking water.

Return the beans to the pan in which they were soaked. Add the water, garlic, onion, carrot, celery, cloves, and bay leaf. Bring the mixture to a boil over high heat. Lower the heat, cover, and simmer the beans for 2 hours to 2 hours and 15 minutes, or until they are very tender and have thickened the soup slightly. Add all the remaining ingredients and stir to mix well. Simmer the soup for an additional 25 to 30 minutes, or until the flavors are well blended. Discard the bay leaf.

Makes 5 to 6 servings.

Beet and Cabbage Borscht

A traditional Russian dish, borscht can be served either hot or cold. This mildly flavored vegetarian version tastes best served piping hot and garnished with a generous dollop of sour cream. Since a combination of shredded vegetables helps give body and flavor to the soup, a food processor will greatly simplify preparation.

1 large onion, finely chopped
2 large garlic cloves, minced
1 tablespoon vegetable oil
9 cups water
2 packets or cubes vegetable bouillon
2 carrots, grated or shredded
2 large celery stalks, thinly sliced
2 medium-sized beets, peeled, trimmed, and grated or shredded
2 cups grated or shredded green cabbage
1 large potato, peeled or unpeeled, grated or shredded
1 small turnip, peeled, trimmed, and grated or shredded
1 small parsnip, peeled, trimmed, and grated or shredded
3 bay leaves
2½ tablespoons apple cider vinegar
1 tablespoon sugar
1 teaspoon dried thyme leaves
1 teaspoon dried basil leaves
¾ teaspoon celery salt
½ teaspoon dried marjoram leaves
½ teaspoon powdered mustard
2 to 3 drops Tabasco sauce
¾ teaspoon salt, or to taste

¼ teaspoon black pepper, preferably freshly ground
7 to 9 tablespoons commercial sour cream

In a large heavy soup pot, combine the onion, garlic, and oil. Cook over medium heat, stirring frequently, for about 4 to 5 minutes, or until the onion is tender. Add all the remaining ingredients *except* the sour cream and stir to mix well. Over high heat, bring the soup to a boil. Then cover, lower the heat, and simmer for about 40 to 45 minutes, or until the vegetables are tender and the potato has thickened the soup slightly. Discard the bay leaves.

Ladle the soup into bowls. Top each serving with a tablespoon of sour cream.

Makes 7 to 9 servings.

Cream of Celery Soup

2 cups diced celery
2 packets or cubes vegetable bouillon
2 cups water
2 tablespoons butter or margarine
1 medium-sized onion, finely chopped
¼ teaspoon dried marjoram leaves
¼ teaspoon powdered mustard
⅛ teaspoon dried thyme leaves
¼ teaspoon white pepper, preferably freshly ground
¼ teaspoon salt
¼ cup cold water
2 tablespoons cornstarch
1 cup light cream or half-and-half
Chopped fresh chives or parsley leaves for garnish (optional)

In a medium-sized saucepan, combine the celery, bouillon, water, butter, onion, marjoram, mustard, thyme, pepper, and salt. Bring the mixture to a boil over high heat. Lower the heat, cover, and simmer for about 20 to 25 minutes, or until the celery is tender.

Meanwhile; in a small cup or bowl, stir together the cold water and cornstarch until smooth and well combined. Add the water-cornstarch mixture to the simmering liquid and stir until it thickens, about 1 minute. Lower the heat. Stir the cream into the mixture. Cook, stirring frequently, for about 2 to 3 minutes longer, or until heated through, *but do not boil.* Garnish individual servings with chopped chives, if desired.

Makes about 4 servings.

Easy Mexican Corn and Bean Soup

This spicy soup is quick and easy to prepare.

   2 tablespoons vegetable oil
   1 large onion, finely chopped
   1 large garlic clove, minced
   1 medium-sized sweet green pepper, diced
   2 cups tomato juice
   2 15-ounce cans tomatoes, including juice, puréed in a blender or food processor
   1 15-ounce can red kidney beans, drained
   2 cups loose-pack frozen corn kernels
   1 tablespoon chili powder, or to taste
   1 teaspoon ground cumin
   1 teaspoon sugar
   ½ teaspoon salt
   ¼ teaspoon black pepper, preferably freshly ground

In a very large saucepan or small Dutch oven, combine the oil, onion, and garlic. Cook over medium-high heat, stirring frequently, for about 4 to 5 minutes, or until the onion is limp. Add all the remaining ingredients. Bring the soup to a boil. Cover, lower the heat, and simmer for about 20 to 25 minutes, or until the corn is cooked and the flavors are well blended.

Makes 4 to 5 servings.

Cream of Green Pea Soup

2½ tablespoons butter or margarine
7 to 8 medium-sized green onions (scallions), including green tops
2 tablespoons all-purpose white flour
4 cups whole milk, divided
1¼ cups peeled and coarsely chopped boiling potatoes
½ to ¾ teaspoon salt
¼ teaspoon white pepper, preferably freshly ground
2 cups loose-pack frozen green peas, preferably "baby" peas, slightly thawed
½ cup light cream or half-and-half

Combine the butter and green onions in a 2- to 3-quart saucepan over medium-high heat. Cook, stirring, for 4 to 5 minutes, or until they are limp. Using a wooden spoon, stir in the flour until well blended and smooth. Cook, stirring, for 2 minutes. Stir in 3 cups of the milk until thoroughly incorporated. Add the potatoes, salt, and pepper. Bring the mixture to a boil; then lower the heat and cover the pan. Simmer, stirring occasionally, for 9 to 12 minutes, or until the potatoes are cooked through but not soft.

Meanwhile, combine the peas and about a tablespoon of water in a small saucepan over medium-high heat. Cover the pan and cook for 3 to 4 minutes, or until the peas are just tender. Remove the pan from the heat and set it aside.

When the green onion-potato mixture is done, transfer it to a food processor. Add all but ½ cup of the cooked peas to the processor. Process the mixture until completely puréed and smooth, scraping down the processor sides several times, if necessary.

Rinse out the pan used to cook the green onion-potato mixture and return the purée to it. Add the remaining 1 cup of milk and the cream, along with the reserved ½ cup of green peas and their cooking liquid. Heat the soup over medium-high heat, stirring occasionally, until piping hot *but not* boiling.

Makes 4 to 6 servings.

East Indian Lentil Soup

This hearty but very easy main-dish soup tastes best made with tiny beige Indian lentils, which are available in Indian specialty food stores. However, regular lentils can also be used.

    2 tablespoons vegetable oil
    1 large onion, finely chopped
    1 garlic clove, minced
    2½ cups (about 1 pound) dry beige Indian lentils or dry
        regular lentils, sorted and washed
    10 cups water
    2 large celery stalks, including leaves, thinly sliced
    1 large carrot, thinly sliced
    2 to 2½ teaspoons curry powder, or to taste
    1 teaspoon sugar
    2 to 2½ teaspoons salt, or to taste
    ¼ teaspoon black pepper, preferably freshly ground

    In a large soup pot, combine the oil, onion, and garlic. Cook over medium-high heat, stirring frequently, for about 5 to 6 minutes, or until the onion is tender. Add all the remaining ingredients and bring to a boil. Cover, lower the heat, and simmer for about 1½ hours, or until the lentils soften and thicken the soup. Stir occasionally to prevent the lentils from sticking to the bottom of the pot.

    Makes 8 to 10 servings.

Savory Vegetarian Mushroom Soup

Rich and creamy, this vegetarian soup is also quite hearty and full-flavored. It's very good for lunch or supper.

    1¼ pounds fresh mushrooms, coarsely sliced (about 7½ to
        8 cups)
    1 tablespoon lemon juice, preferably fresh

¼ cup butter or margarine
1 large onion, coarsely chopped
1 medium-sized celery stalk, coarsely chopped
1 garlic clove, minced
1½ cups water or vegetable stock (see page 302)
1 large potato, peeled and diced
3 tablespoons tomato paste
2½ cups whole milk
⅓ cup drained and finely chopped canned tomatoes
1 tablespoon soy sauce
1 tablespoon chopped fresh chives, *or* 1½ teaspoons dried
    chopped chives
¼ to ½ teaspoon black pepper, preferably freshly ground
Generous ¼ teaspoon dried thyme leaves
1 cup light cream or half-and-half
½ to ¾ teaspoon salt, or to taste
About 1 teaspoon chopped fresh chives for garnish (op-
    tional)

Combine the mushrooms and lemon juice in a large bowl and toss until well mixed. Melt the butter in a large soup pot over medium-high heat. Add the mushrooms and cook, stirring, for 3 to 4 minutes, or until they are limp but have not exuded their juices. Using a slotted spoon, remove about half the mushrooms to a small bowl. Add the onion, celery, and garlic to the pot and continue cooking, stirring, for 4 to 5 minutes longer, or until the onion is soft. Stir the water and potato into the pot and bring the mixture to a boil. Lower the heat and simmer, uncovered, for 8 to 10 minutes, or until the potato is tender. Cool the mixture slightly.

Transfer the mixture to a blender. Add the tomato paste and blend on low speed for 10 seconds. Raise the speed to high and blend until completely puréed and smooth. Rinse out the pot and return the purée to it. Stir in the reserved sliced mushrooms and all the remaining ingredients *except* the cream and salt.

Bring the mixture to a boil; lower the heat and simmer, covered, for 10 minutes. Stir in ¾ cup of the cream and the salt. For a slightly thinner soup, add a bit more cream until the desired consistency is obtained. Continue cooking for 4 to 5 minutes, or until heated through, *but not* boiling. Garnish the soup with a sprinkling of fresh chives, if desired.

Makes 5 to 6 servings.

Santa Fe Potato-Corn Chowder

This is easy, nourishing, and very good.

> 2 tablespoons butter or margarine
> 6 to 7 medium-sized green onions (scallions), including green tops, chopped
> 1 tablespoon all-purpose white flour
> 5½ cups whole milk
> 4 cups peeled and coarsely cubed boiling potatoes (5 to 6 medium sized)
> 1 4-ounce can chopped green chilies, well drained
> ½ teaspoon salt
> ¼ teaspoon black pepper, preferably freshly ground
> 1¾ cups loose-pack frozen corn kernels
> 4 ounces grated mild Cheddar cheese (about 1 cup lightly packed)
> 1 to 2 teaspoons finely chopped fresh parsley leaves for garnish (optional)

Combine the butter and green onions in a 3- to 4-quart soup pot. Cook over medium-high heat, stirring, for 4 to 5 minutes, or until they are limp. Stir in the flour until well blended and smooth; cook for 1½ minutes longer. Add the milk and potatoes and bring the mixture to a boil, stirring occasionally. Lower the heat, cover, and simmer, stirring occasionally, for 10 minutes.

Scoop about 1½ cups of the potato mixture from the pot and transfer it to a blender. Blend on low speed for 10 seconds. Then raise the speed to high and blend until the mixture is thoroughly puréed and smooth. Return the purée to the pot. Stir in the green chilies, salt, pepper, and corn and simmer, covered, for 5 minutes longer. Add all *except* 2 tablespoons of the cheese, stirring, and continue heating until the cheese melts and the soup is piping hot *but not* boiling. Sprinkle the top of the soup with the remaining cheese and chopped parsley, if desired. Serve immediately.

Makes 5 to 6 servings.

Spinach-Pasta Soup with Pesto

1 pound fresh spinach
2 tablespoons olive oil
11 to 12 medium-sized green onions (scallions), including green tops, finely sliced
5½ cups water
3 to 4 leaf lettuce leaves, such as Boston or Bibb lettuce, torn into small bite-sized pieces
1 large boiling potato, peeled and finely diced
1 to 1¼ teaspoons salt
¼ teaspoon black pepper, preferably freshly ground
½ cup 1-inch-long vermicelli pieces

Pesto (Seasoning Paste)

1 cup firmly packed spinach leaves (reserved from the pound of spinach already prepared)
3 tablespoons olive oil
⅓ cup chopped fresh basil leaves, *or* 2½ tablespoons dried basil leaves
⅓ cup chopped fresh parsley leaves
1 large garlic clove, minced
¼ cup grated Parmesan cheese
½ cup water

Garnish

About ¼ cup grated Parmesan cheese

Put the spinach in a large bowl of cool water and swish it back and forth to loosen any grit in the crinkles of the leaves.

Turn out the spinach into a colander and rinse it under cool running water. Then swish the leaves in a large bowl of water once again and turn it out into a colander. Using a sharp knife, trim off the stems and any tough midribs. Tear the leaves into small bite-sized pieces. Thoroughly rinse the leaves under cool running water once more. (If the leaves are especially dirty, a third washing and rinsing may be needed to ensure they are completely grit-free.) Set the spinach aside until thoroughly drained. Put enough spinach (loosely packed) into a measure to make 1 cup and set it aside.

Combine the oil and green onions in a large pot over medium-high heat. Cook, stirring, for 4 to 5 minutes, or until they are limp. Add the water, all (*except* the 1 cup) of the spinach, the lettuce, potato, salt, and pepper. Bring the mixture to a boil; then lower the heat and simmer, covered, for 20 minutes. Set out the vermicelli.

Prepare the pesto as follows: Combine all the ingredients in a blender or food processor. Blend or process until the mixture is completely puréed and smooth. Set the pesto aside.

When the spinach mixture has cooked for 20 minutes, raise the heat to high and bring the pot to a full boil. Stir in the vermicelli. Continue to boil, uncovered, for 4 to 6 minutes, or until the vermicelli is almost cooked through. Add the pesto and continue cooking for about 2 minutes longer, or until the vermicelli is cooked through, but still slightly firm (*al dente*). Serve the soup immediately. Pass the grated cheese in a small bowl at the table so diners can sprinkle some over their soup.

Makes 4 to 6 servings.

Vegetarian Minestrone

The combination of vegetables and herbs is particularly appealing in this meatless version of a traditional Italian favorite.

2 tablespoons vegetable oil
1 medium-sized onion, finely chopped
1 garlic clove, minced

4 cups vegetable stock (see page 302), *or* 2 vegetable bouillon cubes or packets plus 4 cups water
1 15-ounce can tomato sauce
1 15-ounce can garbanzo beans (chick-peas), well drained
1 large celery stalk, diced
1 medium-sized carrot, thinly sliced
1 large boiling potato, peeled or unpeeled, cut into ¾-inch cubes
1 medium-sized zucchini, diced
¼ cup chopped fresh parsley leaves
1 teaspoon dried basil leaves
½ teaspoon dried marjoram leaves
¼ teaspoon dried thyme leaves
¼ teaspoon celery salt
2 to 3 drops Tabasco sauce
¼ teaspoon salt
¼ teaspoon black pepper, preferably freshly ground
½ cup small pasta shells or macaroni

In a Dutch oven or very large saucepan, combine the oil, onion, and garlic. Cook over medium-high heat, stirring frequently, for 4 to 5 minutes, or until the onion is tender. Add the vegetable stock, tomato sauce, garbanzo beans, celery, carrot, potato, and zucchini. Then add the parsley, basil, marjoram, thyme, celery salt, Tabasco sauce, salt, and pepper. Stir to mix well. Cover and bring to a boil. Lower the heat and simmer for about 15 minutes. Add the pasta and gently boil for an additional 15 to 20 minutes, or until the vegetables and pasta are tender.

Makes 5 to 6 servings.

8
CROCK POT SOUPS

If the idea of coming home to a hot meal after a hard day at work sounds appealing, thumb through the recipes in this chapter. They're all intended for slow and no-fuss crock pot cookery.

There's a wide selection to choose from, including Easy Goulash Soup, Workday Bean Soup, Creole-Style Lamb Soup, and Chicken and Barley Soup. All are filling entrées, with generous portions of meat and vegetables.

If you've used a crock pot before, you know there are certain techniques that help ensure success. If you're new to this type of cookery, be sure to read the directions that come with the appliance before proceeding.

In general, soups cooked in the crock pot need less water than conventionally prepared recipes. That's because the low cooking temperature makes for little or no evaporation. Also, meat tends to cook more quickly than vegetables, so carrots, celery, potatoes, and onions need to be diced or cut into small pieces. (When you plan to start a crock pot soup cooking in the morning, but know you're going to be in a hurry, you may want to dice the vegetables the night before and refrigerate them.) When filling the crock pot, remember that vegetables cook best at the bottom of the pot because they are closer to the heat source.

We've also found that crock pot cookery changes the tastes of some foods. A number of seasonings like bay are intensified —so you may want to use less than in a conventional recipe. Others like onion and chili powder actually become more mellow—so you may need more than usual. Also, soups have more flavor if they include broth or bouillon.

Usually it isn't necessary to brown meat before putting it into the crock pot. The one exception is ground beef, which looks more attractive if it is browned first in a frying pan.

Most crock pots have only two temperatures—high and low. But within these settings, we've found considerable variation in the cooking times for pots produced by different manufacturers. That's one reason the cooking directions are fairly flexible in the recipes that follow. Also, it rarely hurts a crock pot soup to cook it an hour or two after the ingredients are tender, if that turns out to be most convenient.

With the majority of crock pots, 2 hours of cooking on low equals 1 hour of cooking on high. So, although most of the recipes in this chapter call for the low setting, you can usually halve the cooking time by simply shifting to the high setting.

Beef and Green Bean Soup with Potatoes

> 1¼ pounds lean stew beef, trimmed and cut into ½-inch cubes
> 2 medium-sized onions, finely chopped
> 1 small smoked pork hock (about ½ pound)
> 4 cups hot tap water
> 2 beef bouillon cubes
> Generous ½ teaspoon ground savory
> Generous pinch of dried thyme leaves
> ¼ teaspoon black pepper, preferably freshly ground
> 4 medium-sized boiling potatoes, peeled and cut into ½-inch cubes
> 2¾ cups 1-inch fresh or loose-pack frozen (thawed) green bean pieces
> ⅛ to ¼ teaspoon salt, or to taste
> 1½ tablespoons finely chopped fresh parsley leaves

Combine all the ingredients *except* the parsley in a crock pot. Cover the pot, turn the setting to low, and cook for 8 to 10 hours. Stir in the parsley. Cover the crock pot and raise the setting to high. Cook for at least 30 minutes, or until the meat and vegetables are tender. Discard the pork hock. Stir the soup briefly and serve.

Makes 5 to 6 servings.

Italian-Style Vegetable-Beef Soup

Add a crusty loaf of garlic bread and, perhaps, a tossed salad and you've got an easy and satisfying meal.

1¼ pounds lean stew beef, trimmed of fat and cut into ½-inch cubes
2 to 3 2-inch diameter chunks salt pork or slab bacon, rind removed (3½ to 4 ounces total weight)
1 large onion, chopped
1 large garlic clove, minced
3 large celery stalks, cut into ¼-inch-thick slices
3 large carrots, cut into ⅛-inch-thick slices
1 cup 1-inch-long fresh or frozen green bean pieces
¾ cup ¼-inch-thick zucchini slices
3 bay leaves
3 cups water
2 beef bouillon cubes
¼ teaspoon black pepper, preferably freshly ground
1 15-ounce can tomato sauce
1 14- to 16-ounce can Great Northern white beans, drained
1 cup canned red kidney beans, drained, *or* 1 cup canned garbanzo beans (chick-peas), drained
½ teaspoon dried oregano leaves
½ teaspoon dried basil leaves
⅛ to ¼ teaspoon salt (optional)
About 1 tablespoon finely chopped fresh parsley leaves for garnish (optional)

Combine all the ingredients *except* the tomato sauce, white beans, kidney beans, oregano, basil, and salt in the crock pot. Cover the pot, turn the setting to low, and cook for 8 to 10 hours.

Stir in all remaining ingredients *except* the salt. Cover the crock pot and raise the setting to high. Cook for at least 45 minutes and up to 1 hour. Add the salt, if necessary. Discard the bay leaves and chunks of salt pork. Sprinkle the soup with chopped parsley, if desired.

Makes 5 to 6 servings.

Chili Bean and Beef Soup

Very easy, very good. For a festive touch, garnish individual servings with shredded Cheddar cheese.

    1 to 1¼ pounds lean stew beef, trimmed and cut into ½-
      inch cubes
    1 large onion, finely chopped
    2 medium-sized celery stalks, thinly sliced
    1½ cups loose-pack frozen corn kernels, rinsed under cool
      water and drained
    2 15- to 16-ounce cans red kidney beans, well drained
    1 14½-ounce can stewed tomatoes, including juice, broken
      up with a spoon
    1 4-ounce can chopped green chilies, well drained
    2 tablespoons long-grain white rice
    2 cups hot tap water
    2 beef bouillon cubes
    1 tablespoon chili powder
    1 8-ounce can tomato sauce
    ¼ teaspoon salt, or to taste
    3 to 4 tablespoons shredded Cheddar cheese for garnish
      (optional)

    Combine all the ingredients *except* the tomato sauce, salt, and Cheddar cheese (if used) in the crock pot. Cover the pot, turn the setting to low, and cook for 8 to 10 hours.
  Stir in the tomato sauce and salt. Cover the crock pot and raise the setting to high. Cook for 15 to 20 minutes longer. Stir briefly. If desired, sprinkle the servings with shredded Cheddar cheese.

    Makes 5 to 6 servings.

Easy Goulash Soup

1 large onion, finely chopped
1 large carrot, thinly sliced
1 large celery stalk, diced
2 large garlic cloves, minced
2 cups peeled and diced potatoes
1 cup ¾-inch-long fresh or frozen green bean pieces
2 tablespoons pearl barley
1½ pounds stew beef, trimmed and cut into ¾-inch cubes
5 cups beef stock or broth
1 bay leaf
2 teaspoons sugar
1½ teaspoons paprika
½ teaspoon powdered mustard
½ teaspoon dried thyme leaves
½ teaspoon salt
¼ teaspoon black pepper, preferably freshly ground
1 15-ounce can tomato sauce
2 tablespoons tomato paste
2 to 3 drops Tabasco sauce

Combine the onion, carrot, celery, garlic, potatoes, green beans, barley, beef, stock, bay leaf, sugar, paprika, mustard, thyme, salt, and pepper in a crock pot. Cover and cook on the low setting for 7 to 8 hours. Remove and discard the bay leaf.

In a medium-sized bowl, stir together the tomato sauce and tomato paste until well combined. Add the mixture to the pot along with the Tabasco sauce. Cook for an additional 1 hour to 1 hour and 30 minutes on the high setting. Stir before serving.

Makes 6 to 8 servings.

Easy Barbecued Beef Soup with Vegetables

Put on a crock pot of this easy soup in the morning and return in the evening to a delicious and filling one-dish meal.

> 1⅓ to 1½ pounds lean stew beef, trimmed and cut into ½-inch cubes
> 1 medium-sized onion, finely chopped
> 1 large celery stalk, finely chopped
> 3 cups water
> 3 beef bouillon cubes
> ½ teaspoon chili powder
> Generous ¼ teaspoon powdered mustard
> Generous ¼ teaspoon dried thyme leaves
> Generous ¼ teaspoon ground allspice
> ¼ teaspoon black pepper, preferably freshly ground
> 2 large carrots, cut into ⅛-inch-thick slices
> 1 large celery stalk, cut into ⅛-inch-thick slices
> 1 medium-sized parsnip, peeled and cut into ⅛-inch-thick slices (optional)
> 3 medium-sized potatoes, peeled and cut into ½-inch cubes
> 1 15-ounce can tomato sauce
> 2 tablespoons packed dark or light brown sugar
> 1 tablespoon apple cider vinegar

Combine all the ingredients *except* the tomato sauce, brown sugar, and vinegar in the crock pot. Cover the pot, turn the setting to low, and cook for 8 to 10 hours.

Stir in the tomato sauce, brown sugar, and vinegar. Cover the crock pot and raise the setting to high. Cook for at least 30 minutes and up to 1 hour. Stir briefly and serve.

Makes 5 to 6 servings.

Ground Beef and Vegetable Soup

1 pound lean ground beef
1 large onion, finely chopped
2 large garlic cloves, minced
1 14½- to 16-ounce can tomatoes, including juice
2 large celery stalks, diced
1 medium-sized potato, peeled or unpeeled, diced
1 large carrot, thinly sliced
2 tablespoons long-grain white rice
4 cups hot tap water
2 beef bouillon cubes
½ cup ketchup
1 cup loose-pack frozen corn kernels
1 cup loose-pack frozen baby lima beans
2 teaspoons packed dark or light brown sugar
½ teaspoon powdered mustard
½ teaspoon celery salt
½ teaspoon dried thyme leaves
1 bay leaf
¼ teaspoon black pepper, preferably freshly ground
¼ teaspoon salt (optional)

In a large frying pan, combine the ground beef, onion, and garlic. Cook over medium-high heat, stirring frequently and breaking up the ground beef with a spoon, until the meat is browned. With a slotted spoon, transfer the mixture to a crock pot. Add all the remaining ingredients to the crock pot, breaking up the tomatoes with a large spoon. Cover and cook on the low setting for 7 to 8 hours. Raise the heat to high and cook an additional 1 or 2 hours, or until the vegetables are tender. Skim any fat from the top of the soup with a large shallow spoon and discard it. Discard the bay leaf. Stir the soup before serving.

Makes 5 to 7 servings.

Hearty Veal and Vegetable Soup

1¼ pounds lean stewing veal, trimmed and cut into ½-inch cubes
2 medium-sized onions, finely chopped
2 medium-sized celery stalks, chopped
2 large carrots, finely diced
1½ cups frozen cut green beans, rinsed under cool water and drained
2 large boiling potatoes, peeled and diced
1 cup diced cauliflower flowerets (optional)
1¼ cups coarsely sliced fresh mushrooms
3 cups hot tap water
3 beef bouillon cubes
2½ teaspoons paprika, preferably imported sweet paprika
Generous ¼ teaspoon dried marjoram leaves
¼ teaspoon dried thyme leaves
1 15-ounce can tomato sauce
1 4-ounce jar sliced pimientos, well drained
¼ to ½ teaspoon salt, or to taste
¼ teaspoon black pepper, preferably freshly ground
1½ tablespoons finely chopped fresh parsley leaves (optional)

Combine all the ingredients *except* the tomato sauce, pimientos, salt, pepper, and parsley in a crock pot. Cover the pot, turn the setting to low, and cook for 8 to 10 hours.

Stir in all the remaining ingredients. Cover the crock pot and raise the setting to high. Cook for 35 to 45 minutes longer, or until the meat and vegetables are tender and the flavors have mingled. Stir the soup briefly and serve.

Makes 5 to 6 servings.

Creole-Style Lamb Soup

1 large onion, finely chopped
2 large garlic cloves, minced
1 large sweet green pepper, diced
1 large celery stalk, diced
1 cup diced zucchini
2 15-ounce cans tomato sauce
4 cups beef stock or broth
1½ pounds stewing lamb, trimmed and cut into ½-inch
    cubes (or lamb leg or shoulder cubes)
⅓ cup chopped fresh parsley leaves
⅓ cup long-grain white rice
1 bay leaf
3 to 4 drops Tabasco sauce
2 teaspoons sugar
1 teaspoon dried marjoram leaves
½ teaspoon dried thyme leaves
½ teaspoon dried basil leaves
¼ teaspoon powdered mustard
¼ teaspoon black pepper, preferably freshly ground
¾ teaspoon salt

Combine all the ingredients in a crock pot. Cover and cook on the low setting for about 7 to 8 hours, or until the meat and vegetables are tender and the flavors are well blended. Discard the bay leaf. Stir before serving.

Makes 6 to 7 servings.

Curried Pork and Apple Soup

1½ pounds fresh country-style pork ribs
1 large onion, finely chopped
3 cups peeled and coarsely sliced tart cooking apples
2 medium-sized carrots, thinly sliced
6 cups chicken stock or broth

1 3-inch-long cinnamon stick
1 bay leaf
½ teaspoon powdered mustard
¼ teaspoon dried thyme leaves
3 to 4 drops Tabasco sauce
1½ to 2 teaspoons curry powder, or to taste
¼ teaspoon salt, or to taste
¼ teaspoon black pepper, preferably freshly ground

Combine all the ingredients in a crock pot. Stir to mix in the seasonings. Cover and cook on the low setting for 6 to 7 hours. Raise the temperature to high and cook an additional 1 or 2 hours. Skim the fat from the top of the mixture, using a large shallow spoon.

Remove the ribs with a slotted spoon and set them aside to cool.

Remove the bay leaf and cinnamon stick and discard them. With a ladle, remove about 2 cups of the apples, onion, and broth from the pot. Cool the mixture slightly; then transfer it to a blender or food processor. If a blender is used, blend on low speed for 10 seconds. Then raise the speed to high and purée until smooth. If a processor is used, purée until smooth. Return the purée to the crock pot.

When the meat is cool enough to handle, cut the lean portion into bite-sized pieces and return them to the pot. Cook for an additional 10 minutes. Stir the soup before serving.

Makes 5 to 6 servings.

Lentil Soup

1 pound dry lentils (2½ cups), sorted and washed
1 large onion, finely chopped
1 large celery stalk, grated or shredded
1 large carrot, grated or shredded
8 cups hot tap water
2 teaspoons sugar
¼ teaspoon powdered mustard
2 to 3 drops Tabasco sauce

1 beef bouillon cube
½ teaspoon dried thyme leaves
¼ teaspoon black pepper, preferably freshly ground
½ teaspoon salt, or to taste
½ pound slab bacon (rind removed), cut into 2 large pieces

Combine all the ingredients in a crock pot and stir to mix in the seasonings. Cover and cook on the high setting for 1 hour. Lower the heat to the low setting and cook for an additional 8 to 9 hours, or until the lentils are very tender and the soup has thickened. Remove the bacon pieces and reserve them. With a large shallow spoon, skim the fat from the surface of the soup and discard it.

When the bacon is cool enough to handle, cut the lean meat into bite-sized pieces and return them to the soup. Cook for an additional 10 minutes. Stir the soup before serving.

Makes 5 to 7 servings.

Workday Bean Soup

This easy crock pot soup recipe is designed to fit into the typical work schedule. The beans are put into the pot at night before going to bed. The next morning the rest of the ingredients are added. Ten to twelve hours later when the cook returns home from work, a savory soup is waiting to be served.

1¼ cups dry pinto or cranberry beans, sorted and washed
1 cup dry Great Northern beans, sorted and washed
1 large smoked pork hock (about 1 pound)
1 large onion, chopped
2 medium-sized celery stalks, coarsely chopped
1 medium-sized carrot, chopped
3 cups water
3 beef bouillon cubes
1 small bay leaf
3 tablespoons ketchup
1½ tablespoons sugar
1 tablespoon apple cider vinegar

¾ teaspoon chili powder
Generous ¼ teaspoon powdered mustard
Generous ¼ teaspoon dried thyme leaves
⅛ teaspoon ground allspice
Scant ½ teaspoon black pepper, preferably freshly ground
1 8-ounce can tomato sauce
1 cup coarsely diced lean country ham (optional)
Salt to taste

Put the beans in the crock pot. Cover them with about 3 inches of hot tap water. Cover the pot, turn the setting to low, and let the beans soak and cook for 8 to 10 hours (or overnight).

Turn out the beans into a colander and discard all but 1 cup of the soaking water. Return the drained beans and the reserved 1 cup of soaking water to the crock pot. Add all the remaining ingredients *except* the tomato sauce, ham, and salt to the pot. Stir the mixture. Cover the crock pot and cook on low for 10 to 12 hours. Stir in the tomato sauce. Discard the bay leaf. The soup may be served "as is," if desired, or for a more substantial meal, ham may be added to it. In this case, stir in the ham, raise the setting to high, and cook for 30 minutes. Add salt to taste before serving. Discard the pork hock.

Makes 5 to 6 servings.

Easy Bean and Barley Soup

1½ cups dry navy beans, sorted and washed
6 cups hot tap water
2 medium-sized smoked pork hocks (about 1½ pounds total weight)
⅓ cup pearl barley
1 15-ounce can tomato sauce
2 tablespoons instant minced onion
2 teaspoons sugar
¾ teaspoon celery salt

½ teaspoon powdered mustard
¼ teaspoon dried thyme leaves
2 to 3 drops Tabasco sauce
¼ teaspoon black pepper, preferably freshly ground
¼ teaspoon salt, or to taste

Put the beans in a crock pot and cover with 5 inches of hot tap water. Cover and cook on the low setting for 7 to 12 hours, or until the beans are tender. Drain the beans in a colander and discard the soaking water. Return the beans to the crock pot along with all the remaining ingredients. Cover and cook on the low setting for 8 to 9 hours.

Remove the pork hocks. When they are cool enough to handle, cut the lean meat into bite-sized pieces and return them to the soup, if desired. Cook for an additional 10 minutes. Stir before serving.

Makes 6 to 8 servings.

Crock Pot Chicken Gumbo

This is a very tasty, as well as convenient, soup.

1 10-ounce package frozen black-eyed peas, rinsed under cool water and drained
1 large onion, finely chopped
1 small smoked pork hock (about ½ pound)
1½ pounds meaty chicken pieces (breasts, thighs, etc.)
2 large celery stalks, chopped
½ medium-sized sweet green pepper, diced
3 tablespoons long-grain white rice
1 large bay leaf
1 small garlic clove, minced (optional)
1 10-ounce package frozen corn kernels, rinsed under cool water and drained
1 cup frozen sliced okra, rinsed under cool water and drained

3½ cups chicken stock or broth
1 cup drained and chopped canned tomatoes
2 tablespoons finely chopped fresh parsley leaves
Generous ¼ teaspoon dried thyme leaves
¼ teaspoon black pepper, preferably freshly ground
¼ to ½ teaspoon salt, or to taste

In the order listed, put the black-eyed peas, onion, pork hock, chicken, celery, green pepper, rice, bay leaf, garlic (if used), corn, okra, and stock into the crock pot. Cover the pot, turn the setting to low, and cook for 8 to 10 hours.

Remove the chicken pieces from the pot and set them aside to cool. Stir in the tomatoes, parsley, and thyme. Cover the crock pot and raise the setting to high. Cook for 45 to 50 minutes.

When the chicken is cool enough to handle, remove the meat from the bones and cut it into bite-sized pieces. Remove the pork hock and bay leaf from the pot and discard them. Return the chicken meat to the pot and add the pepper and salt. Cook for about 5 minutes longer. Stir briefly and serve.

Makes 5 to 6 servings.

Chicken and Barley Soup

3 medium-to-large (bone-in) chicken breast halves, skins removed
4½ cups chicken stock or broth
1 cup water
⅓ cup pearl barley
1 large onion, finely chopped
1 garlic clove, minced
1 large carrot, grated or shredded
1 large celery stalk, grated or shredded
¼ cup chopped fresh parsley leaves
¼ teaspoon dried thyme leaves
¼ teaspoon celery salt
1 large bay leaf

¼ teaspoon black pepper, preferably freshly ground
1 teaspoon salt, or to taste

Combine all the ingredients *except* the salt in a crock pot. Cover and cook on the low setting for 8 to 9 hours, or until the barley is tender and has thickened the soup slightly. Remove the chicken and reserve it in a medium-sized bowl. With a large shallow spoon, skim off and discard the fat from the top of the soup.

When the chicken is cool enough to handle, remove the meat from the bones and cut it into bite-sized pieces. Return the meat to the soup, add the salt, and cook for an additional 10 minutes. Discard the bay leaf. Stir before serving.

Makes 6 to 7 servings.

9
QUICK SOUPS

reat soup doesn't necessarily require a lot of advance preparation or even long, slow cooking—not when you can have Chunky Chicken and Pasta Soup, Celery-Tomato Soup, Chicken and Chilies Soup, or even a smooth and rich Creamy Lettuce and Green Pea Soup in less than half an hour.

Try these and the other streamlined recipes in this chapter. They've been specially designed to save time without skimping on taste appeal. You'll be surprised to find how quickly an honest-to-goodness homemade soup can be set in front of hungry diners, without resorting to a pot full of prepackaged ingredients.

Chunky Chicken and Pasta Soup

This colorful soup always gets an enthusiastic reception, yet it's very quick and easy to make.

    2 tablespoons olive oil, or a little more if needed
    ½ to ¾ pound boned and skinned chicken breast halves,
        cut into ½-inch cubes (meat from 2 medium-to-large
        breast halves)
    1 large onion, finely chopped
    ½ large sweet green pepper, diced
    ½ large sweet red pepper, diced (If unavailable, substitute
        ½ large sweet green pepper.)
    1 garlic clove, minced
    3½ cups chicken stock or broth
    1 16-ounce can tomatoes (preferably Italian-style [plum]
        tomatoes), including juice
    ¼ cup finely chopped fresh parsley leaves
    ¾ teaspoon dried basil leaves
    Scant ½ teaspoon dried oregano leaves
    1 bay leaf
    ¼ teaspoon black pepper, preferably freshly ground
    2 ounces vermicelli or thin spaghetti, broken into 2-inch
        lengths (about 1 cup)

In a Dutch oven or very large saucepan, combine 2 tablespoons of oil and the chicken. Cook over medium-high heat, stirring frequently, until the chicken is cooked through. With a slotted spoon, remove the chicken from the pan and reserve it in a small bowl. Add the onion, green and red pepper, and garlic to the pan. Cook, stirring frequently, until the onion is very tender. If necessary, add a bit more oil to the pan to keep the vegetables from sticking.

Add the stock and tomatoes, breaking up the tomatoes with a large spoon. Return the chicken to the pan. Add the parsley, basil, oregano, bay leaf, and black pepper. Stir to mix well. Lower the heat and simmer the soup, covered, for 5 minutes. Raise the heat so that the soup boils. Add the pasta. Lower the heat again and boil gently, covered, for 12 to 17 minutes, or until the pasta is tender; stir occasionally. Discard the bay leaf.

Makes 5 to 6 servings.

Chicken and Chilies Soup

Green chilies, chicken, and cheese combine to give this extra-easy soup its spicy south-of-the-border flavor. It's good for lunch and also makes a nice first course for a Mexican-style dinner.

2 tablespoons butter or margarine
1 medium-sized onion, finely chopped
1 large garlic clove, minced
1 large celery stalk, diced
3 cups chicken broth
1½ to 2 cups boneless cooked chicken cut into bite-sized pieces
1 4-ounce can chopped green chilies, including liquid
2 tablespoons cornstarch
¼ cup cold water
4 ounces grated mild Cheddar cheese (about 1 cup)
Chopped fresh chives for garnish (optional)

In a medium-sized saucepan, melt the butter over medium heat. Add the onion, garlic, and celery. Cook, stirring frequently, for about 4 to 5 minutes, or until the onion is tender. Add the broth, chicken, and chilies. Bring the mixture to a boil, cover, and simmer for about 10 minutes, or until the celery is crisp tender.

Meanwhile, in a small bowl or cup, stir together the cornstarch and water until well combined. Stir the mixture into the broth, and cook, stirring until the broth thickens, about 1 to 2 minutes. Lower the heat so that the soup simmers gently. In two or three batches, add the cheese to the soup, stirring well with a large spoon after each addition. Stir until the cheese melts. Continue to gently simmer the soup, stirring frequently, about 5 more minutes; *do not* allow it to come to a full boil. Garnish individual servings with chopped fresh chives, if desired.

Makes 4 to 5 servings.

Chicken and Cucumber Soup

Cooked cucumber and tarragon complement each other perfectly in this subtle and pleasing soup.

1½ tablespoons butter or margarine
1 medium-sized onion, finely chopped
1 small garlic clove, minced
1 green onion (scallion), including green top, thinly sliced
2 tablespoons all-purpose white flour
3 cups chicken broth
½ pound boneless cooked chicken meat, cut into bite-sized pieces
1 medium-sized cucumber, peeled, seeded, and diced
2 tablespoons chopped fresh parsley leaves
1 teaspoon lemon juice, preferably fresh
Generous ¼ teaspoon dried tarragon leaves
⅛ teaspoon white pepper, preferably freshly ground
¼ teaspoon salt

In a medium-sized saucepan, melt the butter over medium heat. Add the onion, garlic, and green onion. Cook, stirring occasionally, for about 4 to 5 minutes, or until the onion is tender.

Remove the pan from the heat. With a wooden spoon, stir in the flour until smooth and well blended. Return the pan to the heat and cook the butter-flour mixture, stirring, for 1 minute. Gradually add the broth, stirring until the mixture is smooth. Raise the heat and bring the mixture to a simmer. Add all the remaining ingredients. Lower the heat, cover, and simmer for 8 to 15 minutes, depending on the degree of crispness you prefer in the cucumbers.

Makes about 4 servings.

New England–Style Fish Chowder

2 tablespoons butter or margarine
1 large onion, finely chopped
1 celery stalk, very thinly sliced
1 medium-sized carrot, thinly sliced
2 cups peeled ½-inch potato cubes (about 1 very large potato)
2 cups fish stock (see page 301), or 2 cups water plus 2 packets or cubes vegetable bouillon
¼ cup finely chopped fresh parsley leaves
2 to 3 drops Tabasco sauce
1½ teaspoons dried basil leaves
½ teaspoon dried marjoram leaves
¼ teaspoon celery salt
½ teaspoon salt
¼ teaspoon black pepper, preferably freshly ground
4 cups whole milk, divided
1 tablespoon plus 1 teaspoon cornstarch
1 16-ounce package frozen skinless flounder fillets, partially thawed and cut into 1-inch cubes

In a large saucepan or small Dutch oven, combine the butter, onion, celery, carrot, potatoes, fish stock, parsley, Tabasco sauce, basil, marjoram, celery salt, salt, and pepper. Bring to a boil over medium-high heat, stirring occasionally. Cover the pan. Lower the heat and simmer for about 15 minutes, or until the potatoes are tender.

Stir 3½ cups of the milk into the soup. In a small cup, mix together the cornstarch and the remaining ½ cup of milk. Add to the soup. Raise the heat to medium-high. Cook the soup, stirring frequently, until it boils and thickens, about 3 or 4 minutes. Lower the heat to medium-low. Add the flounder to the soup. Stir to mix well. Cook the soup for an additional 4 to 5 minutes, or until the flounder flakes easily when tested with a fork.

Makes 5 to 6 servings.

Cheddar Cheese Soup with Tomato

2 tablespoons butter or margarine
¼ cup all-purpose white flour
4 cups whole milk
½ teaspoon powdered mustard
½ teaspoon salt
¼ teaspoon white pepper, preferably freshly ground
6 ounces sharp Cheddar cheese, grated (about 1½ cups)
3 canned imported Italian (plum) tomatoes or Italian-style tomatoes, drained and chopped
1 to 2 teaspoons finely chopped fresh chives for garnish (optional)

In a large saucepan, melt the butter over medium heat. Remove the pan from the heat and add the flour, stirring with a wire whisk or wooden spoon to blend well. Return the pan to the heat and cook for 1 minute, stirring. Gradually add the milk, stirring constantly. Continue stirring until the mixture is completely smooth.

Add the mustard, salt, and pepper. Cook over medium to medium-high heat, stirring frequently, until the mixture thickens and begins to boil, about 6 to 8 minutes. (If medium-high heat is used, be particularly careful that the mixture does not stick to the bottom of the pan and burn.) Add the cheese, stirring to blend well. Add the tomatoes and stir well. Cook for an additional 1 to 2 minutes, or until the cheese melts. Garnish individual servings with chopped chives, if desired.

Makes 4 to 5 servings.

Chili-Cheese Soup

Tangy and delicious, this soup makes a nice luncheon entrée or a first course for a Mexican meal.

5 or 6 bacon strips
4 green onions (scallions), including green tops, chopped
1 large garlic clove, minced
1 16-ounce can tomatoes, including juice, puréed in a food processor or blender
1 4-ounce can chopped green chilies, including liquid
2½ cups chicken stock or broth
2 to 3 drops Tabasco sauce
7 ounces sharp Cheddar cheese, grated or shredded (about 1¾ cups)
5 tablespoons all-purpose white flour

In a large frying pan, cook the bacon over medium-high heat until it is crisp and brown. (Reserve the bacon fat.) Transfer the bacon to a double thickness of paper towels to drain. When the bacon is cool enough to handle, finely crumble it and set it aside.

Discard all but about 2 tablespoons of the bacon fat from the pan. Add the green onions and garlic to the remaining bacon fat. Cook over medium-high heat, stirring constantly, for 2 minutes. With a large spoon, remove the onion and garlic to a small Dutch oven or large saucepan. Add the tomatoes, chilies, stock, and Tabasco sauce. Bring to a boil over high heat. Lower the heat, cover, and simmer the mixture for about 10 minutes.

Meanwhile, in a medium-sized bowl, toss the cheese and flour together, making sure the flour evenly coats the cheese. In three or four portions, add the cheese-flour mixture to the simmering soup, stirring well after each addition. Stir until the consistency is smooth. Continue to simmer the soup, stirring frequently, for about 8 to 10 minutes, or until the flour is cooked and the flavors are well blended. Do not boil. Garnish each serving with 1 or 2 tablespoonfuls of the crumbled bacon.

Makes 4 to 5 servings.

Broccoli-Cauliflower Cheese Soup

2 large broccoli stalks (about 1¼ pounds total weight)
2½ cups small cauliflower flowerets
3 tablespoons butter or margarine
2 medium-sized onions, finely chopped
2 tablespoons chopped fresh parsley leaves
½ cup all-purpose white flour, divided
3 cups water
2 chicken bouillon cubes
4 cups whole or lowfat milk
½ teaspoon salt, or to taste
½ teaspoon white or black pepper, preferably freshly ground
Pinch of ground nutmeg
12 ounces grated or shredded very sharp Cheddar cheese (about 3 cups)

Trim the flowerets from the broccoli stalks; reserve the stems. Coarsely chop the flowerets. Using a vegetable peeler or sharp knife, remove and discard the tough outer layer from the reserved broccoli stems. Cut the stems crosswise into ⅛-inch-thick slices. Cut the cauliflower flowerets into ⅛-inch-thick slices. Set the vegetables aside.

Melt the butter in a 4- to 5-quart pot over medium-high heat. Add the onions and parsley and cook, stirring, for 4 to 5 minutes, or until the onions are limp but not browned. Using a wooden spoon, stir in 2 tablespoons of the flour until thoroughly incorporated and smooth. Gradually stir the water and then the bouillon cubes into the pot. Bring the mixture to a boil. Stir in the reserved broccoli and cauliflower. Lower the heat and simmer, uncovered, for 5 minutes. Stir in the milk, salt, pepper, and nutmeg and let the mixture return to a simmer.

In a large bowl, combine all but ¼ cup of the grated cheese with the remaining flour and toss until the cheese is evenly coated with the flour. Stir the cheese-flour mixture into the pot. Cook, uncovered, stirring frequently, for 3 to 4 minutes longer, or until the cheese melts and the soup thickens slightly and is piping hot *but not* boiling. Sprinkle the soup with the remaining grated cheese and serve immediately.

The soup may also be served reheated. Rewarm over low heat, stirring frequently; *do not* let it come to a boil.

Makes 7 to 8 servings.

Creamy Brussels Sprouts Soup

2 tablespoons butter or margarine
1 medium-sized onion, finely chopped
1 small garlic clove, minced
3 cups chicken stock or broth
1 pound medium-sized Brussels sprouts (about 17 to 20), trimmed and shredded
2 tablespoons dry sherry
Generous ¼ teaspoon dried thyme leaves
Generous ¼ teaspoon dried tarragon leaves
¼ teaspoon salt
⅛ teaspoon black pepper, preferably freshly ground
Pinch of ground cloves
2 cups whole milk, divided
1 tablespoon plus 1 teaspoon cornstarch
½ cup light cream or half-and-half

In a large saucepan or small Dutch oven, melt the butter over medium heat. Add the onion and garlic and cook, stirring frequently, for about 4 to 5 minutes, or until the onion is tender. Add the stock, Brussels sprouts, sherry, thyme, tarragon, salt, pepper, and cloves. Bring to a boil over high heat.

Cover, lower the heat, and simmer for about 7 to 8 minutes, or until the Brussels sprouts are tender. Remove the pan from the heat and cool slightly.

In a food processor, purée about 1½ cups of the Brussels sprouts mixture. Return the purée to the pan and stir to mix well. Add 1¾ cups of the milk to the pan and cook over medium heat, stirring occasionally.

In a small cup, stir together the cornstarch and remaining milk, blending well. Stir this mixture into the soup. Raise the heat to medium-high and cook, stirring frequently, until the soup boils and thickens. Remove the pan from the heat and stir to stop the boiling. Stir in the cream. Return the pan to the medium-low heat and cook, stirring, just until hot; *do not boil.*

Makes 5 to 6 servings.

Cauliflower, Pimiento, and Cheese Soup

  1 tablespoon vegetable oil
  4 medium-sized green onions (scallions), including green
    tops, chopped
  3½ cups chicken broth
  1 8-ounce can tomato sauce
  4 cups chopped cauliflower flowerets
  ¼ teaspoon powdered mustard
  ⅛ teaspoon black pepper, preferably freshly ground
  6 ounces grated Monterey Jack cheese (about 1½ cups)
  ¼ cup all-purpose white flour
  1 2-ounce jar chopped pimientos, including juice
  ¼ teaspoon salt (optional)

In a large saucepan or small Dutch oven, combine the oil and green onions. Cook over medium-high heat, stirring frequently, for about 3 to 4 minutes. Add the broth, tomato sauce, cauliflower, mustard, and pepper. Stir to mix well. Bring to a boil over medium-high heat. Cover, lower the heat, and simmer for about 3 minutes.

Meanwhile, in a medium-sized bowl, toss together the cheese and the flour, being sure that the cheese is well coated with flour. In three or four portions, add the cheese mixture to the simmering soup, stirring well after each addition. Continue stirring until the cheese has melted and the consistency is smooth. Gently simmer for 5 minutes, uncovered, stirring frequently. Add the pimientos and salt (if used) and continue gently simmering for an additional 5 minutes, or until the soup has thickened slightly.

Makes 4 to 6 servings.

Celery-Tomato Soup

This recipe showcases the delicate flavor and crisp texture of a vegetable that is usually assigned a supporting, rather than a primary, role in soup cookery.

3 tablespoons butter or margarine
4 cups thinly sliced celery
2 medium-sized onions, finely chopped
3 cups chicken stock or broth
¼ cup finely chopped fresh parsley leaves
½ cup dry white wine
1 teaspoon dried marjoram leaves
Generous ¼ teaspoon dried thyme leaves
¼ teaspoon dried tarragon leaves
⅛ teaspoon black pepper, preferably freshly ground
2 16-ounce cans tomatoes, including juice, puréed in a blender or food processor
1 teaspoon sugar
½ teaspoon salt

In a large saucepan or Dutch oven, melt the butter over medium-high heat. Add the celery and onions and cook, stirring frequently, for 4 to 5 minutes, or until the onions are soft. Add the stock, parsley, wine, marjoram, thyme, tarragon, and pepper. Cover, lower the heat, and simmer, stirring occasionally, for about 20 minutes, or until the celery is just tender. Add the tomatoes, sugar, and salt and stir to combine well. Simmer, covered, for an additional 5 minutes.

Makes 6 to 8 servings.

Easy Corn Soup

2½ tablespoons butter or margarine
1 small onion, coarsely chopped
1 small celery stalk, coarsely chopped
1 small parsnip, peeled and coarsely chopped (optional)
1 cup water
2 chicken bouillon cubes
1 medium-sized potato, peeled and finely diced
1 1-pound bag loose-pack frozen white (shoepeg) or yellow corn kernels (about 4 cups)
1 cup whole or lowfat milk
Generous ¼ teaspoon white pepper, preferably freshly ground
¾ cup light cream or half-and-half
Salt to taste
1 to 2 teaspoons chopped fresh parsley leaves for garnish (optional)

Combine the butter, onion, celery, and parsnip (if used) in a 3-quart saucepan or pot. Cook over medium-high heat, stirring, for 4 to 5 minutes, or until the onion is limp. Stir in the water, bouillon cubes, and potato. Bring the mixture to a boil; then lower the heat and simmer, covered, for 5 minutes. Add 1 cup of the corn kernels and continue to cook, covered, for 6 to 8 minutes, or until the potato is tender; stir occasionally to prevent the potato from sticking to the bottom of the pan. Cool the mixture slightly.

Transfer the mixture to a food processor or blender and purée until completely smooth. Return the purée to the pan and add the milk, remaining corn kernels, and pepper. Simmer, covered, until the corn is cooked through, about 5 minutes. Stir in the cream and reheat the soup until it is piping hot *but not* boiling. Add salt to taste. Garnish the soup with a sprinkling of chopped fresh parsley, if desired.

Makes 4 to 5 servings.

Mexican Corn and Tomato Soup

2 tablespoons vegetable oil
1 medium-sized onion, finely chopped
1 large garlic clove, minced
2½ cups chicken stock or broth, divided
3 cups loose-pack frozen corn kernels
1 small bay leaf
¼ teaspoon dried oregano leaves
⅛ teaspoon white pepper, preferably freshly ground
1 cup drained and chopped canned tomatoes, preferably imported Italian (plum) tomatoes
3 tablespoons drained and chopped canned green chilies
½ to ⅔ cup light cream or half-and-half (approximately)
¼ to ½ teaspoon salt, or to taste
About 2 teaspoons finely chopped fresh parsley leaves for garnish (optional)

Combine the oil, onion, and garlic in a large saucepan. Cook over medium-high heat, stirring, for 3 to 4 minutes, or until the onion is limp. Add 1 cup of the stock, the corn, bay leaf, oregano, and pepper. Bring the mixture to a boil. Cover, lower the heat, and simmer for 10 minutes.

Remove the pan from the heat and discard the bay leaf. Scoop about 1½ cups of the mixture from the pan and transfer it to a blender or food processor. Blend or process until completely puréed and smooth. Return the purée to the saucepan. Stir in the remaining stock, tomatoes, green chilies, ½ cup of the cream, and the salt. Add a bit more cream if a thinner soup is desired. Heat the soup over medium heat for 4 to 5 minutes, or until it is piping hot *but not* boiling. Sprinkle the soup with finely chopped fresh parsley, if desired.

Makes 4 to 5 servings.

Green Onion Soup with Dill

Very easy, but good. If at all possible, use fresh dillweed in the recipe.

> ¼ cup butter or margarine
> 3 cups chopped green onions (scallions), including green tops
> ⅓ cup all-purpose white flour
> 6 cups chicken stock or broth
> 1½ cups peeled and finely cubed boiling potatoes
> ¼ teaspoon black pepper, preferably freshly ground
> 1½ tablespoons finely chopped fresh dillweed, coarse stems removed (If unavailable, substitute 2½ teaspoons dried dillweed.)
> ¼ cup commercial sour cream or regular or lowfat plain yogurt
> ⅛ to ¼ teaspoon salt, or to taste

Combine the butter and green onions in a 3- to 4-quart pot or saucepan over medium-high heat. Cook, stirring, for 4 to 5 minutes, or until they are limp. Using a wooden spoon, stir in the flour until well blended and smooth. Cook, stirring, for 1 minute. Stir in the stock until thoroughly incorporated and smooth. Add the potatoes and pepper. Bring the mixture to a boil; then lower the heat and cover the pot. Simmer, stirring occasionally, for 5 minutes. Stir in the dillweed and continue simmering, covered, for 5 to 7 minutes longer, or until the potatoes are tender.

In a small bowl, combine the sour cream and about ⅓ cup of broth from the soup pot. Using a wire whisk or fork, beat the mixture until completely smooth. Stir the sour cream-broth mixture into the pot and remove it from the heat. Stir in the salt.

The soup may also be served reheated. Heat over medium heat, stirring occasionally; *do not* allow the soup to come to a boil.

Makes 6 to 8 servings.

Creamy Lettuce and Green Pea Soup

1 tablespoon butter or margarine
1 medium-sized onion, finely chopped
2 cups chicken stock or broth
4 cups shredded crisphead ("iceberg") lettuce
1½ cups loose-pack frozen green peas, rinsed in cool water and drained
Scant ½ teaspoon dried tarragon leaves
¼ teaspoon dried thyme leaves
½ teaspoon salt, or to taste
¼ teaspoon white pepper, preferably freshly ground
1 cup light cream or half-and-half
About 1 tablespoon fine lettuce shreds for garnish (optional)

In a large saucepan, melt the butter over medium heat. Add the onion and cook, stirring frequently, for 4 to 5 minutes, or until the onion is tender. Add the stock, lettuce, peas, tarragon, thyme, salt, and pepper. Bring the mixture to a boil over high heat. Cover, lower the heat, and simmer for about 7 to 8 minutes, or until the peas are just tender. Cool the mixture slightly.

In batches, blend in a blender on low speed for 10 seconds. Then raise the speed to high and purée until completely smooth. Return the purée to the pot. Add the cream and stir to mix well. Cook over medium heat for an additional 2 to 3 minutes, stirring frequently, or until the soup is hot. *Do not boil.* Garnish individual servings with a few fine shreds of lettuce, if desired.

Makes 4 to 5 servings.

Cream of Spinach Soup

3 tablespoons butter or margarine
1 medium-sized onion, chopped
1 garlic clove, minced (optional)
2 tablespoons all-purpose white flour
2 cups chicken stock or broth
1 10-ounce package frozen leaf spinach, thawed, drained,
     and coarsely chopped
¼ teaspoon black pepper, preferably freshly ground
⅛ teaspoon dried thyme leaves
⅛ teaspoon dried basil leaves
Pinch of ground nutmeg
1 cup whole milk
1 cup half-and-half or light cream
¼ to ½ teaspoon salt, or to taste

Melt the butter in a large saucepan over medium-high heat. Add the onion and garlic (if used) and cook, stirring, for 3 to 4 minutes, or until the onion is limp. Using a wooden spoon, stir in the flour until thoroughly blended and smooth. Cook, stirring, for about 1 minute longer. Stir in the stock until thoroughly incorporated and smooth. Then stir in the spinach, pepper, thyme, basil, and nutmeg. Bring the mixture to a boil. Then lower the heat and simmer, uncovered, for about 10 minutes; stir occasionally to prevent the spinach from sticking to the bottom of the pan. Remove the pan from the heat and set it aside to cool slightly.

Transfer the mixture to a food processor or blender. If a processor is used, process in on/off bursts; if a blender is used, blend on low speed. Process or blend until the mixture is puréed, but very small flecks of spinach remain. Return the purée to the saucepan previously used. Stir in the milk, half-and-half, and salt. Heat the soup over medium-high heat, stirring occasionally, for 3 to 4 minutes longer, or until it is piping hot *but not* boiling.

Makes 4 to 5 servings.

Creole Tomato Soup

Here's a nice, quick alternative to vegetable soup. It can be served as a first course or as part of a soup and sandwich meal.

> 2 tablespoons butter or margarine
> 1 medium-sized sweet green pepper, diced
> 1 medium-sized onion, finely chopped
> 1 medium-sized garlic clove, minced
> 2 16-ounce cans tomatoes (preferably Italian-style [plum] tomatoes), including juice, puréed in a blender or food processor
> 2 chicken bouillon cubes or 2 vegetable bouillon packets or cubes
> 2 cups water
> Scant 1 teaspoon dried marjoram leaves
> ½ teaspoon dried basil leaves
> ¼ teaspoon dried thyme leaves
> 2 bay leaves
> 1 to 2 drops Tabasco sauce, or to taste
> ¼ teaspoon black pepper, preferably freshly ground
> ½ teaspoon salt

In a Dutch oven over medium-high heat, melt the butter. Add the green pepper, onion, and garlic. Cook, stirring, for about 4 to 5 minutes, or until the onion is soft. Add all the remaining ingredients. Cover and bring to a boil. Lower the heat and simmer the soup for about 15 minutes, or until the green pepper is tender and the flavors are well blended. Discard the bay leaves.

Makes about 4 servings.

Creamy Tomato Soup with Chunky Vegetables

> 2 tablespoons butter or margarine
> 1 medium-sized onion, finely chopped

1 large garlic clove, minced
3 cups chicken stock or broth
1 large celery stalk, diced
1½ cups ¾-inch unpeeled new potato cubes (2 small potatoes)
1 medium-sized turnip, peeled and diced
1 medium-sized sweet green pepper, diced
¼ cup dry sherry
¼ cup finely chopped fresh parsley leaves
¾ teaspoon dried basil leaves
¼ teaspoon dried thyme leaves
¼ teaspoon dried marjoram leaves
⅛ teaspoon powdered mustard
2 drops Tabasco sauce
⅛ teaspoon black pepper, preferably freshly ground
1½ tablespoons cornstarch
¼ cup cold water
1 8-ounce can tomato sauce
¾ cup light cream or half-and-half
⅛ teaspoon salt, or to taste

In a large saucepan or small pot, melt the butter over medium-high heat. Add the onion and garlic. Cook, stirring frequently, for about 5 minutes, or until the onion is soft. Add the stock, celery, potatoes, turnip, green pepper, sherry, parsley, basil, thyme, marjoram, mustard, Tabasco sauce, and black pepper. Bring the mixture to a boil. Cover, lower the heat, and simmer for about 15 to 20 minutes, or until the vegetables are tender. (The celery will be crisp-tender.)

Meanwhile, in a small bowl, stir the cornstarch and water together until thoroughly blended. Add the cornstarch-water mixture to the liquid in the pot. Raise the heat slightly and cook, stirring frequently, until the stock thickens and boils, about 1 to 2 minutes.

Lower the heat again. Stir in the tomato sauce, cream, and salt (if used). Heat the soup for an additional 4 to 5 minutes; *do not boil.*

Makes 4 to 5 servings.

Bloody Mary Soup

Good as a first course at brunch, this soup is a real eye-opener. If you prefer your Bloody Marys "virgin," omit the vodka.

    2 tablespoons butter or margarine
    1 medium-sized onion, finely chopped
    1 small garlic clove, minced
    2 teaspoons sugar
    1 28-ounce can tomatoes (preferably Italian-style [plum]
        tomatoes), including juice, partially puréed in a blender
        or food processor
    2 teaspoons Worcestershire sauce
    1 teaspoon lemon juice, preferably fresh
    ⅛ teaspoon black pepper, preferably freshly ground
    Scant ½ teaspoon salt, or to taste
    2 to 4 tablespoons vodka, or to taste
    Finely chopped fresh parsley leaves or chives for garnish
        (optional)

In a medium-sized saucepan, melt the butter over medium heat. Add the onion and garlic and cook, stirring frequently, for about 4 to 5 minutes, or until the onion is tender. Add the sugar, tomatoes, Worcestershire sauce, lemon juice, pepper, and salt. Stir to mix well. Bring to a boil over high heat. Cover, lower the heat, and simmer for 15 to 17 minutes, or until the flavors are well blended. Add the vodka and simmer for an additional 2 to 3 minutes. Garnish individual servings with chopped parsley leaves, if desired.

Makes about 4 servings.

Fiesta Vegetable Soup

Rice is teamed up with colorful bits of carrot, celery, pimiento, parsley, and corn in this light and festive soup. Served along with a basket of nacho chips, it makes a good and easy first course for a Mexican-style meal. Or try it for lunch, along with grilled cheese sandwiches.

¼ cup long-grain white rice, very well washed and drained
3 tablespoons peanut or vegetable oil
1 small onion, chopped
1 tablespoon finely diced celery
1 tablespoon finely diced carrot
2 garlic cloves, minced
5½ cups chicken stock or broth
1 small bay leaf
¼ teaspoon black pepper, preferably freshly ground
Scant ⅛ teaspoon chili powder
Pinch of dried marjoram leaves
2 to 3 drops Tabasco sauce
1 cup loose-pack frozen corn kernels
1 2-ounce jar chopped pimientos, well drained
2 tablespoons finely chopped fresh parsley leaves

Turn out the rice onto paper towels and pat it dry. Combine the rice and oil in a large saucepan or small pot over medium-high heat. Cook the rice, stirring constantly, for 3 to 4 minutes, or until it begins to turn golden; lower the heat slightly if the rice begins to brown. Stir the onion, celery, carrot, and garlic into the rice. Cook, stirring, for 3 to 4 minutes, or until the onion is limp. Add the stock, bay leaf, pepper, chili powder, marjoram, and Tabasco sauce. Bring the mixture to a boil; then lower the heat and simmer, covered, for 12 minutes. Add the corn and pimientos and continue simmering, covered, for about 5 minutes longer, or until the rice and corn are just tender. Discard the bay leaf. Stir in the parsley.

The soup is particularly attractive served in an earthenware pot or deep bowl. Or present it in individual bowls, if desired.

Makes 5 to 6 servings.

Oriental Vegetable Soup

This makes a quick, yet very appealing beginning to an Oriental-style meal.

> 2 dried Chinese black mushrooms, *or* dried Japanese shi-itake mushrooms
> ¼ cup boiling water
> 2 medium-sized green onions (scallions)
> 4 cups chicken stock or broth
> 3 cups coarsely chopped celery cabbage
> 1 small sliver peeled gingerroot, very finely minced
> 1 teaspoon soy sauce
> ⅛ teaspoon white pepper, preferably freshly ground
> 7 to 8 fresh snow pea pods, trimmed and halved on the diagonal

Put the mushrooms in a small bowl with the boiling water and set them aside to soak for 15 minutes.

Meanwhile, trim the green tops from the green onions. Coarsely chop the tops and set them aside. Cut the green onion white parts crosswise into ¼-inch pieces. Combine the stock, green onion white pieces, celery cabbage, gingerroot, soy sauce, and pepper in a 2- to 3-quart saucepan. Bring the mixture to a boil over medium-high heat. Then cover the pan, lower the heat, and simmer the mixture for 10 minutes.

Trim off and discard the tough stems from the soaked mushrooms. (Reserve the soaking liquid.) Using a sharp knife, cut the mushrooms into very thin slices. Add the mushroom slices, reserved soaking liquid, and snow peas to the pan. Simmer the soup, covered, for 2 minutes longer. Sprinkle the chopped green onion tops over the soup and serve immediately.

Makes 4 to 5 servings.

10
ELEGANT SOUPS

Soup represents a wonderful opportunity to set the tone for the rest of the meal. A small, beautifully presented serving of a sumptuous soup can mark an occasion as special, or announce that the cook has taken extra care to please.

With this in mind, we've assembled a collection of recipes especially suited for serving at an elegant luncheon, dinner, or late-night supper. Included are such offerings as Creamy Seafood Bisque, Velvety Fennel Velouté, Asparagus-Cheese Potage, and Oyster and Mushroom Soup Florentine.

Some—but not all—of the soups which follow do require a bit more time to make than most in this book. However, they can often be partially or completely prepared in advance and simply assembled or reheated at serving time. And there are some recipes included here—Potage Vert, Good Wife Soup, and Curried Broccoli-Crab Soup, for example—that make a grand impression, but are really rather easy to prepare.

As you thumb through this chapter, you'll notice that some of the recipes feature "gourmet" ingredients, such as lobster, crab, imported dried mushrooms, and that outrageously expensive golden-yellow spice, saffron. While these are undeniably indulgences, soup represents perhaps the best way to "stretch" modest quantities of pricey items and feature them in a meal. Our luxurious Cream of Lobster Soup, for example, calls for only one 2-pound lobster and serves 5 to 6.

Besides the recipes presented here, there are others in *Soup's On!* suitable for important occasions. In particular, look through the chapters on cold soups and fish and shellfish soups for ideas.

Creamy Seafood Bisque

A smooth, richly flavored bisque featuring succulent bits of shrimp, crabmeat, and bay scallops.

> 8 or 9 medium-sized top quality, very fresh white mushrooms
> 1 tablespoon lemon juice, preferably fresh
> 2½ tablespoons butter or margarine

1 small onion, coarsely chopped
3 tablespoons all-purpose white flour
3 cups whole milk, divided
½ teaspoon soy sauce
Scant 1 teaspoon salt, or to taste
¼ teaspoon white pepper, preferably freshly ground
⅓ pound fresh or frozen (thawed) bay scallops (see Note),
  large ones cut in half
¼ pound fresh or frozen (thawed) peeled shrimp, cut into
  ½-inch pieces
⅓ pound fresh or frozen (thawed) crabmeat
½ cup light cream or half-and-half
2 teaspoons chopped fresh chives, *or* 1 teaspoon dried
  chives for garnish

Coarsely chop the mushrooms and toss them with the lemon juice. Melt the butter in a 3- to 4-quart soup pot or saucepan over medium-high heat. Add the onion and mushrooms and cook, stirring, for 5 to 6 minutes, or until the vegetables are limp and the mushrooms begin to release their juices. Using a wooden spoon, stir in the flour until well blended and smooth. Cook, stirring, for 1½ minutes longer.

Transfer the vegetable mixture to a blender. Add 1 cup of the milk to the blender. Blend the mixture until completely puréed and smooth. Return the purée to the pot. Stir in the remaining milk, soy sauce, salt, and pepper. Bring the mixture to a simmer over medium-high heat. Stir in the scallops and shrimp and allow the mixture to return to a simmer. Simmer, uncovered, stirring occasionally, for 4 to 6 minutes longer, or until the scallops and shrimp pieces are just cooked through. Add the crabmeat and cream and heat for about 2 to 3 minutes longer, or until the mixture is piping hot and the crabmeat is heated through.

Ladle the bisque into soup cups or bowls. Garnish each serving with a light sprinkling of chives.

Makes 4 to 5 servings.

Note: If bay scallops are unavailable, sea scallops may be substituted. In this case, cut each scallop into 4 or 5 bite-sized pieces.

Curried Broccoli-Crab Soup

The combination of ingredients may be unusual, but they provide a welcome change from the more typical crab soup. This soup tastes best when made just before serving, as the curry flavor intensifies upon refrigeration and tends to overwhelm the crab. We like to use frozen Alaskan king crabmeat or snow crabmeat because the red exterior color contrasts so nicely with the green of the broccoli.

> 2 tablespoons butter or margarine
> 2 tablespoons all-purpose white flour
> 4 cups whole milk
> 1 teaspoon salt
> ½ teaspoon curry powder
> ¼ teaspoon black pepper, preferably freshly ground
> ¼ teaspoon onion powder
> ⅛ teaspoon garlic powder
> 3 cups small broccoli flowerets
> ¾ cup cooked fresh or frozen (thawed) crabmeat, all shell removed
> 1 cup light cream or half-and-half

In a large saucepan, melt the butter over medium-low heat. Blend in the flour with a wooden spoon or wire whisk. Cook, stirring, for 1 to 2 minutes, or until the mixture is smooth. Gradually add the milk, stirring to blend well. Raise the heat to medium. Cook, stirring frequently with a wooden spoon, until the mixture thickens and boils, about 6 to 8 minutes. Add the salt, curry powder, pepper, onion powder, garlic powder, and broccoli. Cover and cook for about 10 minutes, or until the broccoli is tender.

If the crabmeat is in large chunks, flake it with a fork. Stir in the crabmeat and the cream. Heat the soup until piping hot, *but do not* let it boil.

Makes about 4 servings.

Variation

Curried Broccoli-Crab Soup also tastes delicious cold. To

serve chilled, reduce the amount of curry powder to ¼ teaspoon and increase the amount of salt to 1¼ teaspoons, or to
taste. Chill, covered, for at least 4 hours before serving.

Cream of Lobster Soup

Making this is a big production, but for an important occasion
few soups can match it.

5¼ cups fish stock (see page 301)
¼ cup dry white wine
1 2-pound live lobster, rinsed
1 cup coarsely chopped leek green parts, well washed and
    drained (see page 13), *or* ½ cup coarsely chopped green
    onions (scallions) and ½ cup coarsely chopped onion
4 parsley sprigs
1 ¼-inch-thick lemon slice
Generous ¼ teaspoon whole black peppercorns
Scant ¼ teaspoon dried thyme leaves
⅛ teaspoon white pepper, preferably freshly ground
⅛ teaspoon dried crushed red (hot) pepper
6½ tablespoons butter or margarine, divided
2 tablespoons Cognac
7 tablespoons all-purpose white flour
2 tablespoons tomato paste
2 cups heavy cream
½ teaspoon salt, or more to taste
About ½ cup lightly salted unsweetened whipped cream
    for garnish, *or* about 2 teaspoons very finely chopped
    fresh parsley leaves

In a large soup pot, bring the stock and wine to a rolling
boil over high heat. Add the lobster and tightly cover the pot;
boil for 6 minutes. Remove the pot from the heat. Using tongs,
remove the lobster from the stock and set it aside to cool. Add
the leek green parts, parsley, lemon slice, peppercorns, thyme,
white pepper, and dried red pepper to the stock; set it aside.

When the lobster is cool enough to handle, remove the meat as follows: Crack the claws and joint shells which connect to them using a nutcracker or mallet. Extract the meat with a small fork or the point of a small knife. (Don't worry if the meat seems underdone.) Reserve the meat in a small bowl. Return the empty shell pieces and any juices exuded by the lobster to the pot with the stock. Split the lobster in half lengthwise using a sharp knife. Discard the stomach sac and feathery gills in the area directly under the head. Also discard the narrow intestinal tube that runs down the length of the tail. Remove the tail meat and any pink roe and reserve with the claw meat; cover and refrigerate. Return the remainder of the lobster, including the paste-like, greenish-gray tomalley to the stock. Bring the ingredients to a boil over medium-high heat. Lower the heat and gently simmer, covered, for 45 to 50 minutes.

Turn out the mixture into a colander set over a large bowl to catch the stock; drain well. Then discard the solids. Strain the stock through a *very fine* sieve (or a fairly fine sieve lined with a triple thickness of lightly dampened cheesecloth). There should be about 3¾ cups; if there is less, add enough water to make this amount. (If there are more than 4 cups, return it to a saucepan and boil it over high heat, uncovered, for a few minutes, or until it is reduced to between 3¾ and 4 cups.) At this point, the stock may be refrigerated and final preparations can be made up to 24 hours later, if desired. Or preparations can be continued as follows: Coarsely dice the reserved lobster meat. Melt 2 tablespoons of the butter in a large saucepan over medium-high heat. Add the lobster meat and cook, stirring gently, for 1½ to 2 minutes, or until it is coated with butter. Pour the Cognac over the meat and ignite it with a match; then stir until the flames die out. Using a slotted spoon, transfer the meat to the bowl in which it was previously reserved. Add the remaining 4½ tablespoons of butter to the saucepan and melt over medium-high heat. Using a wooden spoon, vigorously stir in the flour until thoroughly incorporated and smooth. Cook, stirring, for 1½ minutes longer. Stir in the tomato paste and mix well. Gradually stir in the reserved stock until well blended and smooth. Bring the mixture to a boil over medium-high heat. Lower the heat and simmer for 3 to 4 minutes, or until the mixture thickens slightly. Stir in the cream and the reserved lobster meat. Add the salt. At this point, the soup may be slowly reheated to piping hot and served, although it is even better if first refrigerated for several hours (or overnight) so the flavors can mingle.

Gently reheat the soup to piping hot over medium-low heat, stirring occasionally; *do not* allow it to boil.

To serve, divide the liquid and lobster meat among very small bowls or soup cups. Garnish each serving with a dollop of whipped cream (or a decorative swirl of cream piped through a pastry tube). Or for a simpler garnish, top each serving with a pinch or two of freshly chopped parsley leaves.

Makes 5 to 6 servings.

Shrimp and Mushroom Soup Under Puff Pastry

If you're looking for a first course with razzle-dazzle, this is it! The recipe features a rich, velvety shrimp and mushroom soup tucked into individual ovenproof soup bowls or ramekins and then topped with puff pastry and baked. Although the presentation is quite dramatic and impressive, the use of commercial puff pastry makes the "show" fairly easy to pull off.

Ideally, six 1-cup ovenproof soup bowls or pots that are no wider than 4 to 5 inches across at the top should be used for this recipe. (Many of the French onion soup bowls sold are too big.) If suitably sized ramekins or mini-soufflé dishes are available, these will do, too. (In this case, most on the market are too small!) You need ones that will hold about 1 cup each and are about 4 inches across at the top.

> ½ pound very fresh unpeeled shrimp (If unavailable, substitute top-quality unpeeled frozen shrimp, thawed.)
> 2 cups bottled clam juice
> 2 cups chicken stock or broth

¼ cup dry white wine
1 medium-sized onion, chopped
1 ¼-inch-thick lemon slice
½ teaspoon dried thyme leaves
½ teaspoon whole black peppercorns
⅛ teaspoon dried crushed red (hot) pepper
5 tablespoons butter or margarine
1½ cups sliced fresh mushrooms
¼ cup all-purpose white flour
1 teaspoon tomato paste
¾ to 1 cup light cream or half-and-half (approximately)
¼ to ½ teaspoon salt, or more to taste
⅛ teaspoon white pepper, preferably freshly ground
1 17½-ounce package frozen puff pastry, thawed and then
   refrigerated until needed
1 large egg
1 tablespoon water

Rinse and drain the shrimp. Peel them, reserving the shells in one bowl and the shrimp in another. Dice the shrimp; then cover and refrigerate them.

Combine the shrimp shells, clam juice, stock, wine, onion, lemon slice, thyme, peppercorns, and dried red pepper in a 2- to 3-quart saucepan. Bring the mixture to a boil over medium-high heat. Lower the heat and simmer, uncovered, for about 30 minutes.

Strain the liquid through a *very fine sieve* (or a fairly fine sieve lined with a triple thickness of lightly dampened cheesecloth) into a bowl. Press down on the solids to force through as much liquid as possible; then discard them. There should be about 2¾ to 3 cups of broth. If there is less, add enough water to bring the amount to 2¾ cups. If there is more, boil it down to 3 cups or a little less. Set it aside.

Rinse out and dry the pan previously used. Add 2½ tablespoons of the butter to the pan and melt it over medium-high heat. Stir in the diced shrimp and mushrooms and cook, stirring, for about 2½ to 3 minutes, or until the shrimp turn pink and the mushrooms are slightly soft. Using a slotted spoon, remove the shrimp and mushrooms from the pan and reserve them in a bowl. Melt the remaining 2½ tablespoons of butter in the pan. Using a wooden spoon, stir in the flour until well blended and smooth. Cook, stirring, for 1½ minutes longer. Remove the pan from the heat and stir in the tomato paste until well blended. Vigorously stir the strained broth into the soup until completely incorporated and smooth. Return the pan to the heat. Bring the mixture to a simmer over medium-high heat; simmer for 2 minutes. Add the reserved shrimp and mushrooms and simmer for 1½ minutes longer. Stir in ¾ cup of cream, the salt, and pepper. If the soup seems too thick, stir in a bit more cream until the desired consistency is obtained. Remove the pan from the heat; set aside while the puff pastry is prepared. (Alternatively, cover and refrigerate the soup for up to 8 hours before completing final preparations. Then heat the soup to barely lukewarm *but not hot* again before using it.)

Complete preparations as follows: Preheat the oven to 425 degrees. Remove one sheet of the puff pastry dough from the refrigerator and unfold it on a lightly floured work surface. Using a lightly floured rolling pin, roll out the sheet to about 15 by 12 inches, or until it is large enough for three 5- to 6-inch-diameter rounds to be cut from it. (To determine the size needed, simply lay the soup bowls upside down on the pastry sheet, allowing a 1-inch margin around each.) Using a small sharp knife, form a round by cutting around a bowl *leaving a 1-inch margin.* Lift up the cut round from the work surface and use it as a pattern to cut out two more rounds. Cover and refrigerate the rounds; save the dough scraps for another use or discard them. Remove the second sheet of dough from the refrigerator and cut out three more pastry rounds. Return them to the refrigerator.

Divide the soup among the six soup bowls, filling them *no more than a scant two-thirds full.* (Don't overfill them, as the soup might erupt through the crust during baking.) In a small bowl or cup, beat together the egg and water until blended. Brush some of the egg-water wash around the rims of the soup bowls. Remove the pastry rounds from the refrigerator. Cover each bowl with a round, pressing the dough edges firmly against the edges of the bowl. Form a decorative edging by pressing the tines of a fork against the pastry edge all the way around. Brush the egg-water wash over the pastry tops and edges. Transfer the soup bowls to a baking sheet. Bake in a preheated 425 degree oven for 13 to 16 minutes, or until the pastry tops are puffy and golden. Serve immediately.

Makes 6 servings.

Oyster and Mushroom Soup Florentine

The idea of combining oysters and spinach in a soup came from a recipe served at the Seasons restaurant in Boston. Including mushrooms—which complement the other two ingredients beautifully—was an addition we devised. This is an elegant, subtly flavored soup.

> 1 pound fresh spinach
> 12 ounces shucked fresh oysters, including their liquor (about 1½ cups)
> 1¾ cups coarsely chopped fresh white mushrooms (about ⅓ pound)
> 1½ teaspoons lemon juice, preferably fresh
> 4½ tablespoons butter or margarine, divided
> ⅓ cup chopped onion
> 2½ tablespoons all-purpose white flour
> 2½ cups chicken stock or broth
> Generous ¼ teaspoon dried thyme leaves
> Generous ¼ teaspoon black pepper, preferably freshly ground
> 1⅔ cups whole milk
> 1 cup light cream
> ¼ to ½ teaspoon salt

Put the spinach in a large bowl or tub of cool water and swish back and forth to loosen any grit in the crinkles of the leaves. Turn out the spinach into a colander and rinse under cool running water. Then, swish the leaves in a large bowl of cool water once again and turn out into a colander. Thoroughly rinse under cool running water once more. (If the leaves are especially dirty, a third washing and rinsing may be needed to ensure they are completely grit-free.) Set the spinach aside until thoroughly drained.

Drain the oysters, reserving their liquor in a small bowl or cup. Quarter the oysters and set them aside. Toss the mushrooms and lemon juice together until well mixed.

Melt 1½ tablespoons of the butter in a large saucepan over medium-high heat. Add the mushrooms and lemon juice and cook, stirring, for about 2 minutes, or until the mushrooms are slightly soft but not exuding their juices. Using a slotted spoon, transfer the mushrooms to a large bowl.

Melt 1 tablespoon more of the butter in the saucepan. Add the oysters and cook, stirring, for about 3 minutes, or until they shrink slightly and curl at the edges. Using the slotted spoon, transfer the oysters to the bowl with the mushrooms.

Melt the remaining 2 tablespoons of the butter in the saucepan. Add the onion and cook, stirring, for 4 to 5 minutes, or until they are limp. Using a wooden spoon, stir in the flour until well blended and smooth. Stir in the stock until thoroughly incorporated and smooth. Add the spinach, thyme, and pepper. Bring the mixture to a boil; then lower the heat and simmer, uncovered, stirring occasionally, for 5 minutes. Remove the pan from the heat and let cool slightly.

Transfer the mixture to a food processor and process in on/off bursts until the spinach is puréed, but distinct flecks of it remain visible. Return the mixture to the saucepan previously used. Stir in the liquor from the oysters, the milk, cream, and reserved oysters and mushrooms. Place over medium heat and heat, covered, until piping hot *but not* boiling. Stir in the salt.

The soup may also be made ahead and reheated over medium heat, if desired. Do not allow it to come to a full boil.

Makes 5 to 6 servings.

Scallop Soup Suprême

Deliciously rich and velvety smooth, this soup showcases the delicate flavor and toothsome texture of scallops.

1½ pounds fresh bay scallops, *or* 1½ pounds fresh sea scallops, quartered
5 tablespoons butter or margarine, divided
1 large onion, coarsely chopped
1½ tablespoons chopped celery
1½ tablespoons all-purpose white flour
¼ teaspoon powdered mustard
1½ cups bottled clam juice
¾ cup peeled and finely chopped boiling potatoes
2½ to 2¾ cups whole milk (approximately), divided
¼ to ½ teaspoon salt, or to taste
Scant ½ teaspoon white pepper, preferably freshly ground
1½ cups light cream or half-and-half
2½ teaspoons lemon juice, preferably fresh
About 2 teaspoons chopped fresh parsley leaves for garnish

Rinse and thoroughly drain the scallops. Combine them with 3 tablespoons of the butter in a 3-quart saucepan over medium-high heat. Cook, stirring, for about 2 minutes, or until the scallops are just cooked through. Using a slotted spoon, transfer a generous half of the scallops to a bowl. Transfer the other half to a blender; set it aside.

Add the remaining 2 tablespoons of butter, the onion, and celery to the saucepan. Cook, stirring, for 4 to 5 minutes, or until the onion is limp. Using a wooden spoon, stir in the flour until well blended and smooth. Continue cooking, stirring, for 1½ minutes longer. Transfer the onion-celery mixture and the mustard to the blender with the reserved scallops.

Add the clam juice and potatoes to the pan previously used and bring them to a boil. Lower the heat and simmer, uncovered, for 9 to 12 minutes, or until the potatoes are tender but not mushy; stir occasionally to prevent them from sticking to the bottom of the pan. Transfer the potatoes and the clam juice to the blender. Add 1½ cups of the milk to the blender. Blend on low speed for 10 seconds. Then raise the speed to high and blend until completely puréed and smooth.

Return the purée to the saucepan, along with the reserved whole scallops. Stir in the salt, pepper, cream, and lemon juice. Stir in 1 more cup of milk. If the soup seems too thick, thin it with additional milk until the desired consistency is obtained. Heat the mixture, uncovered, over medium heat until piping hot *but not* boiling; stir occasionally.

Ladle the soup into bowls. Garnish each serving with a light sprinkling of parsley.

Makes 5 to 6 servings.

Artichoke Soup

An elegant and subtly flavored soup. It's a wonderful treat for artichoke lovers.

> 2 medium-sized artichokes, stems trimmed off even with the base
> 1 large garlic clove, mashed with a fork
> 3 tablespoons butter or margarine
> 1 small onion, finely chopped
> ⅓ cup all-purpose white flour
> 2½ cups whole milk
> 1½ cups chicken stock or broth
> ⅛ teaspoon ground nutmeg
> ¼ teaspoon white pepper, preferably freshly ground
> ¼ teaspoon salt
> ½ cup light cream or half-and-half
> 2 teaspoons lemon juice, preferably fresh

Put the artichokes and garlic in a large saucepan or small pot and add 4 or 5 inches of water. Cover and bring to a boil over high heat. Lower the heat and simmer the artichokes for about 35 to 40 minutes, or until an outer leaf pulls away from the base very easily. Drain the artichokes well in a colander and set them aside. Discard the garlic.

When the artichokes are cool enough to handle, discard the outermost leaves around the base. Begin removing the additional leaves, scraping the flesh from the inside bottom of each, using a teaspoon. Put the flesh in a small bowl. Each of the outer leaves will yield only about ¼ teaspoon. However, more flesh can be removed from the interior leaves. Also, the whole bottom of each of the tender innermost leaves can be cut off and used. You should have about 1 cup of total scrapings and leaf bottoms. Discard the chokes, the coarse fibers covering the artichoke hearts. Coarsely dice the hearts. Reserve the meat from the leaves and the hearts separately.

In a large saucepan, melt the butter over medium heat. Add the onion and cook, stirring frequently, for about 4 to 5 minutes, or until the onion is tender. Remove the pan from the heat. With a wire whisk or wooden spoon, stir in the flour, blending until it is smooth. Return the pan to the heat and cook for 1 minute. Add the milk, stirring until the mixture is smooth. Stir in the stock, nutmeg, and white pepper. Cook over medium to medium-high heat, stirring frequently, until the soup boils and thickens, about 6 to 8 minutes. If the higher heat is used, stir almost constantly. Remove the pan from the heat and let cool slightly. In a blender, purée the meat from the artichoke leaves with 2 cups of the milk-stock mixture. Return the purée to the pan and stir to mix well. Stir in the artichoke hearts. Add the salt and cream and stir to blend. Stir in the lemon juice. Cook the soup over medium-low heat for an additional 4 or 5 minutes, *but do not* allow it to boil.

Makes 4 to 5 servings.

Asparagus-Cheese Potage

A rich, creamy-gold soup brightened with tender bits of asparagus, this makes a nice luncheon entrée.

> 1 pound fresh asparagus spears, washed and drained
> 2 tablespoons butter or margarine
> 1 medium-sized onion, finely chopped
> 6½ tablespoons all-purpose white flour, divided
> 3¾ cups chicken stock or broth
> ⅛ teaspoon white pepper, preferably freshly ground
> 4 ounces grated mild Cheddar cheese (about 1 cup packed)
> 1 cup half-and-half or whole milk
> 2 egg yolks
> ⅓ cup diced peeled, seeded, and chopped tomato, preferably vine ripened (optional)

Gently break off the tough woody ends of the asparagus spears and discard them. Cut the spears crosswise into ¼-inch-long pieces; if desired, reserve the tips separately to use as a garnish.

Combine the butter and onion in a 2- to 3-quart saucepan. Cook the onion over medium-high heat, stirring, for 4 to 5 minutes, or until it is limp. Using a wooden spoon, stir in 3½ tablespoons of the flour until well blended and smooth. Stir in the stock, asparagus pieces, and pepper and bring the mixture to a boil. Lower the heat and simmer the mixture, covered, for 7 to 10 minutes, or until the asparagus is just tender.

Meanwhile, if the asparagus tips are reserved for a garnish, combine them with a tablespoon or two of water in a small saucepan over medium-high heat. Cook them for about 3 minutes, or until they are almost tender. Turn out the tips into a colander and cool them under cold running water. Set aside to drain.

Toss together the cheese and the remaining 3 tablespoons of flour until the cheese is evenly coated with the flour. Beat the half-and-half into the egg yolks in a small deep bowl.

When the asparagus pieces are cooked through, stir the cheese-flour mixture into the saucepan. Cook, stirring, for 3 to

4 minutes, or until the cheese melts and the mixture is smooth and hot *but not* boiling. Stir in the milk-egg yolk mixture and the tomatoes (if used). Continue cooking, stirring constantly, for 5 to 6 minutes longer, or until the soup is slightly thickened and piping hot; *do not* allow it to come to a boil. Ladle the soup into individual soup bowls. If the asparagus tips were prepared, garnish the center of each soup bowl with 2 or 3 of them.

Asparagus-Cheese Potage is best served immediately, but it may be made ahead and reheated, if desired. Rewarm over low heat, stirring frequently; do not let the soup come to a boil or it will curdle.

Makes 4 to 5 servings.

Velvety Fennel Velouté

In this recipe, long, slow cooking brings out the intense anise-celery taste of the fennel. The soup makes a perfect first course for a special dinner.

2 medium-sized fennel bulbs
⅓ cup olive oil
6 medium-sized green onions (scallions), including green tops, coarsely chopped
1 large garlic clove, minced
4 cups chicken stock or broth, divided
3 tablespoons butter or margarine
3½ tablespoons all-purpose white flour
3 large egg yolks
1 cup light cream or half-and-half
½ teaspoon salt, or more to taste
¼ teaspoon white pepper, preferably freshly ground

If the fennel bulbs are purchased untrimmed, cut off all but the bottom 4½ inches. Reserve the tenderest leaves; then discard the remaining leaves and the tops. Cut a ¼-inch-thick slice from the root end and discard it. Complete preparation of untrimmed or pretrimmed bulbs by discarding the two tough outer stalks from each. Coarsely chop the bulbs. Reserve several sprigs of fennel leaves for the garnish; coarsely chop the remainder. Add them to the chopped fennel bulbs. Put the chopped fennel pieces in a colander and rinse them well; let stand until thoroughly drained.

Combine the oil, green onions, and garlic in a large heavy skillet. Cook over medium-high heat, stirring, for 3 minutes. Add the chopped fennel and cook, stirring, for 2 to 3 minutes, or until the pieces are coated with the oil. Lower the heat and cover the skillet. Very gently cook the vegetables for 25 to 30 minutes, or until they are soft and golden, but not browned. Set the skillet aside to cool slightly.

Transfer the fennel-green onion mixture to a blender container. Add 1 cup of the stock to the blender. Blend on low speed for 10 seconds. Then raise the speed to high and blend for several minutes, or until the mixture is completely puréed. Set it aside.

Melt the butter in a medium-sized saucepan over medium-high heat. Using a wooden spoon, stir in the flour until well blended and smooth. Cook, stirring, for 1 minute. Stir in the remaining stock until thoroughly incorporated. Remove the pan from the heat. Strain the puréed fennel mixture through a very fine sieve into the saucepan; press down on the solids to force through as much liquid as possible. Return the pan to the heat and bring the mixture to a boil, stirring. Cover and simmer for 2 to 3 minutes.

Meanwhile, rinse out the blender container. Combine the egg yolks, cream, salt, and pepper in the blender and blend until very smooth. Stir the egg yolk-cream mixture into the saucepan. Heat the mixture, stirring constantly, for 4 to 6 minutes, or until it thickens slightly and coats the spoon; *do not* allow it to come near the simmering point or the soup may curdle. (If the soup starts to overheat, lift it from the heat, stirring, and cool slightly before continuing.)

Ladle the soup into soup cups or small bowls. Garnish each serving with a small sprig of fennel.

Makes 4 to 6 servings.

Fennel and Sweet Pepper Soup

Fennel seeds combine with sweet peppers and chilies to give this unusual soup its distinctive and pleasing flavor.

1 cup diced sweet red pepper (If unavailable, substitute sweet green pepper.)
¼ cup olive oil, divided
1 cup coarsely chopped onion
1 large garlic clove, minced
5 large sweet green peppers, seeded and coarsely chopped
¼ cup all-purpose white flour
5 cups chicken stock or broth
2 teaspoons fennel seeds
1 4-ounce can chopped green chilies, well drained
1 large bay leaf
½ teaspoon dried thyme leaves
3 canned Italian-style (plum) tomatoes, drained and coarsely chopped
1½ cups light cream or half-and-half
1 teaspoon salt, or to taste
¼ teaspoon black pepper, preferably freshly ground

In a Dutch oven or large saucepan, combine the sweet red pepper and 1 tablespoon of the oil. Cook over medium heat, stirring, for about 4 to 5 minutes, or until the pepper is tender. Remove the pepper with a slotted spoon and reserve it.

Add the rest of the oil to the Dutch oven along with the onion, garlic, and sweet green peppers. Cook over medium heat, for 10 to 12 minutes, stirring frequently, or until the vegetables are tender. Add the flour and stir with a wooden spoon to mix well. Cook for an additional 1 minute, stirring.

Add the stock and stir until completely combined and smooth. Add the fennel seeds, chilies, bay leaf, thyme, and tomatoes. Bring the mixture to a boil. Lower the heat, cover, and simmer for about 20 minutes. Remove the bay leaf. Cool the mixture slightly.

In batches, blend in a blender on low speed for 10 seconds.

Then raise the speed to high and purée until completely smooth. Strain the purée through a moderately fine strainer to remove the fennel seeds. Discard the contents of the strainer.

Return the purée to the pan. Stir in the cream, salt, black pepper, and reserved diced sweet red pepper. Cook for an additional 3 or 4 minutes, *but do not boil.*

Makes 5 to 7 servings.

Fresh and Dried Mushroom Soup

In this recipe, the deep woodsy flavor and aroma of dried imported mushrooms accents and enhances the taste of ordinary commercial ones. Specifically, the kind of dried mushroom needed is *Boletus edulis:* Cêpes, Steinpilze, and porcini are all members of this family and can be used interchangeably in the following soup. Dried *Boletus* mushrooms can be found in gourmet and specialty food shops.

> ½ to ¾ ounce dried *Boletus* mushrooms (about ⅓ cup)
> ⅓ cup boiling water
> 4½ cups chicken stock or broth
> 1 small whole onion
> ¼ cup finely chopped fresh parsley leaves
> ⅛ teaspoon dried thyme leaves
> Generous ¼ teaspoon white pepper, preferably freshly ground
> ½ pound fresh white mushrooms, sliced (about 1¾ to 2 cups)
> 1 teaspoon lemon juice, preferably fresh
> 3 tablespoons butter or margarine
> 3 tablespoons cold water
> 1½ tablespoons dry sherry
> ¼ cup cornstarch
> 1 cup heavy or light cream
> About 2 teaspoons finely chopped fresh parsley leaves for garnish (optional)

With your hands, break the *Boletus* mushrooms into very small pieces. Transfer them to a colander; rinse briefly and drain. Combine the *Boletus* mushrooms and boiling water in a small bowl. Set aside to soak for at least 30 minutes and up to 1 hour.

Bring the stock to a boil in a 3-quart saucepan over medium-high heat. Add the onion, parsley, thyme, and pepper. Using a slotted spoon, transfer the *Boletus* mushrooms from the bowl to the pan; reserve the soaking liquid. Allow the mixture to return to a boil and cook over medium-high heat, uncovered, for 5 minutes. Then lower the heat and simmer, covered, for 30 minutes.

Meanwhile, toss the fresh mushrooms with the lemon juice. Melt the butter in a medium-sized frying pan over medium-high heat. Add the mushrooms and cook, stirring, for 4 to 5 minutes, or until they are almost cooked through and begin to exude their juices. Remove the pan from the heat and set it aside.

In a small deep bowl, combine the cold water and sherry. Strain the reserved *Boletus* mushroom soaking liquid through a very fine sieve (or a moderately fine sieve lined with a triple thickness of slightly dampened cheesecloth) into the bowl containing the water and sherry. Stir in the cornstarch until well mixed and smooth.

When the *Boletus* mushroom pieces have simmered for 30 minutes, remove the onion from the pan and discard it. Add the reserved sautéed mushrooms to the saucepan. Briefly stir the cornstarch mixture and add it to the pan. Bring the mixture to a boil over medium-high heat and boil for 2 to 3 minutes, or until it thickens. Stir in the cream and heat for about 5 minutes longer, stirring occasionally, or until the soup is piping hot *but not* boiling. Garnish each serving with some finely chopped fresh parsley leaves, if desired.

Makes 5 to 6 servings.

Potage Vert

This is a smooth and rich cream soup featuring a delightful blend of fresh herbs. As the translation of its French name (Green Soup) indicates, the soup is a bright, beautiful shade of green.

> 3½ tablespoons butter or margarine
> 2 cups lightly packed chopped fresh parsley leaves
> ¼ cup chopped fresh chives
> 2 tablespoons all-purpose white flour
> 4 cups whole milk
> 1½ cups peeled and cubed boiling potatoes
> 1 teaspoon salt, or more to taste
> ¼ teaspoon white pepper, preferably freshly ground
> 1½ cups lightly packed fresh watercress leaves
> ½ cup light cream or half-and-half, or a little more, if desired
> Parsley sprigs or watercress sprigs for garnish (optional)

Combine the butter, parsley, and chives in a 2- to 3-quart saucepan. Cook over medium-high heat, stirring, for 4 to 5 minutes, or until the herbs are limp. Using a wooden spoon, stir in the flour until well blended and smooth. Stir in the milk, potatoes, salt, and pepper. Bring the mixture to a boil; then lower the heat and cover the pan. Simmer, stirring occasionally, for 12 minutes. Stir in the watercress and continue simmering, covered, for 3 to 4 minutes, or until the watercress is limp but retains its bright color.

In batches, transfer the mixture to a blender. Blend on low speed for 10 seconds. Then raise the speed to high and blend until the mixture is thoroughly puréed and smooth. Stop the motor and scrape down the sides of the container several times. Rinse out the pan previously used and return the purée to it. Add the ½ cup of cream to the pan. If the soup seems too thick, add a bit more cream until the desired consistency is obtained. Heat the soup over medium-high heat, stirring occasionally, until piping hot *but not* boiling. Garnish individual servings with a parsley sprig, if desired.

Makes 4 to 5 servings.

Saffron Soup

This makes a fine beginning to an elegant meal. The saffron and egg yolks lend the soup a creamy yellow hue, as well as a rich taste. Serve the soup with garlic croutons for a pleasant textural contrast.

2 tablespoons olive oil
1 large onion, coarsely chopped
1 garlic clove, minced
1 small carrot, chopped
2 tablespoons sweet red pepper, chopped (If unavailable, substitute sweet green pepper.)
¼ cup coarsely chopped fresh parsley leaves
2 tablespoons all-purpose white flour
4½ cups chicken stock or broth
¼ cup dry white wine
1 bay leaf
¼ teaspoon saffron threads, very finely crumbled
¼ teaspoon whole black peppercorns
⅛ teaspoon dried thyme leaves
⅛ teaspoon dried crushed red (hot) pepper
2 teaspoons tomato paste
⅔ cup light cream or half-and-half, divided
2 large egg yolks
¼ to ½ teaspoon salt, or to taste
Paprika for garnish (optional)
Garlic croutons for garnish (see page 315)

Combine the oil, onion, garlic, carrot, sweet pepper, and parsley in a 2- to 3-quart saucepan. Cook over medium-high heat, stirring, for 4 to 5 minutes, or until the onion is limp. Using a wooden spoon, stir in the flour until thoroughly incorporated and smooth. Cook, stirring, for 1 minute longer. Stir in the stock and wine until well blended and smooth. Add the bay leaf, saffron, peppercorns, thyme, and dried red pepper. Bring the mixture to a boil; then lower the heat and simmer, covered, for 45 minutes.

Strain the mixture through a very fine sieve; discard the

solids. (The stock may be covered and refrigerated for up to 8 hours at this point.)

To complete preparations, return the strained stock to a 2- to 3-quart saucepan. In a small bowl or cup, stir together the tomato paste and a tablespoon or two of the cream until well blended and smooth. Add the mixture to the stock. Using a fork or whisk, beat the remaining cream together with the egg yolks until smooth and slightly frothy. Stir the cream-yolk mixture into the stock. Season with salt.

Carefully heat the soup over medium heat, stirring constantly, until it is piping hot, thickens slightly, and coats the spoon; *do not* allow it to come even near a simmer. (If it appears to be nearing a simmer, lift it from the heat, stirring, and let it cool slightly before continuing to cook.)

Ladle the soup into soup cups or small bowls. Garnish each serving with a light sprinkling of paprika and 2 generous tablespoons of croutons. Serve immediately.

Makes 5 to 6 servings.

Good Wife Soup

This is our updated version of a very old Scottish recipe. The soup is quite delicious and also quick and rather easy to prepare. Do take care to follow the directions on adding and cooking the egg yolks, however. If the temperature is too high, the soup may curdle.

3 tablespoons butter or margarine
1½ cups peeled, seeded, and finely diced cucumber
4 medium-sized green onions (scallions), coarsely
   chopped
1½ tablespoons all-purpose white flour
3¾ cups chicken stock or broth
1½ cups finely shredded green leaf lettuce, such as Boston
   or Bibb lettuce
2 tablespoons chopped watercress leaves
Generous ¼ teaspoon dried tarragon leaves

Generous pinch of white pepper, preferably freshly
   ground
½ cup light cream or half-and-half
3 large egg yolks
⅛ to ¼ teaspoon salt, or to taste
Small watercress sprigs for garnish (optional)

Melt the butter in a large saucepan over medium-high heat. Add the cucumber and green onions and cook, stirring, for 6 to 7 minutes, or until the green onions are limp and the cucumber is slightly softened. Using a wooden spoon, stir in the flour until thoroughly incorporated and smooth. Cook, stirring, for 1 minute longer. Stir in the stock until well blended and smooth. Bring the mixture to a boil. Lower the heat and simmer, covered, for about 3 minutes. Stir in the lettuce, watercress, tarragon, and pepper and continue simmering for 2 minutes longer.

Using a fork, beat together the cream and egg yolks in a small deep bowl. Lower the heat to medium and stir the cream-egg yolk mixture into the pan. Heat the soup, stirring constantly, for 3 to 4 minutes longer, or until it thickens very slightly and forms a slight film on the spoon; *do not* allow it to come even near the simmering point or it will curdle. (If steam rises and the mixture appears to be overheating, immediately lift it from the heat and continue stirring to cool it.) Add the salt.

Ladle the soup into small bowls or soup cups. Garnish each with a watercress sprig, if desired.

The soup may also be served reheated. This is best done in a double boiler over medium-high heat; stir the soup occasionally and watch to make sure it does not overheat.

Makes 4 to 6 servings.

High Summer Soup with Salsa

This festive, seasonal soup features vegetables bountiful in high summer—yellow squash, fresh corn, and tomatoes. The mild flavor of the squash and corn acts as an appealing foil for the zesty tomato salsa. A pretty shade of yellow, the soup also sets off the color of the tomato quite nicely. For best results, use very fresh, firm, unblemished squash and a juicy, fully ripe summer tomato.

The soup makes a nice first course for a summer dinner party.

Salsa

    1 large fully ripe, vine-ripened tomato, peeled, seeded, and finely diced
    2 teaspoons finely chopped fresh chives, *or* green onion (scallion) tops
    ¾ teaspoon red wine vinegar or apple cider vinegar
    Generous ¼ teaspoon salt
    Pinch of dried basil leaves
    2 to 3 drops Tabasco sauce

Soup

    3 tablespoons butter or margarine
    2 large onions, coarsely chopped
    2 garlic cloves, minced
    ¼ cup finely chopped carrot
    1¼ pounds yellow squash (3 to 4 medium sized), chopped
    ½ cup peeled and chopped potato
    3 cups chicken stock or broth, divided
    1½ teaspoons lemon juice, preferably fresh
    ½ teaspoon sugar
    ¼ teaspoon powdered mustard
    ⅛ teaspoon white pepper, preferably freshly ground
    Generous pinch of cayenne pepper
    2 to 3 drops Tabasco sauce
    1 cup fresh corn kernels, cut from 2 large ears yellow corn, *or* 1 cup loose-pack frozen corn kernels

1 tablespoon finely chopped fresh chives, *or* ½ tablespoon dried chopped chives

¼ cup light cream or half-and-half

½ to ¾ teaspoon salt, or to taste

At least 1 hour prior to serving time prepare the salsa as follows: Combine all the ingredients in a noncorrosive bowl and toss until well mixed. Cover and refrigerate at least 1 hour and up to 12 hours before serving to allow flavors time to mingle.

To prepare the soup: Melt the butter in a 3-quart saucepan over medium-high heat. Add the onions, garlic, and carrot and cook, stirring, for 6 to 7 minutes, or until the onions are tender but not browned. Stir in the squash, potato, 2 cups of the stock, the lemon juice, sugar, mustard, white pepper, cayenne pepper, and Tabasco. Bring the mixture to a boil over medium-high heat. Lower the heat and simmer the mixture, covered, for 8 to 10 minutes, or until the vegetables are soft; stir occasionally to prevent the potato from sticking to the bottom of the pan. Cool the mixture slightly.

In batches, transfer the mixture to a blender and blend on low speed for 10 seconds. Then raise the speed to high, and blend until completely puréed and smooth. Rinse out the pan previously used, and return the purée to it. Stir in the remaining 1 cup stock, the corn, and chives. Bring to a boil over medium-high heat. Simmer the soup, uncovered, for 9 to 10 minutes longer, or until the corn is tender. Stir in the cream and the salt. Reheat the soup to piping hot *but not* boiling.

To serve the soup, ladle it into bowls and garnish each serving with a tablespoon or two of the salsa. Serve immediately.

Makes 4 to 6 servings.

Winter Garden Bisque with Carrot Cream

Winter vegetables often tend to be overlooked by American cooks, but they shouldn't be, as this elegant, subtly delicious soup proves. This recipe actually features two components—a smooth, pale green soup and a garnish of a golden carrot cream. The effect is pleasing to both the palate and the eye.

1 small leek, trimmed of root and all but 3 inches of green top
2 tablespoons butter or margarine
1 medium-sized parsnip, peeled and coarsely chopped
2 tablespoons coarsely chopped celery
1 tablespoon all-purpose white flour
2½ cups chicken stock or broth
1 small kohlrabi (about 2½ inches in diameter), peeled and coarsely diced (If unavailable, substitute 1 small turnip.)
1 cup coarsely chopped cauliflower flowerets
5 to 6 Brussels sprouts, trimmed and quartered
1 medium-sized boiling potato, peeled and coarsely cubed
1 tablespoon chopped fresh chives, *or* 1½ teaspoons dried chives
¼ teaspoon salt, or more to taste
⅛ teaspoon dried tarragon leaves
⅛ teaspoon white pepper, preferably freshly ground
¾ cup light cream or half-and-half

Carrot Cream

½ cup chopped carrot
⅓ cup peeled and chopped parsnip
¾ cup chicken stock or broth, divided
⅛ teaspoon salt
⅛ teaspoon white pepper, preferably freshly ground
⅓ cup light cream or half-and-half

To prepare the soup: Quarter the leek lengthwise. Separate the layers and thoroughly wash under cool running water to remove any traces of grit. Drain the leek well and coarsely chop it. Turn out the chopped leek into a colander. Rinse and drain well.

Melt the butter in a 2- to 3-quart saucepan over medium-high heat. Add the leek, parsnip, and celery and cook, stirring, for 4 to 5 minutes, or until the leek is slightly soft. Using a wooden spoon, stir in the flour until thoroughly incorporated and smooth. Cook, stirring, for 1 minute. Stir in the stock until well blended and smooth. Add the kohlrabi, cauliflower, Brussels sprouts, potato, chives, salt, tarragon, and pepper and bring the mixture to a boil. Lower the heat and simmer the mixture, covered, for 12 to 13 minutes, or until the potato is cooked through but not soft. Remove the pan from the heat and let it cool slightly.

In batches, transfer the mixture to a blender. Blend on low speed for 10 seconds; then raise the speed to high and blend until completely puréed and smooth. Rinse out and dry the pan previously used and return the purée to it. Add the cream. Set the soup aside while the carrot cream is prepared. (Alternatively, at this point, cover and refrigerate the soup for up to 24 hours before serving.)

To prepare the carrot cream: In a small saucepan, combine the carrot, parsnip, ½ cup of the stock, the salt, and pepper. Bring the mixture to a boil over medium-high heat. Lower the heat. Simmer the mixture, uncovered, stirring occasionally, for 12 to 15 minutes, or until the carrot is cooked through and much of the liquid has evaporated from the pan. Set it aside to cool slightly.

Wash out the blender container. Combine the cooked carrot mixture, the remaining ¼ cup stock, and the cream in the blender. Blend on low speed for 10 seconds. Raise the speed to high and blend until the mixture is completely puréed and smooth; stop the motor and scrape down the container sides with a rubber spatula once or twice during blending. Rinse out the saucepan previously used and return the carrot cream to it. (At this point, the carrot cream may be reheated or refrigerated for up to 24 hours before serving.)

To complete preparations of the soup and carrot cream, re-heat them (separately) over medium heat, stirring occasionally, until piping hot *but not* boiling.

Ladle the soup into small bowls. Add a large dollop of the carrot cream to the center of each serving and swirl once through the mixtures.

Makes 5 to 6 servings.

11
COLD SOUPS

For some people, the idea of cold soups takes a bit of getting used to. But a cup or bowl of chilled soup on a hot day can be every bit as appealing as a hot soup on a cold day! Try our West African Curried Chicken Soup, Summer Garden Bisque, or Easy Gazpacho and see for yourself.

The techniques for making the recipes that follow are similar to those employed in other chapters of *Soup's On*. Most of the soups are cooked first and then cooled. This means they're perfect for make-ahead entertaining as they can be prepared up to a day in advance. On the other hand, because it takes longer than you might imagine to chill hot ingredients, cold soups can't be produced on the spur of the moment. Most taste best well chilled and, therefore, should be refrigerated for at least 4 or 5 hours before serving. However, it's possible to speed things up a bit by starting the process in the freezer. Soups placed in the freezer should be checked and stirred often to make sure they don't inadvertently freeze.

Because cooling tends to mellow flavors, the best soups to serve chilled are generally those with strong and very distinctive seasonings. For the same reason, we've also found it necessary to add a bit more salt to cold soups than to those served piping hot.

West African Curried Chicken Soup

Pineapple and curry team up to give this soup its pleasing flavor. We like to serve it as a first course to a summer dinner or luncheon.

    2 tablespoons butter or margarine
    2 celery stalks, diced
    1 small onion, finely chopped
    1 medium-sized garlic clove, minced
    1½ to 2 teaspoons curry powder, or to taste
    3½ tablespoons all-purpose white flour
    3½ cups chicken stock or broth
    1 cup crushed pineapple, well drained

1 large chicken breast half, cooked, boned, skinned, and
cut into ½-inch pieces
1 cup light cream or half-and-half

In a Dutch oven or very large saucepan, melt the butter
over medium heat. Add the celery, onion, and garlic and cook,
stirring frequently, for about 5 minutes, or until the onion is
soft. Remove the pan from the heat.

In a small bowl, blend together the curry powder and flour.
Add this mixture to the butter and stir with a wooden spoon to
blend well.

Return the pan to the heat. Cook, over medium heat, stirring, for 1 minute. Gradually add the stock, stirring constantly
with a wire whisk or wooden spoon, until the mixture is
smooth. Bring the mixture to a boil, stirring occasionally. Then
cover, lower the heat, and simmer for about 20 minutes. Remove the pan from the heat. Add all the remaining ingredients
and stir to mix well. Cover and chill the soup for at least 5
hours, or overnight.

Makes 5 to 6 servings.

Avocado Soup

A velvety texture, pale green color, and the subtle, smooth taste
of ripe avocados lend this recipe its appeal. The attractive
green hue tends to fade fairly rapidly, however, so for best
results, don't store the soup more than the time required for
chilling.

Avocado Soup is very rich, so plan on serving only small
portions.

1 tablespoon olive oil
4 to 5 green onions (scallions), including green tops,
coarsely chopped
1 large garlic clove, minced
2 large ripe avocados, peeled, pitted, and cut into chunks
2¾ to 3 cups chilled chicken stock or broth (approximately)

2 teaspoons lemon juice, preferably fresh

¼ teaspoons salt, or more to taste

¼ teaspoon white pepper, preferably freshly ground

Thin half-slices of freshly sliced avocado for garnish (optional)

Small dollops of commercial sour cream for garnish (optional)

Combine the oil, green onions, and garlic in a small saucepan. Cook over medium-high heat, stirring, for 4 to 5 minutes, or until the green onions are limp.

Transfer the mixture to a blender. Add the avocado chunks, 2 cups of the stock, the lemon juice, salt, and pepper. Begin blending the mixture on low and then raise the speed to medium. As the mixture thickens, gradually add ½ cup more stock through the hole in the lid until the purée is very smooth. Transfer the soup to a bowl or storage container and stir in enough more stock to yield a "soupy" consistency. Refrigerate, covered, for about 1 to 1½ hours, or until chilled but not icy cold. Serve the soup in small bowls. Garnish each serving with several thin half-slices of avocado and a small dollop of sour cream, if desired.

Makes 4 servings.

Borscht

4 cups beef stock, brown stock, or broth

2 cups water

4 cups peeled and grated beets

2 large onions, grated or very finely chopped

2 large carrots, grated or shredded

2 large celery stalks, very finely chopped

1 large garlic clove, minced

2 large bay leaves

1 teaspoon packed dark or light brown sugar

½ teaspoon dried marjoram leaves

½ teaspoon dried thyme leaves

⅛ teaspoon ground ginger
¼ to ½ teaspoon salt, or to taste
¼ teaspoon black pepper, preferably freshly ground
2 medium-sized beets
1 tablespoon lemon juice, preferably fresh
4 to 5 tablespoons commercial sour cream for garnish

In a Dutch oven or very large saucepan, combine the stock, water, 4 cups grated beets, onions, carrots, celery, garlic, bay leaves, brown sugar, marjoram, thyme, ginger, salt, and pepper. Bring to a boil over medium-high heat. Cover, lower the heat, and simmer for about 40 to 45 minutes, stirring occasionally, or until the vegetables have flavored the soup.

While the soup is cooking, place the 2 medium-sized beets in a small saucepan and cover them with water. Bring to a boil over high heat. Cover, lower the heat, and simmer for 20 to 30 minutes, or until the beets are tender when pierced with a fork. Drain them in a colander; then peel, chop, and reserve them.

Strain the soup through a sieve. Discard the vegetables cooked with the soup. Add the reserved chopped beets. Cover and chill the soup for at least 4 hours, or overnight. Stir in the lemon juice. Float 1 tablespoon of sour cream on top of each serving.

Makes 4 to 5 servings.

Iced Carrot Soup with Dill

Light and slightly tangy, this colorful, healthful soup is refreshing on a sultry summer day.

2 tablespoons butter or margarine
1 cup coarsely chopped onion
1 tablespoon all-purpose white flour
3¼ cups chicken stock or broth, divided
2½ to 2¾ cups thinly sliced carrots (about 1 pound)
¾ cup peeled and diced potato
¼ to ½ teaspoon salt

⅛ teaspoon white pepper, preferably freshly ground
½ cup commercial sour cream
1 tablespoon chopped fresh dillweed, coarse stems removed
Small sprigs of dillweed for garnish (optional)

Melt the butter in a 2- to 3-quart saucepan over medium-high heat. Add the onion and cook, stirring, for 4 to 5 minutes, or until the onion is limp. Stir in the flour until well blended and smooth. Cook, stirring, for 2 minutes longer. Stir in 1½ cups of the stock, the carrots, potato, salt, and pepper. Bring the mixture to a boil; then lower the heat and cover the pan. Simmer, stirring occasionally, for 11 to 14 minutes, or until the carrots are just cooked through. Remove the pan from the heat and cool it slightly.

Transfer the mixture to a blender and purée until completely smooth. (Add a little of the reserved chicken stock if the mixture is too thick to purée easily.) Transfer the mixture to a 2-quart storage container or bowl. Combine the sour cream and about ½ cup more of the stock in the processor or blender and purée until completely smooth. Add the sour cream-stock mixture, the remaining stock, and dillweed to the carrot purée. Stir the soup well and refrigerate, covered, for at least 4½ hours and up to 12 hours before serving.

Serve the soup very cold in small bowls or cups. Garnish each serving with a small sprig of dill, if desired.

Makes 5 to 6 servings.

Summertime Celery Soup

Delicious, refreshing, and very easy to prepare, this is great on a hot day. The intriguing taste of fennel seeds brings out the flavor of the celery.

1¼ teaspoons fennel seeds
⅓ cup boiling water
3 tablespoons olive or vegetable oil

3 cups coarsely chopped celery (about 7 to 8 medium-sized stalks)

7 to 8 green onions (scallions), including green tops, coarsely chopped

1 small garlic clove, minced

4 cups chicken stock or broth, divided

Generous 1½ tablespoons long-grain white rice

2 tablespoons finely chopped fresh chives, *or* 1 tablespoon dried chopped chives

Scant ⅛ teaspoon white pepper, preferably freshly ground

Salt to taste

About 2 teaspoons finely chopped fresh chives for garnish (optional)

Small dollops of commercial sour cream for garnish (optional)

Combine the fennel seeds and boiling water in a small cup. Set aside so the seeds can steep while the rest of the preparations are completed.

Combine the oil, celery, green onions, and garlic in a large saucepan. Cook over medium-high heat, stirring, for 3 to 4 minutes, or until the green onions are slightly soft. Add 2½ cups of the stock, the rice, chives, and pepper to the pan. Bring the mixture to a boil over medium-high heat. Lower the heat and simmer, covered, for about 20 minutes, or until the celery and rice are tender. Remove the pan from the heat and let the mixture cool slightly.

In batches, transfer the mixture to a blender. Blend for 10 seconds on low speed. Then raise the speed to high and blend until completely smooth. Transfer the purée to a large bowl or storage container. Stir in the remaining stock. Add salt to taste. Strain the fennel seed soaking water through a fine sieve into the soup; discard the fennel seeds. Cover and refrigerate the soup for at least 3 hours, or overnight, before serving.

Garnish each serving with a light sprinkling of chives, if desired. The servings may also be topped with small dollops of sour cream, if desired.

Makes 4 to 6 servings.

Cucumber Soup

Cooked cucumbers, leek, and bay leaf combine to give this creamy cold soup its distinctive flavor.

    2 tablespoons butter or margarine
    4 medium-sized cucumbers, peeled, seeded, and chopped,
        divided
    1 medium-sized leek, white part only, well washed (see
        page 13) and cut into thin slices   ·
    3½ tablespoons all-purpose white flour
    3½ cups chicken broth
    1 large bay leaf
    ⅛ teaspoon white pepper, preferably freshly ground
    1 cup light cream or half-and-half
    1 tablespoon lemon juice, preferably fresh
    Thin unpeeled cucumber slices for garnish

In a large saucepan, melt the butter over medium-high heat. Add half of the cucumbers and the leek and cook, stirring frequently, until the leek is tender but not browned. Remove the pan from the heat. Stir in the flour with a wooden spoon, blending well. Return the pan to the heat. Cook, stirring, for about 1 minute. Stir in the broth, blending well. Bring the mixture to a boil. Add the bay leaf and pepper. Cover, lower the heat, and simmer for about 20 minutes, or until the leek is very tender and the flavors are well blended. Remove the bay leaf. Remove the pan from the heat and let cool slightly.

In batches, if necessary, transfer the mixture to a blender. Blend on low speed for 10 seconds. Then raise the speed to high and blend until the mixture is thoroughly puréed and smooth.

Transfer the soup to a glass or ceramic bowl. Cover and chill for at least 4 hours. Stir in the cream, the remaining 2 chopped cucumbers, and the lemon juice.

Serve in chilled cups or small bowls. Garnish individual servings with a slice of unpeeled cucumber. The soup can be stored in the refrigerator for several days but must be stirred well after standing.

Makes 6 to 7 servings.

Vichyssoise

A favorite summer soup of many, Vichyssoise is really quite simple to make. For an interesting variation, you can substitute sour cream for the light cream called for in the recipe.

3 pounds leeks (6 to 7 medium sized)
3 tablespoons butter or margarine
5 cups chicken stock or broth
2 pounds boiling potatoes, peeled and diced (about 5½ cups diced potatoes)
¾ teaspoon salt
¼ teaspoon white pepper, preferably freshly ground
1½ cups light cream or half-and-half
Parsley sprigs or minced chives for garnish (optional)

Trim off and discard the root end of the leeks and all but about 1 inch of the green tops. Peel off and discard one or two layers of tough outer leaves. Then, beginning at the green end, slice down about 1 inch into the leeks. Put the leeks into a colander. Wash them thoroughly under cool running water, separating the layers to remove any grit trapped between them; wash again to remove all traces of grit. Then set them aside until well drained. Cut the leeks into ½-inch pieces.

In a very large saucepan or small soup pot, melt the butter over medium heat. Add the leeks and cook, stirring frequently, for about 10 minutes, or until the leeks are tender but not browned. Lower the heat slightly, if necessary, to prevent them from browning. Add the stock and potatoes. Bring to a boil over high heat. Lower the heat, cover, and simmer for about 10 to 11 minutes, or until the potatoes are tender. Remove the pan from the heat and let cool slightly. Add the salt and pepper.

In batches, transfer the mixture to a blender. Blend on low speed for 10 seconds. Then raise the speed to high and blend until the mixture is thoroughly puréed and smooth.

Transfer the purée to a medium-sized glass or ceramic bowl. Chill in the refrigerator for at least 5 hours, or overnight. Add the cream and stir to mix well. If desired, garnish each serving with a parsley sprig or a sprinkling of minced chives.

Makes 7 to 9 servings.

Curried Onion-Potato Soup

2 tablespoons butter or margarine
1 tablespoon vegetable oil
1 medium-sized garlic clove, minced
3 cups coarsely chopped onion
1¼ teaspoons ground cumin
1¼ teaspoons ground turmeric
1 teaspoon curry powder, or to taste
¼ teaspoon black pepper, preferably freshly ground
3½ cups chicken stock or broth
2 to 3 drops Tabasco sauce
2 cups peeled and diced potatoes
¾ cup light cream or half-and-half
½ teaspoon salt, or to taste
1 to 2 teaspoons finely chopped fresh parsley leaves or chives for garnish (optional)

In a large saucepan or small soup pot, melt the butter over medium-low heat. Add the oil, garlic, onion, cumin, turmeric, curry powder, and pepper and stir to blend well. Raise the heat to medium-high and cook, stirring frequently, for about 7 to 8 minutes, or until the onion is very soft. Add the stock, Tabasco sauce, and potatoes. Cover and simmer the mixture for about 15 to 18 minutes, or until the potatoes are very tender. Remove the pot from the heat. Let the mixture cool slightly.

In batches, blend in a blender on low speed for 10 seconds. Then raise the speed to high and purée until completely smooth. Transfer the purée to a large glass or ceramic bowl. Stir in the cream. Add the salt as needed and stir well. Cover and chill for at least 5 hours, or overnight. Stir before serving.

Serve in small bowls or soup cups. Garnish individual servings with a sprinkling of parsley, if desired.

Makes 4 to 5 servings.

Orange-Tomato Soup

2 tablespoons finely chopped onion
1 cup chicken bouillon (reconstituted from 1 chicken bouillon cube or packet)
2 tablespoons packed dark or light brown sugar
4 cups tomato juice
⅓ cup frozen orange juice concentrate
2 tablespoons lemon juice, preferably fresh
3 to 4 drops Tabasco sauce, or to taste
Thin orange half-slices for garnish (optional)

In a medium-sized saucepan, combine the onion and bouillon. Bring to a boil over high heat. Cover, lower the heat, and simmer for about 6 to 7 minutes, or until the onion is tender.

Meanwhile, combine all the remaining ingredients *except* the orange slices in a glass or ceramic bowl. Add the onion-bouillon mixture. Cover and refrigerate for 4 to 5 hours.

Serve the soup in cups or small bowls. If desired, cut a ½-inch slit in the diameter of each orange slice so that a slice can be positioned over the side of each cup.

Makes 4 to 5 servings.

Pimiento Soup

Zesty and pleasantly smooth at the same time, this easy, appetizing soup makes a colorful first course to a warm-weather luncheon or supper. It's particularly nice at a meal featuring grilled chicken or shrimp.

2½ tablespoons olive or vegetable oil
1 medium-sized onion, coarsely chopped
2 4-ounce jars sliced pimientos, well drained
6 tablespoons tomato paste
Generous ½ cup commercial sour cream

3 to 4 drops Tabasco sauce
3⅓ cups chicken stock or broth, divided
½ teaspoon salt, or more to taste
Finely chopped fresh parsley leaves, dillweed, or chives for
    garnish
Small dollops of commercial sour cream for garnish (op-
    tional)

Combine the oil and onion in a large saucepan. Cook over medium-high heat, stirring, for 5 to 6 minutes, or until the onion is limp. Transfer the onion-oil mixture to a blender or food processor. Add the pimientos, tomato paste, sour cream, Tabasco sauce, and ¾ cup of the stock to the onion mixture. Blend or process until completely smooth. (If necessary, add a bit more of the stock to the blender to facilitate the puréeing.)

Transfer the purée to a large bowl or storage container. Stir in the remaining stock and the salt until well blended. Cover and refrigerate for at least 3 hours, or overnight, before serving.

Ladle the soup into small bowls. Garnish each serving with a light sprinkling of chopped parsley, dillweed, or chives. The servings may also be topped with small dollops of sour cream, if desired.

Makes 4 to 6 servings.

Zesty Tomato-Vegetable Soup

3 tablespoons olive oil
1 medium-sized onion, coarsely chopped
1 large celery stalk, coarsely chopped
1 medium-sized carrot, coarsely chopped
¾ cup chopped sweet red pepper
1 cup beef stock, brown stock, or broth
1 35-ounce can imported Italian (plum) tomatoes, includ-
    ing juice, puréed in a blender or food processor
¼ cup dry red wine

1 teaspoon lemon juice, preferably fresh
1 teaspoon celery salt
Generous pinch of dried crushed red (hot) pepper, or to
   taste
3 to 4 drops Tabasco sauce, or to taste
1 tablespoon finely chopped fresh chives or parsley leaves
   for garnish (optional)

Combine the olive oil, onion, and celery in a 2- to 3-quart saucepan. Cook over medium-high heat, stirring, for 4 to 5 minutes, or until the onion is soft. Add the carrot and sweet pepper and cook, stirring, for 3 to 4 minutes longer. Stir in all the remaining ingredients *except* the chives and bring the mixture to a boil over medium-high heat. Lower the heat and simmer, covered, for 10 minutes. Remove the pan from the heat and let it cool slightly.

In batches, transfer the mixture to a blender container. Blend on low speed for 10 seconds. Then raise the speed to high and blend until completely puréed and smooth. Transfer the soup to a noncorrosive bowl or storage container and chill for at least 4 hours and up to 24 hours before serving.

Ladle the soup into small bowls or soup cups. Garnish each serving with a light sprinkling of chopped chives, if desired.

Makes 4 to 6 servings.

Easy Gazpacho

If the yen for gazpacho strikes and fresh tomatoes are unavailable, try this version. The secret of success is in using good-quality canned tomatoes and puréeing them along with the garlic before the other vegetables are added.

1 28-ounce can imported Italian (plum) tomatoes, including juice
1 small garlic clove, minced
1 to 2 tablespoons finely minced fresh onion, or to taste
1 medium-sized cucumber, peeled, seeded, and diced

1 celery stalk, diced
½ large sweet green pepper, diced
1 tablespoon olive oil
2 to 3 drops Tabasco sauce, or to taste
½ teaspoon salt
¼ teaspoon black pepper, preferably freshly ground
4 to 6 fresh parsley sprigs for garnish (optional)

In a food processor or blender, purée the tomatoes and the garlic. Transfer the tomatoes to a medium-sized glass or ceramic bowl. Add all the remaining ingredients and stir to mix well. Cover and refrigerate for at least 4 hours, or overnight. Stir well before serving. If desired, garnish each individual serving with a fresh parsley sprig.

Makes 4 to 6 servings.

Gazpacho with Marinated Shrimp and Olives

Colorful and delicious, this makes a refreshing and festive first course for a summer company meal.

Marinade and Condiments

3 tablespoons olive oil
1½ tablespoons red wine vinegar
1 teaspoon finely chopped onion
Generous ¼ teaspoon salt
⅛ teaspoon black pepper, preferably freshly ground
Pinch of cayenne pepper, or to taste
1¼ cups coarsely chopped, peeled cooked shrimp
⅔ cup diced sweet green pepper
½ cup well-drained, pitted and sliced ripe (black) olives

Soup

    1½ cups tomato juice
    1½ tablespoons red wine vinegar
    1½ tablespoons olive oil
    1 garlic clove, finely minced
    2 tablespoons finely chopped onion
    ¼ to ½ teaspoon salt
    ¼ teaspoon black pepper, preferably freshly ground
    ⅛ teaspoon dried marjoram leaves
    Generous pinch of cayenne pepper
    3 medium-sized vine-ripened tomatoes, finely chopped
    1½ cups peeled and finely chopped cucumber
    ¼ cup drained finely chopped canned pimiento
    1 tablespoon finely chopped celery
    About 1 tablespoon finely chopped fresh parsley leaves or
      chives for garnish (optional)

To prepare the marinade and condiments: In a medium-sized noncorrosive bowl beat together the olive oil, vinegar, onion, salt, black pepper, and cayenne pepper until well blended. Toss the cooked shrimp, green pepper, and olives in the marinade until thoroughly coated. Cover and refrigerate the mixture for at least 3½ hours and up to 12 hours before serving.

To prepare the soup: Combine the tomato juice, vinegar, olive oil, garlic, onion, salt, black pepper, marjoram, and cayenne pepper in a large noncorrosive bowl and stir until well blended. Gently stir in all the remaining soup ingredients *except* the parsley or chives. Refrigerate the gazpacho, covered, for at least 3½ hours and up to 12 hours before serving.

To serve, ladle the gazpacho into soup bowls. Drain off and discard the marinade from the shrimp-olive mixture. Sprinkle about ¼ cup of the shrimp-olive mixture over each individual serving. Garnish each bowl with a light sprinkling of parsley or chives, if desired.

Makes 4 to 5 servings.

Chilled Watercress Soup

Here's a soup that celebrates the pungent, peppery taste of fresh watercress. The watercress itself is not cooked, which preserves the characteristic flavor of the fresh herb.

2 pounds leeks (about 3 large)
2 tablespoons butter or margarine
1½ cups peeled and diced potatoes
3 cups chicken stock or broth
1 teaspoon lemon juice, preferably fresh
⅛ teaspoon white pepper, preferably freshly ground
1 cup coarsely chopped watercress leaves and tender stems
1 cup light cream or half-and-half
¼ teaspoon salt, or to taste

Trim off and discard the root end of the leeks and all but about 1 inch of the green tops. Peel off and discard one or two layers of tough outer leaves. Then, beginning at the green end, slice down about 1 inch into the leeks. Put the leeks into a colander. Wash them thoroughly under cool running water, separating the layers to remove any grit trapped between them. Wash again to remove all traces of grit. Then set them aside until well drained. Cut the leeks into ½-inch pieces.

In a medium-sized saucepan, melt the butter over medium heat. Add the leeks and cook, stirring frequently, for about 5 or 6 minutes, or until they are tender. If necessary, lower the heat to prevent them from burning. Add the potatoes and stock. Bring the mixture to a boil over medium-high heat. Cover, lower the heat, and simmer for about 12 to 14 minutes, or until the potatoes and leeks are very tender. Cool the mixture slightly. Add the lemon juice and pepper and stir well.

In batches, blend in a blender on low speed for 10 seconds. Then raise the speed to high and purée until completely smooth. Stir in the watercress and blend on low in on/off bursts just enough to break up the leaves and stems. Remove the mixture to a medium-sized bowl. Stir in the cream and salt. Cover and chill for at least 5 hours. Serve in small bowls or cups.

Makes 4 to 5 servings.

Tangy Zucchini-Buttermilk Soup

Buttermilk is a subtle addition to this unusual cold soup. For an even tangier version, omit the light cream and increase the buttermilk to 1 cup.

1 medium-sized onion, finely chopped
1 small garlic clove, minced
1 tablespoon butter or margarine
2 cups diced zucchini
½ cup peeled and diced potato
3 cups chicken bouillon (reconstituted from 3 cubes or packets)
2 tablespoons chopped fresh parsley leaves
⅛ teaspoon white pepper, preferably freshly ground
¼ teaspoon powdered mustard
½ cup commercial buttermilk
½ cup light cream or half-and-half
2 to 3 drops of Tabasco sauce
¼ teaspoon salt, or to taste
Small parsley sprigs for garnish (optional)

In a medium-sized saucepan, combine the onion, garlic, butter, zucchini, potato, and bouillon. Bring to a boil over high heat. Cover, lower the heat, and simmer for 12 to 15 minutes, or until the potato is very tender. Remove the pan from the heat. Cool the mixture slightly.

In batches, blend in a blender on low speed for 10 seconds. Then raise the speed to high and purée until almost completely smooth but some parsley flecks remain. Transfer the purée to a medium-sized glass or ceramic bowl. Stir in all the remaining ingredients. Cover and chill for 4 to 5 hours.

Serve in cups or small bowls. If desired, garnish each serving with a small parsley sprig.

Makes 4 to 5 servings.

Summer Garden Bisque

In this easy recipe, an interesting combination of summer garden vegetables yields wonderfully savory results.

3 tablespoons butter or margarine
2 cups coarsely chopped onion
1 large garlic clove, minced
2 tablespoons coarsely chopped celery
4 cups chicken stock or broth, divided
1¾ cups peeled and coarsely cubed eggplant
1⅓ cups unpeeled coarsely chopped yellow squash
1⅓ cups peeled and coarsely chopped zucchini
Generous ⅛ teaspoon white pepper, preferably freshly ground
⅓ cup water
1 cup diced unpeeled yellow squash
1 cup diced unpeeled zucchini
1 cup peeled, seeded, and diced vine-ripened tomato
⅛ to ¼ teaspoon salt (optional)
Chopped fresh parsley leaves for garnish

Combine the butter, onion, garlic, and celery in a 2- to 3-quart saucepan. Cook over medium-high heat, stirring, for 5 to 6 minutes, or until the onion is soft. Stir in 1½ cups of the stock, the eggplant, chopped yellow squash, chopped zucchini, and pepper and bring the mixture to a boil. Lower the heat and simmer the mixture, covered, for 5 minutes, or until the eggplant is soft. Remove from the heat and cool slightly.

In batches, if necessary, transfer the mixture to a blender. Blend on low speed for 10 seconds. Then raise the speed to high and blend until the mixture is thoroughly puréed and smooth.

Rinse out the pan previously used and return the purée to it. Add the water, remaining stock, and diced yellow squash and zucchini. Bring the soup to a boil over medium-high heat. Lower the heat and simmer for 4 to 6 minutes, or until the yellow squash and zucchini are tender but not soft. Remove the pan from the heat and stir in the tomato.

Refrigerate the mixture, covered, for 4 to 5 hours, or until thoroughly chilled. Add the salt, if needed.

Ladle the soup into small bowls or soup cups. Garnish each serving with a sprinkling of fresh chopped parsley.

Makes 5 to 6 servings.

12
FRUIT SOUPS

A lmost everyone welcomes fruit on a menu. So it's not surprising that even folks who find the idea of fruit soups exotic discover they like these dishes very much. And little wonder, since they add appealing color, delicious flavor, and a touch of sweetness to the meal.

When do you serve a fruit soup? This depends partly on the specific soup, of course, so we've provided helpful suggestions in the introductions to a number of the recipes.

For example, try some of our light and zesty soups such as Iced Strawberry-Buttermilk Soup, Cranberry Madrilène, or Iced Mandarin Cantaloupe Soup as a nice change of pace from an ordinary fruit cup appetizer at a luncheon or dinner. Consider serving some of the mellow, fairly sweet soups, like Dried Fruit and Wine Soup or Blueberry Soup as a smooth and soothing first course to a brunch or fancy breakfast. Some of our very rich and sumptuous recipes—Raspberry 'n' Cream Soup or Apricot Soup, for instance—make a simple, elegant dessert. And many of the fruit soups here can be offered as "refreshers" and special snacks.

Golden Apple-Pear Soup

This appealing cold fruit soup is mild and slightly sweet. It's good served in place of stewed fruit at a fancy brunch or breakfast.

> 1 12-ounce can frozen unsweetened apple juice concentrate
> 4 cups water
> ¼ to ⅓ cup sugar
> 2 ¼-inch-thick orange slices
> 2 ⅛-inch-thick lemon slices
> 2 3-inch-long cinnamon sticks
> 10 whole cloves
> 1⅓ cups peeled and diced firm, tart cooking apples (Winesap, Granny Smith, etc.)
> ¼ cup apple brandy or blackberry-flavored brandy

¼ cup cornstarch
1⅓ cups peeled and diced ripe Bartlett or Bosc pears
About ½ cup regular or lowfat vanilla yogurt for garnish

Stir together the apple juice concentrate, water, sugar, orange and lemon slices, cinnamon sticks, and cloves in a 3-quart saucepan or pot over medium-high heat. Bring the mixture to a boil; lower the heat and simmer, covered, for 20 to 25 minutes. Strain the mixture through a fine sieve and return it to the pan previously used. Discard the spices and fruit slices.

Add the diced apple to the pan and allow the mixture to return to a simmer. Simmer, covered, for 3 minutes.

Stir together the brandy and cornstarch in a small cup or bowl until well blended and smooth. Stir the brandy-cornstarch mixture and pears into the pan. Simmer for 2 to 3 minutes longer, or until the soup is clear and slightly thickened.

Refrigerate the soup, covered, for 3½ to 4 hours, or until well chilled. Garnish individual servings with generous dollops of vanilla yogurt.

Makes 4 to 6 servings.

Spicy Apple-Wine Soup

Serve this sweet, spicy soup on a cold day as a first course featuring game or pork. It also works well as a luncheon first course.

2 ¼-inch-thick lemon slices, seeds removed
6 whole cloves
½ cup red Burgundy wine
2 cups white grape juice, divided
2 cups peeled and coarsely chopped tart apples
1 3-inch-long cinnamon stick
2 tablespoons mild honey
1 tablespoon sugar
1½ tablespoons cornstarch

About ¼ cup coarsely chopped pecans or walnuts for garnish

Commercial sour cream for garnish (optional)

Stud the lemon slices with the cloves. In a small saucepan, combine the wine, 1¾ cups of the grape juice, the apples, cinnamon stick, honey, sugar, and clove-studded lemon slices. Bring the mixture to a boil over medium-high heat. Lower the heat, cover, and simmer for about 11 to 13 minutes, or until the apples are tender when pierced with a fork. Remove and discard the lemon slices and cloves.

Meanwhile, stir together the cornstarch and remaining ¼ cup grape juice. When the apples are tender, add the cornstarch-grape juice mixture and cook, stirring, until the liquid thickens, about 1 to 2 minutes.

To serve, ladle the hot soup into cups or small bowls. Sprinkle about 2 teaspoons of chopped nuts on top of each serving. Alternatively, first garnish each serving with a small dollop of sour cream. Then sprinkle with the nuts.

Makes 4 to 5 servings.

Apricot Soup

This is a rich and velvety dessert soup featuring dried apricots, a splash of wine, orange juice, and cream. It makes a simple, yet elegant ending to a dinner.

1½ cups chopped dried apricots (about 7½ to 8 ounces)
2½ cups orange juice
½ cup dry white wine
Generous ⅓ cup sugar
1 3-inch-long cinnamon stick
1 tablespoon plus 1 teaspoon cornstarch
¼ cup water
1¼ cups whole milk
1 teaspoon vanilla extract

1 tablespoon Amaretto or other almond-flavored liqueur (optional)

1½ to 1⅔ cups light cream or half-and-half (approximately)

Dollops of very lightly sweetened whipped cream for garnish

Combine the apricots, orange juice, wine, sugar, and cinnamon stick in a 2- to 3-quart saucepan. Bring to a boil over medium-high heat, stirring. Lower the heat and simmer, covered, for about 15 minutes, or until the apricots are very tender. Discard the cinnamon stick.

Stir together the cornstarch and water in a cup or small bowl until well blended and smooth. Stir the mixture into the saucepan and continue simmering for 1 to 2 minutes, or until the apricot mixture thickens slightly. Remove the pan from the heat and cool slightly.

Transfer the apricot mixture to a blender. Blend on low speed for 10 seconds. Then raise the speed to medium and blend for 1½ to 2 minutes, or until thoroughly puréed and smooth; stop the motor and scrape down the sides of the container several times during blending. Turn out the purée into a large storage container or bowl. Stir in all the remaining ingredients *except* the cream and whipped cream. Stir in 1½ cups of the cream. If the soup seems too thick, thin it with a bit more cream until the desired consistency is obtained.

Refrigerate the soup, covered, for at least 4 hours and up to 24 hours before serving. (The soup tends to thicken on standing; thin it with a little milk before serving, if necessary.)

Stir the soup. Serve it very cold in small, prechilled soup cups or small bowls. Add a generous dollop of whipped cream to the center of each serving.

Makes 5 to 6 servings.

Cherry Soup

Cranberry juice cocktail provides the bright red color for this cold soup and also contributes to the full-bodied cherry taste.

> 2 cups dark sweet red cherries, stemmed and pitted (about ½ pound)
> 3¾ cups commercial cranberry juice cocktail, divided
> 2 tablespoons sugar
> 1 tablespoon lemon juice, preferably fresh
> ⅛ teaspoon ground allspice
> Pinch of ground cinnamon
> ¼ teaspoon salt
> 2 tablespoons cornstarch
> ½ teaspoon vanilla extract
> 2 tablespoons kirsch (cherry-flavored liqueur)
> Commercial sour cream for garnish

In a medium-sized saucepan, combine the cherries, 3½ cups of the cranberry juice, the sugar, lemon juice, allspice, cinnamon, and salt. Bring to a boil over high heat. Cover, lower the heat, and simmer for 5 minutes.

Meanwhile, stir together the remaining ¼ cup of the cranberry juice and the cornstarch until well mixed. Raise the heat so that the liquid in the pan begins to boil. Add the juice-cornstarch mixture, and stir until the liquid thickens and becomes clear, about 1 minute. Stir in the vanilla and kirsch. Simmer for an additional 2 to 3 minutes.

Transfer the soup to a medium-sized bowl, cover, and chill for at least 4 to 5 hours and preferably 7 to 8 hours so the flavors can mingle.

Serve in small bowls or cups. Garnish individual servings with a dollop of sour cream.

Makes about 4 servings.

Fresh Peach Soup with Amaretto

A supremely simple combination that lets the wonderful flavor of the fresh peaches come through. The soup is also light and silky smooth.

For best appearance, serve this soup as soon as it is prepared. It tends to lose its pretty peach color and fresh taste if allowed to stand very long.

> 2¼ pounds fresh, fully ripe peaches, well chilled (about 7 to 8 medium sized)
> ⅓ cup sugar
> ¼ cup Amaretto or similar almond-flavored liqueur
> 1 teaspoon lemon juice, preferably fresh
> ½ teaspoon vanilla extract
> ½ cup plain regular or lowfat yogurt

Peel and pit all the peaches except one; it will be used for garnish. Combine the peeled and pitted peaches, the sugar, Amaretto, lemon juice, and vanilla in a blender or food processor. Blend or process the mixture until completely puréed and smooth. Add the yogurt and blend or process a few seconds longer, or until it is thoroughly incorporated and the mixture is smooth.

Divide the soup among 4 prechilled small glass bowls, sherbet dishes, or bouillon cups. Peel and pit the remaining peach and cut it into thin slices. Arrange 4 or 5 slices pinwheel fashion in the center of each bowl and serve immediately.

(If absolutely necessary, the soup may be covered and refrigerated for up to 1 hour. In this case, do not add the garnish until just before serving. Stir the soup before serving.)

Makes 4 small servings.

Plum Soup

Depending on the variety of plum used, this soup will vary from quite tart and robust to almost, but not quite tame. Although it may be served plain, the appealing sweet-sour taste makes it a perfect foil for our smooth and soothing Fruit Soup Dumplings (see page 316). The combination not only tastes wonderful but looks very attractive as well.

For the best soup, choose very flavorful plums with a slight bite to them. Red Beaut, Black Beaut, and Dorado are all good choices, although any other summer or fall plums suitable for cooking will do.

> 1½ pounds fully ripe, tart purple or red plums, washed, pitted, and halved
> 1 cup water, divided
> ½ cup dry red wine
> 2 ¼-inch-thick lemon slices, seeds removed
> 1 3-inch-long cinnamon stick
> Generous pinch of ground cloves
> ⅔ to 1 cup sugar, depending on the sweetness of the plums
> 1 tablespoon cornstarch
> ¾ cup light cream or half-and-half
> Fruit Soup Dumplings, *or* dollops of slightly sweetened whipped cream for garnish

Combine the plum halves, ¾ cup of the water, the wine, lemon slices, cinnamon stick, cloves, and sugar in a large saucepan. Bring to a boil over medium-high heat. Lower the heat and gently simmer, uncovered, for 8 to 15 minutes, or until the plums are tender. (The time will vary considerably, depending on the variety of plum.) Discard the lemon slices and cinnamon stick.

Stir the remaining ¼ cup water and the cornstarch together in a small cup until well blended and smooth. Stir the mixture into the saucepan. Continue simmering for 1½ to 2 minutes, or until the liquid thickens slightly and becomes clear. Remove the pan from the heat and let it cool slightly. Stir in the cream.

In batches, transfer the plum mixture to a blender. Blend on low speed for 10 seconds. Then raise speed to high and blend for 1½ to 2 minutes, or until the mixture is completely puréed and smooth. Transfer the purée to a noncorrosive bowl or storage container. Cover and refrigerate the soup, covered, for 2 to 3 hours until lightly chilled.

If it is to be garnished with dumplings, allow the soup to warm up almost to room temperature. If garnished with whipped cream, it may be served lightly chilled. Serve in small bowls or soup cups.

Makes 5 to 6 servings.

Blueberry Soup

A light and pretty soup featuring whole blueberries in a blueberry-wine "broth." This is great served as a brunch or luncheon first course, or as a refreshing dessert. The soup may be served with either the sour cream garnish presented below, or with our Fruit Soup Dumplings on page 316.

> 4 cups fresh or loose-pack frozen (thawed) blueberries, divided
> Generous ¼ cup lemon juice, preferably fresh
> Generous ½ to ⅔ cup sugar, depending on the sweetness of the berries
> 2 tablespoons cornstarch
> Generous ⅛ teaspoon ground cinnamon
> 1 cup water
> 1 cup dry white wine
> 1 ½-inch-thick lemon slice, seeds removed
> ½ teaspoon vanilla extract

Garnish

> ⅔ cup commercial sour cream
> 1 tablespoon sugar
> ½ teaspoon vanilla extract

Combine 2 cups of the blueberries and the lemon juice in a 2- to 3-quart saucepan. Bring to a simmer over medium-high heat. Cook, stirring, for about 2 minutes, or until the berries begin to exude their juices. Transfer the berry mixture to a blender container. Add the sugar, cornstarch, and cinnamon to the blender. Blend on low speed for 10 seconds. Then raise the speed to high and blend until completely puréed.

Rinse out the saucepan previously used. Strain the blueberry purée through a very fine sieve into the saucepan; press down hard with the back of a spoon to force through as much of the juice and pulp as possible. Stir the water, wine, and lemon slice into the pan.

Bring the blueberry mixture to a boil, stirring, over medium-high heat. Boil, stirring, for 2 to 3 minutes, or until it thickens slightly and becomes clear. Remove the pan from the heat and stir in the vanilla. Set the mixture aside to cool to room temperature.

Discard the lemon slice. Stir in the remaining 2 cups of whole blueberries and refrigerate the soup, covered, for at least 4 hours and up to 12 hours.

At serving time, stir together the garnish ingredients until well blended and smooth. Divide the soup among soup cups or small bowls. Add a generous dollop of the sour cream mixture to the center of each serving.

(Alternatively, omit the sour cream garnish and serve the soup with Fruit Soup Dumplings. In this case, allow the soup to come to room temperature. Place two freshly poached dumplings in the center of each serving and serve.)

Makes 4 to 5 servings.

Cranberry Madrilène

This beautiful, jewel-like jellied soup makes an elegant, yet light and easy first course for a summer luncheon featuring chicken or turkey. It also makes a nice introduction for a dinner during the Thanksgiving and Christmas holidays.

Note that what might seem an excessive amount of gelatin is required due to the acidity of the cranberries.

3⅓ cups water, divided
3 packets plus ¾ teaspoon unflavored gelatin
1 12-ounce can frozen cranberry-apple juice concentrate
1 cup dry white wine
1 tablespoon plus 2 teaspoons lemon juice, preferably fresh
3 ½-inch-thick lemon slices
3 ½-inch-thick orange slices
2 whole cloves
5 or 6 orange wedges for garnish

Put 1⅓ cups of the water in a small bowl. Sprinkle the gelatin over the water and set aside to soften.

Meanwhile, combine the remaining 2 cups of water, cranberry-apple juice concentrate, wine, lemon juice, lemon and orange slices, and cloves in a 2- to 3-quart saucepan over medium-high heat. Bring the mixture to a boil; then lower the heat and simmer, covered, for 15 minutes. Stir in the softened gelatin mixture and continue simmering for about 2 minutes longer, or until the gelatin dissolves.

Strain the madrilène through a very fine sieve into a storage container or bowl. Refrigerate, covered, for 4 to 5 hours, or until very cold and jellied.

Spoon the madrilène into prechilled small glass dishes or soup cups. (For a particularly attractive presentation, serve the dishes in larger bowls of cracked ice.) Make a ½-inch-deep crosswise cut into the flesh of the orange wedges; then secure the wedges over the rims of the dishes or cups.

Makes 5 to 6 servings.

Raspberry 'n' Cream Soup

This one's for raspberry lovers.

> 3 cups bottled cran-raspberry juice, divided
> 1 tablespoon plus 1 teaspoon cornstarch
> ⅓ cup commercial sour cream
> 1 10-ounce package juice-packed frozen raspberries, in-
> cluding juice, thawed
> Additional commercial sour cream for garnish (optional)

In a small cup or bowl, combine ¼ cup of the cran-raspberry juice and the cornstarch and stir to mix well. In a small saucepan, heat 1¼ cups of the cran-raspberry juice over medium-high heat. Stir in the juice-cornstarch mixture and cook, stirring, until the juice thickens and boils, about 1 to 2 minutes. Transfer the juice to a medium-sized bowl.

Combine the remaining 1½ cups of the cran-raspberry juice and the ⅓ cup sour cream in a blender container. Process on medium speed for about 15 seconds, or until well blended. Add this mixture to the thickened juice and stir to blend. Skim the foam from the top of the mixture, using a large shallow spoon. Refrigerate for at least 5 hours. Stir in the raspberries and their juice. Before serving, stir to distribute the raspberries.

Serve in small bowls or cups. Garnish each serving with a dollop of sour cream, if desired.

Makes 4 to 5 servings.

Iced Strawberry-Buttermilk Soup

Pretty, as well as zesty and refreshing, this soup is a great addition to a warm-weather brunch or luncheon menu. Though the soup is smooth and creamy, it is actually quite light and low in calories.

The rhubarb and buttermilk in the recipe lend welcome tartness and enhance the flavor of the strawberries, without being identifiable on their own.

  3 cups loose-pack frozen cut rhubarb, partially thawed
  ¾ cup sugar, or a little more to taste
  ½ cup water, divided
  1 tablespoon lemon juice, preferably fresh
  1½ tablespoons cornstarch
  2½ cups hulled ripe strawberries, or frozen (partially thawed) loose-pack whole strawberries
  1½ cups fresh commercial buttermilk (approximately), divided
  1 teaspoon vanilla extract
  3 tablespoons Grand Marnier or other orange-based liqueur, or cherry brandy, or orange juice
  Fresh or frozen strawberry slices for garnish

Combine the rhubarb, sugar, and ¼ cup of the water in a medium-sized saucepan. Bring to a simmer, stirring, over medium heat. Stirring occasionally, simmer, uncovered, for 7 to 9 minutes, or until the rhubarb is very tender.

Stir together the remaining ¼ cup water, lemon juice, and cornstarch in a small cup until well blended and smooth. Stir the water-cornstarch mixture into the rhubarb mixture until thoroughly incorporated. Cook, stirring, for about 2 to 3 minutes longer, or until the mixture thickens and becomes clear. Remove the pan from the heat and cool it slightly.

In batches, if necessary, transfer the mixture to a blender. Blend on low speed for 10 seconds. Then raise the speed to high and blend for 2 to 3 minutes, or until completely puréed. If the purée looks and tastes very smooth at this point, transfer it to a medium-sized storage container or bowl. If small bits of the rhubarb remain, strain the mixture through a fine sieve into the storage container or bowl.

Combine the strawberries, 1¼ cups of the buttermilk, the vanilla, and liqueur in the blender. Blend until completely puréed. Strain the purée through a very fine sieve, pressing down on the solids with a large spoon to force through as much of the juice and pulp as possible; discard the seeds. Stir together the sieved strawberry mixture and the rhubarb mixture.

Cover and chill in the freezer for 2 to 2½ hours, or until the soup is very cold and a few ice crystals have formed around the edges but the mixture *is not frozen.* Be very careful that the soup does not freeze inadvertently.

Stir the soup to break up the ice crystals and divide among prechilled bowls or soup cups. Pour about 2 teaspoons of buttermilk into the center of each bowl. Using a small spoon, stir once through the soup and buttermilk to produce a swirled effect. Garnish each serving with several strawberry slices and serve immediately.

Makes 4 to 5 servings

Strawberry-Pear Soup

Pears are a subtle yet pleasing addition to this chilled soup. The recipe also utilizes the liquid from the juice-packed canned pears. If there isn't quite enough juice in the can to make 1 cup, add a little bit of water.

    4 cups hulled and coarsely sliced strawberries
    ½ cup water
    1 cup juice from juice-packed canned pear halves
    4 juice-packed canned pear halves
    2 teaspoons lemon juice, preferably fresh
    ¼ cup sugar, or more to taste

In two batches, combine the strawberries and water in a blender container. Blend until the strawberries are completely puréed. Press the mixture through a fine sieve. Discard the strawberry seeds. In batches, if necessary, return the purée to the blender container. Add all the remaining ingredients and blend until the soup is completely smooth. Transfer the soup to a glass or ceramic bowl. Cover and chill for 3 to 4 hours before serving.

Makes 4 to 5 servings.

Iced Mandarin Cantaloupe Soup

A pretty cantaloupe-orange color, wonderfully refreshing and tasty, *and* incredibly quick to make, this soup is nice as a first course or as a light dessert on a hot, humid day. It can be prepared and on the table in less than 5 minutes!

> 1 11-ounce can chilled mandarin oranges (packed in light syrup), drained
> Generous ¼ teaspoon peeled and finely chopped ginger-root
> 2½ to 3 tablespoons sugar
> ¾ cup chilled orange juice
> 3 tablespoons light or dark rum
> 2 tablespoons lemon juice, preferably fresh
> 1 1-pound bag loose-pack *frozen* cantaloupe balls
> Mint or lemon balm leaves for garnish (optional)

Combine the mandarin oranges, gingerroot, and sugar in a blender. Blend until completely puréed and smooth. Add the orange juice, rum, and lemon juice. Blend on low speed for 10 seconds. Raise the speed to medium and then high and gradually add the frozen cantaloupe balls through the hole in the blender cap. Continue blending until all have been added and the mixture is ice cold and completely smooth. Divide the mixture among prechilled small glass bowls, sherbet dishes, or bouillon cups. Garnish each serving with a small sprig of mint or lemon balm, if desired, and serve immediately.

(Alternatively, store the soup, covered, in the freezer for up to 1½ to 2 hours. Be very careful that the soup does not freeze inadvertently. Then thoroughly stir the mixture to break up any ice crystals and divide among individual serving dishes.)

Makes 4 small servings.

Easy Lime and Cantaloupe Soup

So easy to whip up, this is a tangy refresher on a hot day. The soup tends to separate on standing, so it's best to serve it the day it's made.

 1 medium-to-large cantaloupe, peeled, seeded, and cut into 1-inch chunks
 1 6-ounce can frozen limeade concentrate
 ¼ cup frozen orange juice concentrate
 1 cup water
 Small mint sprigs for garnish (optional)

Combine all the ingredients *except* the mint in a blender container and blend until puréed. Transfer the soup to a glass or ceramic bowl. Cover and chill for 2 to 3 hours. Stir before serving.

Serve in small bowls or cups. If desired, garnish individual portions with a small sprig of mint.

Makes 4 to 5 servings.

Watermelon "Gazpacho"

Instead of using puréed tomatoes as a base and adding zesty vegetables to make a soup, in this fanciful creation we use puréed watermelon and a bounty of delectable fruits to the same end. The result is a light and beautiful fruit soup that can be served as a first course, a side dish, or even a simple dessert. This fruit "gazpacho" is very refreshing and not too sweet.

 4¾ to 5 pounds fresh watermelon (about one quarter of a medium-large watermelon)
 Generous ¼ teaspoon peeled and very finely minced gingerroot
 2 tablespoons sugar, or a little more to taste
 1½ tablespoons lemon juice, preferably fresh

½ cup peeled and finely diced ripe mango *or* fresh peach
½ cup pitted and diced dark sweet cherries
⅓ cup quartered green seedless grapes
⅓ cup fresh or loose-pack frozen blueberries
½ teaspoon finely chopped fresh lemon balm leaves (If unavailable, substitute 1 pinch of grated lemon rind.)
1 teaspoon finely chopped fresh mint leaves for garnish (optional)

Seed and cut enough chunks from the watermelon to make 2¾ cups. Combine the seeded watermelon chunks, gingerroot, sugar, and lemon juice in a blender or processor and purée until completely smooth. Transfer the purée to a large noncorrosive bowl. Seed and dice the remainder of the flavorful watermelon flesh; discard the rind and lighter-colored flesh. Add the diced watermelon to the purée. Stir in the mango, cherries, grapes, blueberries, and lemon balm. Cover and refrigerate for 3 to 4 hours, or until well chilled.

Divide the "gazpacho" among prechilled small glass bowls or soup cups. If desired, top each serving with a pinch or two of finely chopped fresh mint leaves.

Makes 4 to 5 servings.

Dried Fruit and Wine Soup

Serve this good and easy soup at a brunch or luncheon. Or try it in place of stewed fruit for breakfast.

⅔ cup chopped dried apricots
½ cup chopped dried pears
½ cup chopped pitted prunes
⅓ cup finely chopped dried apples
Generous ⅓ cup sugar
3¼ cups water (approximately)
2 ¼-inch lemon slices, seeds removed
2 3-inch-long cinnamon sticks

½ cup fruity white table wine, such as Moselle or Rhine
   wine
1 tablespoon cornstarch
2 to 3 tablespoons commercial sour cream for garnish

Combine the dried fruits, sugar, water, lemon slices, and cinnamon sticks in a 2- to 3-quart saucepan. Bring the mixture to a boil over medium-high heat; then lower the heat and simmer, covered, for 12 minutes. Remove and discard the lemon slices and cinnamon sticks.

In a small bowl or cup, stir together the wine and cornstarch until well blended and smooth. Stir the wine-cornstarch mixture into the pan. Allow the soup to return to a simmer and cook for 3 to 4 minutes longer, or until the fruit is tender but not mushy. (If the fruit has absorbed most of the liquid, stir in enough more water to yield a "soupy" consistency.)

Serve the soup warm or at room temperature. Ladle servings into small bowls or soup cups. Garnish each serving with a dollop of sour cream. The soup may be made ahead and refrigerated, if desired. If it becomes too thick during storage, thin it with a bit of orange juice or water before serving.

Makes 4 to 6 servings.

13

STOCKS AND CLEAR SOUPS

It's no accident that the French word for stock is *fonds,* or foundation. Stock provides an essential flavor base upon which the rest of the ingredients build in a recipe. It also lends dishes body and underlying character.

Certainly, this is true in soupmaking. The foundation of good soup is good stock or broth. It can mean the difference between a soup that is slightly watery or somehow lacking and one that truly satisfies the soul.

Fortunately, most stocks are extremely simple creations. Preparation usually involves nothing more than combining water and a few seasonings with bones (or in the case of crustaceans, shells) and vegetables, and then gently simmering the ingredients until their essential flavors are released into the liquid.

For some stocks, particularly beef, the simmering process takes quite a while, but little of the cook's time and attention is actually required. And other stocks involve much less time. Fish stock, for example, simmers for about 30 minutes, and ham stock for an hour. (On those occasions when it's inconvenient or completely impractical to prepare stock at home, keep in mind that there are a number of flavorful commercial broths and bouillons which can be successfully substituted. For information on these, see page 11, in the "Ingredients" section in Chapter 1.)

While the stocks presented here are used to enrich many of the recipes in the book, stocks and broths can also serve as soups themselves. These, including consommé, bouillon, and several light broths, appear in this chapter as well. Often, preparation of such recipes involves enhancing a stock with seasonings and boiling it down to concentrate the flavor. Sometimes, the liquid is also strained or "clarified," an easy, yet remarkable, process that draws out sediment and leaves the liquid very clear. For your convenience, specific directions for clarifying are included wherever this step is required.

Beef Stock

This is a basic, versatile beef stock which can be used to enrich many of the recipes in *Soup's On.* Since the bones are not browned (caramelized) prior to simmering, the stock has a lighter color and less pronounced "beefy" flavor than brown stock or most commercial beef bouillons. It comes in particularly handy when a subtle richness is desired or when a brown-colored stock would make a soup look unattractive.

Like our other stocks, this one is lightly salted so it can be used more or less interchangeably with commercial broths and bouillons. If you wish to use the stock for other purposes besides soupmaking, the salt can be reduced or even omitted from it, and each individual dish can be salted as needed.

Though this stock benefits from long simmering (up to 6 hours, if convenient), it needs virtually no attention from the cook during most of that time. A quick check now and then to make sure the pot isn't simmering too rapidly is about all that is required.

> 3 to 3½ pounds beef bones, preferably marrow bones sawed into 2-inch-long pieces
> 2 pounds meaty beef bones from shin, plate, etc.
> 14 cups water
> 4 large onions, cut into eighths
> 2 large celery stalks, coarsely sliced
> 2 large carrots, coarsely sliced
> 2 medium-sized parsnips, peeled and coarsely sliced
> 1 small turnip, peeled and cut into eighths
> ⅓ cup coarsely chopped fresh parsley leaves
> 2 large bay leaves
> 1 teaspoon whole black peppercorns
> ½ teaspoon dried thyme leaves
> 2 whole cloves
> 2½ teaspoons salt

Rinse the bones and drain them well. Combine them in a very large (8-quart minimum) pot with enough cold water to cover. Bring the water to a boil over medium heat; gently boil the bones for 3 minutes. Turn out the bones into a colander; rinse them well. Rinse out the pot and return the bones to it, along with the water. Bring the water to a boil over medium heat. Cover the pot and adjust the heat so that the mixture boils very gently for about 1 hour; as scum rises to the surface, occasionally skim it off with a large shallow spoon. Also skim off and discard any fat on the surface.

Add the onions, celery, carrots, parsnips, and turnip to the pot. Cover the pot and simmer the mixture for 1 hour longer. Stir in all the remaining ingredients and continue simmering, covered, for at least 2 hours and up to 6 hours.

Strain the stock through a fine sieve, discarding the bones and vegetables. Skim off any fat from the stock surface, using a large shallow spoon. (Alternatively, chill the stock and then lift off and discard the hardened fat from the surface.)

The stock may be stored in the refrigerator for 3 to 4 days. It may also be frozen for up to 3 months.

Makes about 2½ to 3 quarts.

Brown Stock

Like plain beef stock, brown stock is made with beef bones and meat. The difference is in the preparation. For brown stock, the bones, meat, and vegetables are roasted before they are simmered. The roasting process not only intensifies the flavor of the ingredients but also contributes to the color of the stock. This is because the caramelized bits which form on the bottom of the pan turn the liquid a rich, beefy brown.

Notice that the last ingredient listed in this recipe is optional tomato paste. Although it does help bring out flavor, it introduces sediment and should not be added if you plan to clarify your stock and use it for consommé or other clear soups. In this case, simply omit the tomato paste and continue on with preparations.

> 3 pounds beef bones, preferably knuckle and marrow bones, sawed into 1½- to 2-inch-long pieces
> 2 pounds beef plate ribs or short ribs
> 3 large onions, cut into eighths
> 2 large celery stalks, coarsely sliced
> 3 large carrots, coarsely sliced
> 1 medium-sized parsnip, peeled and coarsely sliced
> 15 cups water

½ cup coarsely chopped fresh parsley leaves
3 large bay leaves
1 teaspoon whole black peppercorns
½ teaspoon dried thyme leaves
1 tablespoon salt
¼ cup tomato paste (optional)

Preheat the oven to 400 degrees. Rinse the soup bones and ribs under cold water. Pat them dry with paper towels. Spread out the bones, ribs, and vegetables in a very large roasting pan. (If a very large roasting pan is not available, use two smaller ones.) Roast the mixture in the preheated oven for 1 hour and 20 to 30 minutes; stir frequently to ensure that the ingredients brown evenly and do not burn. If necessary, lower the oven temperature slightly to prevent burning.

Transfer the contents of the roasting pan to a very large soup pot or stock pot. Add 2 cups of the water to the roasting pan. Using a large wooden spoon, carefully scrape up any browned bits sticking to the bottom. Transfer the water and browned beef bits from the pan to the stock pot. Add the remaining water and the parsley to the pot. Bring the mixture to a boil over medium heat. Cover the pot and adjust the heat so that the mixture simmers very gently for about 1 hour; as scum rises to the surface, skim it off with a large shallow spoon.

Stir in the bay leaves, peppercorns, thyme, and salt, and continue simmering, covered, for at least 2 hours and up to 6 hours longer.

When the simmering process is completed, remove the pot from the heat. If the tomato paste is to be used, stir it together with ½ cup of liquid removed from the pot until well blended and smooth. Stir the mixture back into the pot.

Strain the stock through a fine sieve, discarding the bones and vegetables. Skim off any fat from the surface of the stock, using a large shallow spoon; refrigerate the stock immediately. (Alternatively, the stock can be chilled before the fat is removed. In this case, the fat will harden on the surface of the cold stock and can then be lifted off and discarded.)

The stock may be stored in the refrigerator for 3 to 4 days. It may also be frozen for up to 3 months.

Makes 2½ to 3 quarts.

Chicken Stock

Rich in flavor, this stock is far superior to commercial chicken broth or bouillon. It can be kept in the refrigerator for 2 to 3 days and frozen for up to 6 months. It's not necessary to use expensive chicken parts to make the stock. Backs, wings, and necks are fine. In fact, these parts can be saved when you buy whole chickens and then stored in the freezer. If you don't have a pot large enough to make the whole recipe, it can easily be halved.

Note that the amount of salt called for yields a stock that tastes about as salty as commercial chicken broth. Naturally, less can be used, if desired.

> About 7 pounds bony chicken parts, such as backs, wings, and necks
> 16 cups water
> 4 medium-sized carrots, coarsely sliced
> 4 large celery stalks, coarsely sliced
> 5 to 6 fresh parsley sprigs
> 2 parsnips, *or* 2 small turnips, peeled and diced
> 2 large onions, coarsely chopped
> 2 bay leaves
> ½ teaspoon dried thyme leaves
> 2 teaspoons salt
> Generous ½ teaspoon black pepper, preferably freshly ground

In a large stock pot, combine the chicken, water, carrots, celery, parsley, parsnips, and onions. Bring to a boil over medium-high heat. Cover, lower the heat, and simmer gently for 1½ hours, skimming the foam from the top of the stock frequently during the first 20 to 30 minutes. Add all the remaining ingredients. With the cover of the pot slightly ajar, simmer the stock over low heat for an additional 1½ hours, stirring occasionally. Remove the chicken and vegetables with a slotted spoon and discard them. With a large shallow spoon, skim the fat from the top of the stock and discard it.

Strain the stock through a sieve and measure it. You should

have about 10 cups of liquid. If more has evaporated, add a bit of water. If there is too much liquid, wash out the pot in which the stock was prepared, return the stock to the pot, and boil it down until only 10 or 11 cups remain.

The stock may be refrigerated for 2 or 3 days and frozen for up to 6 months.

Makes about 2½ quarts.

Ham Stock

Although quick and easy to make, this stock gives a wonderful smoked meat flavor to soups. Several recipes in *Soup's On!* call for ham stock. You may also want to try using it as a base for lentil, split pea, or vegetable soups. Because the salt content of ham hocks varies, you may have to adjust the amount of salt in recipes when using this stock.

2 to 3 smoked pork hocks (about 1⅓ to 1½ pounds total weight)
6 to 7 cups water
1 medium-sized onion, coarsely chopped
1 large garlic clove, minced
1 large bay leaf

In a small Dutch oven or large saucepan, combine all the ingredients. Cover and bring to a boil over high heat. Lower the heat and simmer for approximately 1 hour, or until the stock is nicely flavored. Remove the pot from the heat. Remove and discard the pork hocks. Using a large shallow spoon, skim off and discard any fat from the surface of the stock.

Strain the stock through a sieve and measure. If there are fewer than 6 cups of liquid, add enough water to yield this amount.

Makes about 6 cups.

Fish Stock

Of all stocks, fish is the easiest and most economical to prepare. Fresh fish frames and heads can usually be obtained free or for just a small service charge from seafood markets and fishmongers. Moreover, the ingredients need simmer for only 30 minutes to yield a flavorful, gelatin-rich stock.

Be sure to use only very fresh and clean, non-oily, white-fleshed fish. The oily, darker-fleshed varieties make a stock too strong. Also, do not prepare the mixture in an aluminum pot, as it may add a metallic taste or cause discoloration of the stock.

> 4 to 4½ pounds frames and heads from flounder, sole, haddock, etc.
> 8 cups water
> ½ cup dry white wine
> 1 medium-sized onion, coarsely chopped
> 1 small celery stalk, coarsely sliced
> 1 small carrot, coarsely sliced
> 7 to 8 fresh parsley sprigs
> 1 small bay leaf
> 1½ teaspoons lemon juice, preferably fresh
> ½ teaspoon whole black peppercorns
> ⅛ teaspoon dried thyme leaves
> Pinch of fennel seeds (optional)
> 1¼ teaspoons salt

Thoroughly rinse the fish frames and drain them. Rinse the heads, being careful to wash out any blood. (If they seem bloody, soak them in cold water for a few minutes. Then drain them, rinse them well, and place in water again. If the water discolors, repeat the soaking process until it stays clear.) Combine the frames and heads in a large (6-quart minimum) pot with all the remaining ingredients *except* the salt. Bring to a boil over medium heat. Cover, lower the heat, and simmer for about 30 minutes.

Strain the stock through a fine sieve, discarding the bones and vegetables. Stir in the salt. The stock may be stored in the refrigerator for 1 to 2 days. It may also be frozen for up to 3 months.

Makes about 2 quarts.

Vegetable Stock

A nice base for vegetarian soups, this flavorful stock can be substituted in many recipes that call for vegetable bouillon or vegetable bouillon reconstituted from cubes or powder. However, the homemade stock is not as concentrated as vegetable bouillon. In general, use 2 cups of homemade vegetable stock for every 1 cup of vegetable bouillon plus 1 cup of water.

Because this homemade stock has a modest amount of salt, you may need to increase the salt slightly in recipes when using it. Or, if you are on a low-salt diet, you can omit the salt from the stock entirely.

As vegetable stocks do not keep well, use the mixture within 24 hours if stored in the refrigerator. The stock can also be frozen for 4 to 6 weeks.

3 tablespoons vegetable oil
2 large onions, finely chopped
1 large garlic clove, minced
1 large potato, well scrubbed and diced
3 large celery stalks, including leaves, thinly sliced
1 large carrot, well scrubbed and thinly sliced
1 large turnip, well scrubbed, root and stem end removed, and diced
½ cup finely chopped fresh parsley leaves
2 large bay leaves
¼ teaspoon black pepper, preferably freshly ground
Scant ¾ teaspoon salt
5 cups water

In a large heavy saucepan, combine the oil, onions, garlic, potato, and celery. Over medium to medium-low heat, cook the vegetables in the oil for about 10 minutes, being careful not to brown them. Stir frequently and, if necessary, lower the heat to prevent the vegetables from browning. Add all the remaining ingredients and stir to mix well. Cover and bring to a boil over high heat. Lower the heat and simmer the stock for about 1 hour.

Strain the stock through a sieve and discard the vegetables. Measure the stock. If there are fewer than 4 cups of liquid, add water as necessary to yield 4 cups.

Makes 4 cups.

Beef Consommé

The clarification process involved in making consommé is not difficult, but the directions must be followed carefully. Pay particular attention to skim any fat from the surface of the stock before beginning. Also, try not to disturb or break up the thick layer of solids which forms on the consommé surface during cooking.

5½ cups thoroughly degreased brown stock or top-quality canned beef broth, divided
3 to 4 ounces very lean, minced or finely chopped beef, preferably shin beef
½ cup canned Italian-style (plum) tomatoes, including juice, finely chopped
1 large onion, finely chopped
1 large celery stalk, finely chopped
1 large carrot, finely chopped
¼ teaspoon whole black peppercorns
½ teaspoon dried thyme leaves
2 large egg whites
2 tablespoons Cognac or dry sherry
¼ to ½ teaspoon salt, or to taste

Combine 4½ cups of the stock, the beef, tomatoes, onion, celery, carrot, peppercorns, and thyme in a completely grease-free 2½- to 3-quart saucepan. Bring to a boil over medium-high heat.

Meanwhile, combine the remaining 1 cup of the stock with the egg whites in a large bowl. Beat the mixture with a wire whisk or fork until well blended and frothy. Set it aside.

When the stock-beef mixture comes to a boil, slowly add it to the stock-egg white mixture, beating with a wire whisk or fork. Return the mixture to the saucepan and bring it to a simmer, stirring, over medium-high heat. Immediately lower the heat and very gently simmer the consommé, uncovered, for 1 hour; do not stir or otherwise disturb it. (During cooking, the egg whites and other solids will form a thick layer on the top, while the clear consommé will be on the bottom.)

Line a colander or large sieve with a layer of slightly dampened unbleached muslin (or a triple thickness of dampened cheesecloth). Set the colander over a large completely grease-free bowl. Gently turn out the mixture into the lined colander. Let stand for 10 to 15 minutes, or until the broth has drained through. For an even clearer consommé, repeat the straining through a colander or sieve lined with a clean piece of dampened unbleached muslin.

Reheat the consommé in a clean saucepan over medium-high heat. Stir in the Cognac. Add salt to taste.

Ladle the consommé into consommé cups or small bowls and serve.

(Alternatively, the consommé may be covered and chilled in the refrigerator, then reheated at serving time. In this case, carefully skim off and discard any hardened fat from the consommé surface before heating.)

Makes 4 servings.

Cucumber Broth

A beautifully clear chicken broth with translucent slices of cucumber floating in it. (Note: The basic directions which follow can also be used to clarify plain chicken broth. In this case, simply omit the soy sauce, gingerroot, and cucumber. Once the broth has been clarified, it may be served plain or garnished with a bit of chopped fresh parsley leaves. Cooked noodles or lightly poached vegetables may also be added, if desired.)

4¾ cups completely degreased chicken stock or broth, divided

1 small onion, chopped
½ teaspoon soy sauce
Generous pinch of finely minced gingerroot
2 large egg whites
½ small firm cucumber

Combine 3 cups of the stock, the onion, soy sauce, and gingerroot in a completely grease-free 2-quart saucepan. Bring to a boil over medium-high heat.

Meanwhile, combine the remaining 1¾ cups of stock with the egg whites in a large, completely grease-free bowl. Beat the mixture with a wire whisk or fork until well blended and frothy. Set it aside.

When the stock-seasoning mixture comes to a boil, slowly add it to the stock-egg white mixture, beating with a wire whisk or fork. Return the mixture to the saucepan and bring it to a simmer, stirring, over medium-high heat. As soon as bubbles begin breaking the surface, immediately lower the heat and very gently simmer, uncovered, for 15 to 20 minutes; do not stir or otherwise disturb the stock. (During cooking, the egg whites and other solids will form a thick layer on the top, while the clear broth will be on the bottom.)

Meanwhile, peel the cucumber half. Seed it by carefully hollowing out the center using a sharp knife. Cut the cucumber half into ⅛-inch-thick slices and set them aside.

Line a colander or large sieve with a layer of slightly dampened unbleached muslin (or a triple thickness of dampened cheesecloth). Set the colander over a large grease-free saucepan.

When the chicken stock mixture has simmered for at least 15 minutes, gently turn it out into the lined colander. Let stand for about 5 minutes, or until the broth has drained into the saucepan; discard the solids.

Add the cucumber slices to the broth. Bring to a boil over high heat. Lower the heat and simmer for 2 to 3 minutes, or until the cucumber slices become translucent. Serve immediately.

Makes 4 to 5 servings.

Mushroom Broth

The essence of mushrooms enriches this simple but elegant clear soup. A few thin slices of button mushrooms floated on the top make an attractive garnish.

4½ cups clarified beef stock, brown stock, or bouillon
1½ cups water
4½ cups coarsely sliced fresh mushrooms (about 1¼ pounds)
3 medium-sized green onions (scallions), including green tops, coarsely chopped
9 to 10 fresh parsley sprigs
1½ teaspoons lemon juice, preferably fresh
1½ teaspoons soy sauce
½ teaspoon whole black peppercorns
⅛ teaspoon dried thyme leaves
6 to 7 unblemished, firm fresh button mushrooms for garnish

Combine all the ingredients *except* the button mushrooms in a medium-sized saucepan. Bring the mixture to a boil over medium-high heat. Tightly cover the pan, lower the heat, and gently simmer the mixture for about 45 minutes.

Strain the mixture through a fine sieve, pressing down on the solids with a spoon to extract as much juice as possible. Discard the solids. Divide the broth among soup cups or small bowls.

Carefully cut the button mushrooms into paper-thin slices and float 5 or 6 slices on each serving.

(Alternatively, the broth may be prepared ahead and refrigerated. At serving time, reheat the broth; then slice the mushroom and garnish the soup with them just before serving.)

Makes 5 to 6 servings.

Tomato Bouillon

Serve this attractive, zesty bouillon hot or cold.

3 cups tomato juice
¾ cup dry red wine
3 cups completely degreased beef stock, *or* brown stock, *or*
  bouillon (reconstituted from cubes or granules), divided
1 large onion, chopped
1 large celery stalk, chopped
1 large carrot, chopped
6 to 7 fresh parsley sprigs
Generous ½ teaspoon whole black peppercorns
1 to 2 drops Tabasco sauce
Pinch of dried thyme leaves
3 large egg whites

Combine the tomato juice, wine, and 1½ cups of the
beef stock in a completely grease-free 3-quart saucepan. Bring
to a boil over medium-high heat.

Meanwhile, combine the remaining 1½ cups of beef stock,
the onion, celery, carrot, parsley, peppercorns, Tabasco,
thyme, and egg whites in a large completely grease-free bowl.
Beat the mixture with a wire whisk or fork until well blended
and frothy. Set it aside.

When the tomato juice mixture comes to a boil, slowly add it
to the beef stock-egg white mixture, beating with a wire whisk
or fork. Return the mixture to the saucepan and bring it to a
simmer, stirring, over medium-high heat. As soon as bubbles
begin breaking the surface, immediately lower the heat and
simmer very gently, uncovered, for 25 to 30 minutes; do not
stir or otherwise disturb the stock. (During cooking, the egg
whites and other solids will form a thick layer on the top, while
the clear broth will be on the bottom.)

Line a colander or large sieve with a layer of slightly
dampened unbleached muslin or a triple thickness of
dampened cheesecloth. Set the colander over a grease-free

saucepan or bowl. Gently turn out the mixture into the lined colander. Let stand for about 10 minutes, or until the bouillon has drained through; discard the solids.

Reheat the bouillon over high heat until piping hot.

(Alternatively, it may be covered and refrigerated for 3 to 4 hours, or overnight, if desired, and served cold, or reheated and served hot.)

Makes 4 servings.

Clam-Tomato Broth with Chives

A clear soup enlivened with bits of fresh tomato and chives, this whets the appetite quite nicely. It may be served hot or cold, and makes a light (and low-calorie) first course for a dinner or luncheon.

Since there is virtually no fat in the ingredients, the clarification process yields a sparkling clear broth. Clarifying the broth is not at all difficult; just be sure to follow the directions carefully.

3 cups bottled clam juice
2 cups tomato juice
1 teaspoon lemon juice, preferably fresh
1 medium-sized onion, chopped
1 small celery stalk, chopped
¼ cup coarsely chopped fresh parsley, including stems
2 tablespoons coarsely chopped fresh chives, *or* 2½ teaspoons dried chopped chives
1 small bay leaf
Generous ¼ teaspoon whole black peppercorns
¼ teaspoon dried thyme leaves
Pinch of fennel seeds (optional)
2 to 3 drops Tabasco sauce
2 large egg whites
3 tablespoons peeled, seeded, and finely diced fresh tomato

1 teaspoon finely chopped fresh chives, *or* ½ teaspoon dried chopped chives

Combine 2 cups of the clam juice and the tomato juice in a completely grease-free 2- to 3-quart saucepan. Bring to a boil over medium-high heat.

Meanwhile, combine the remaining 1 cup of clam juice, the lemon juice, onion, celery, parsley, coarsely chopped chives, bay leaf, peppercorns, thyme, fennel seeds (if used), Tabasco, and egg whites in a large completely grease-free bowl. Beat the mixture with a wire whisk or fork until well blended and frothy. Set it aside.

When the clam and tomato juice mixture comes to a boil, slowly add it to the clam juice-egg white mixture, beating with a wire whisk or fork. Return the mixture to the saucepan and bring it to a simmer, stirring, over medium-high heat. As soon as bubbles begin breaking the surface, immediately lower the heat and very gently simmer, uncovered, for 30 minutes; do not stir or otherwise disturb the stock. (During cooking, the egg whites and other solids will form a thick layer on the top, while the clear broth will be on the bottom.)

Line a colander with a layer of dampened unbleached muslin (or a triple thickness of dampened cheesecloth). Set the colander over a large grease-free bowl. Gently turn out the mixture into the colander. Let stand for about 5 minutes, or until the broth has drained through; discard the solids.

Reheat the broth in a clean saucepan over medium-high heat until piping hot. Stir in the tomato and finely chopped chives.

Ladle the broth into consommé cups or small bowls and serve immediately.

(Alternatively, the broth may be covered and refrigerated for 3 to 4 hours or up to 8 hours, if desired, and served cold. In this case, add the chopped tomato and finely chopped chives shortly before the soup is served.)

Makes 4 servings.

Wine Consommé

Use a smooth, yet dry, good-quality red wine in this recipe. Also be sure the beef stock or broth has been thoroughly degreased (skimmed of all traces of fat).

> 4½ cups completely degreased beef stock, brown stock, or broth, divided
> ¾ cup dry red wine
> ¼ cup coarsely chopped fresh parsley leaves
> Generous ¼ teaspoon whole black peppercorns
> 2 ¼-inch-thick lemon slices
> 3 whole cloves
> 1 1½-inch piece cinnamon stick
> 2 large egg whites
> 4 to 5 paper-thin half-slices of lemon for garnish (optional)

Combine 3 cups of the stock and the wine in a completely grease-free 2-quart saucepan. Bring to a boil over medium-high heat.

Meanwhile, combine the remaining 1½ cups of the stock, the parsley, peppercorns, ¼-inch-thick lemon slices, cloves, cinnamon stick, and egg whites in a large completely grease-free bowl. Beat the mixture with a wire whisk or fork until well blended and frothy. Set it aside.

When the stock-wine mixture comes to a boil, slowly add it to the stock-egg white mixture, beating with a wire whisk or fork. Return the mixture to the saucepan and bring it to a simmer, stirring, over medium-high heat. As soon as bubbles begin breaking the surface, immediately lower the heat and very gently simmer, uncovered, for 30 to 35 minutes; do not stir or otherwise disturb the stock. (During cooking, the egg whites and other solids will form a thick layer on the top, while the clear broth will be on the bottom.)

Line a colander or large sieve with a layer of slightly dampened unbleached muslin (or a triple thickness of dampened cheesecloth). Set the colander over a large grease-free saucepan. Gently turn out the mixture into the lined colander. Let stand for about 10 minutes, or until the consommé has drained through; discard the solids.

Reheat the consommé over high heat until piping hot and divide among 4 or 5 bouillon cups or small bowls. Garnish individual servings by floating a thin half-slice of lemon in each, if desired.

Makes 4 to 5 servings.

14

THE FINAL TOUCH

ere is an assortment of simple recipes—from croutons and dumplings to seasoning paste and noodles—which we occasionally call for in *Soup's On*. They represent the final touch that may not be essential, but that makes a good soup a truly memorable one.

Croutons

¼ cup butter or margarine
2½ cups ¼-inch cubes (crustless) day-old French bread

Melt the butter in a medium-sized frying pan over medium-high heat. Add the bread cubes, tossing until evenly coated with the butter. Toast the cubes, stirring, for 4 to 5 minutes, or until they are golden brown and crisp. Remove the pan from the heat and continue stirring for 30 seconds. The croutons may be used immediately, or cooled and stored in an airtight container for a day or two.

Makes about 2½ cups.

Garlic Croutons

1½ tablespoons olive oil
1½ tablespoons butter
1 large garlic clove, split in half lengthwise
2 cups ¼-inch cubes (crustless) day-old Italian or French bread

Heat the olive oil and butter in a medium-sized frying pan over medium heat until the butter melts. Add the garlic clove halves and cook, stirring frequently and pressing down on the pieces, for 3 to 4 minutes; do not allow the garlic to brown. Discard the garlic. Add the bread cubes to the pan. Cook, stirring, for 4 to 5 minutes, or until they are nicely browned and crisp. They can be used immediately or cooled and stored in an airtight container for a day or two.

Makes about 2 cups.

Croûtes

Croûtes are well-toasted slices of French bread used to garnish some French soups. Unlike croutons, they are not sprinkled over the top of the soup, but, rather, placed in the bowl and the soup is ladled over them.

> 5 to 6 large ¾-inch-thick slices day-old French bread
> 3 to 4 tablespoons olive oil (approximately)

Preheat the oven to 325 degrees. Generously brush both sides of the bread slices with olive oil. Lay the slices on a baking sheet. Bake the slices on one side for 12 to 15 minutes. Then turn them over and bake on the second side for 12 to 15 minutes, or until they are very dry and crisp.

The croûtes may be used immediately, if desired, or cooled and packed in an airtight plastic bag. They can be kept in a cool, dry spot for 3 or 4 days.

Makes 5 to 6 croûtes, enough to garnish 5 or 6 soup servings.

Fruit Soup Dumplings

> 2 large eggs
> 1 tablespoon sugar
> 3 tablespoons butter or margarine at room temperature
> Generous ⅛ teaspoon ground mace
> ⅔ cup farmer cheese
> ¾ cup fine fresh white bread crumbs
> 1 tablespoon all-purpose white flour

In a medium-sized bowl, lightly beat the eggs and sugar together with a fork or wire whisk. Add the butter and mace and beat until well blended. Stir in the farmer cheese, bread crumbs, and flour until thoroughly incorporated and smooth. Set aside, uncovered, at room temperature for 2 to 3 hours.

To complete preparations, bring 2 quarts of water to a boil in a large saucepan over high heat. Adjust the heat so the water simmers very gently.

With moistened hands, one at a time, form the dough into 10 to 12 round dumplings and slip them into the pot, using a slotted spoon. Stir once very gently to lift them from the bottom of the pot. Poach the dumplings, uncovered, for 9 to 12 minutes, or until they are slightly firm and cooked through. (They will rise to the surface during cooking.) Remove the dumplings using a slotted spoon and arrange them, two to a bowl, on the soup. The dumpling may also be covered and held in a warm oven for up to 30 minutes, if desired.

Makes 10 to 12 dumplings.

Homemade Egg Noodles

Commercial noodles can, of course, be used in the soups in this book, but if you wish to make your own, here is a good recipe. The noodles can be cooked as directed below and added to plain or clarified chicken stock or broth, or used in our Chicken Noodle Soup, page 65. They can also be used in other soups calling for egg noodles.

    2 cups all-purpose white flour
    Generous 1 teaspoon salt
    2 tablespoons cold butter or margarine
    2 large eggs, lightly beaten
    3 to 4 teaspoons water (approximately)

Stir together the flour and salt in a medium-sized bowl. Cut in the butter with a pastry blender or fork until the mixture has the consistency of coarse meal. Make a well in the center of the mixture and add the eggs and 2 teaspoons of water to it. Using your hands, mix the eggs and water into the flour until well combined. If the dough seems too dry to hold together smoothly, add a bit more water, but be careful not to add too much. When the dough forms a smooth, cohesive ball, transfer it to a very lightly floured work surface. Vigorously knead the dough, pushing it back and forth and slapping it on the work surface until it is smooth and elastic, about 5 minutes. Let the dough rest on the work surface for 5 minutes. Divide the dough in half. Wrap one half in wax paper and set it aside.

Using a rolling pin dusted with flour, roll out the other half of the dough to a nearly transparent rectangle approximately 18 inches long and 11 inches wide. (At first the dough will be very springy and resistant to rolling, but will become easier to manage as the layer gets thinner.) Lift the rectangle from the surface several times to make sure it isn't sticking. Trim off and discard the uneven edges of the rectangle. Working from a shorter side, gently fold the dough in thirds as though folding a business letter. Transfer the folded dough to a large cutting board. Using a sharp knife, make clean cuts *across* the folds at ¹⁄₁₆-inch intervals to yield long, thin strips. Gently unfold the dough. Working with 10 to 12 strips at a time, grasp them at one end and lift them from the cutting board. Gently shake the strips to separate them. Then cut them crosswise into 1¼-inch-long noodles. Continue separating and cutting the strips until all the noodles are formed. Spread them one layer thick on a long sheet of wax paper. Repeat the process with the second half of the dough.

Let the noodles dry, uncovered, for at least 45 minutes and up to 2 hours before using. Or let them dry until completely hard, about 8 hours. Transfer the noodles to a plastic bag and refrigerate for several days, or freeze for several months. If using frozen noodles, don't thaw them first.

To cook the noodles: Bring a very large pot of lightly salted water to a rolling boil over high heat. Measure out as many noodles as desired. Drop the noodles into the water and boil, uncovered, over high heat for 5 to 8 minutes, or until the noodles are cooked through but still slightly firm; be careful not to overcook them. Turn them out into a colander until well drained; then add them to your broth or soup. (Alternatively, add uncooked noodles directly to the soup and cook as instructed in the recipe.)

Makes about 4 cups dry, uncooked egg noodles.

Pistou (Seasoning Paste)

¼ teaspoon salt
1 to 2 large garlic cloves, minced
2 tablespoons tomato paste
6 tablespoons grated Parmesan cheese, divided
About ⅔ to ¾ cup olive oil, divided
3 tablespoons finely chopped fresh basil leaves, *or* 1½ table-
    spoons dried basil leaves

Combine the salt and garlic in a mortar or a small heavy bowl. Pound them together with a pestle or mash them together with the back of a spoon. Add the tomato paste and 2 tablespoons of the cheese. Pound or vigorously stir the mixture until well blended and smooth. A drop or two at a time, pound or stir in 2 tablespoons of the olive oil until a smooth paste is formed.

Transfer the paste to a blender container. Sprinkle the remaining 4 tablespoons of cheese over the paste. Sprinkle the basil over the cheese. Open the feed hole in the blender cap. Turn the blender on low speed and immediately begin feeding more olive oil through the hole *a few drops at a time*. As the oil is incorporated and the paste becomes smoother, gradually add it at a slightly faster rate, in a slow, thin stream. Continue blending and slowly adding oil until the pistou is smooth and about the consistency of light mayonnaise; immediately stop adding oil and turn off the blender.

Transfer the pistou to a small serving bowl. It may be used immediately or covered and refrigerated for 3 or 4 days. (As storage time lengthens, the pistou may begin to discolor slightly, but the taste will not be affected.)

Makes a scant 1 cup.

LIST OF MAIN-DISH SOUPS

The following soups are all substantial enough to be the main dish for a meal, especially when the menu includes bread and butter, a salad, and dessert.

SOUPS FROM AROUND THE WORLD:

Goulash Soup (page 17)

Corn and Bean con Carne Soup (page 19)

Albóndigas (Mexican Meatball Soup) (page 20)

Danish-Style Oxtail Soup with Dumplings (page 22)

Spanish-Style Vegetable Soup (page 24)

Scotch Broth (page 25)

Frankfurt Bean Soup (page 27)

Cock-a-Leekie (page 29)

Chicken and Vegetable Soup Provençal (page 31)

Waterzooi (Belgian Chicken and Vegetable Soup) (page 33)

Mulligatawny (page 36)

French Onion Soup (page 41)

MEAT AND POULTRY SOUPS:

Old-Fashioned Beef and Vegetable Soup (page 49)

Beefy Minestrone (page 51)

Hunter's Beef and Mushroom Soup (page 53)

Alphabet Beef and Vegetable Soup (page 54)

Meatball and Vegetable Soup (page 55)

Favorite Oxtail Soup (page 58)

Three-Meat Soup (page 59)

Veal and Sweet Pepper Soup (page 61)

Hearty Ham Soup (page 62)

Country Pork Ribs and Cabbage Soup (page 63)

Chunky Vegetable and Sausage Soup (page 64)

Chunky Chicken and Vegetable Soup with Little Dumplings (page 68)

Pimiento-Chicken Soup with Chives (page 70)

Home-Style Chicken and Vegetable Chowder (page 71)

Chicken and Curly Endive Soup (page 73)

Spicy North African–Style Chicken Soup (page 75)

Country-Style Turkey Vegetable Soup (page 77)

FISH AND SHELLFISH SOUPS:

Bouillabaisse (page 82)

Cioppino (page 84)

Portuguese-Style Fisherman's Pot (page 86)

Bermuda Fish Chowder (page 88)

Scandinavian-Style Fish Chowder with Dill (page 90)

Manhattan-Style Fish Chowder with Vegetables (page 91)

New England–Style Clam Chowder (page 92)

Manhattan-Style Clam Chowder (page 93)

Maryland Crab Soup (page 95)

Snow Crab and Shrimp Chowder (page 97)

Shrimp and Chicken Gumbo (page 100)

Scallop Chowder (page 103)

Oyster, Sausage, and Ham Gumbo (page 106)

BEAN AND GRAIN SOUPS:

Eastern European–Style Beef and Bean Soup (page 149)

Lamb and White Bean Soup (page 151)

Tuscan White Bean Soup (page 152)

Black Bean Soup (page 154)

Red Bean and Sausage Soup (page 155)

Split Pea and Ham Soup (page 155)

Bean with Bacon Soup (page 157)

Lentil-Barley Soup with Beef (page 158)

Savory Brown Rice and Lentil Soup (page 161)

Beef and Barley Soup (page 162)

Lima Bean and Barley Soup (page 163)

Peanut Soup Gold Coast Style (page 165)

VEGETARIAN SOUPS:

Hearty Barley Soup (page 169)

Cuban Black Bean Soup (page 170)

Tangy Three-Bean Soup (page 172)

Easy Mexican Corn and Bean Soup (page 175)

Santa Fe Potato-Corn Chowder (page 179)

Vegetarian Minestrone (page 181)

CROCK POT SOUPS:

Beef and Green Bean Soup with Potatoes (page 186)

Italian-Style Vegetable-Beef Soup (page 187)

Chili Bean and Beef Soup (page 188)

Easy Goulash Soup (page 189)

Easy Barbecued Beef Soup with Vegetables (page 190)

Ground Beef and Vegetable Soup (page 191)

Hearty Veal and Vegetable Soup (page 192)

Creole-Style Lamb Soup (page 193)

Curried Pork and Apple Soup (page 193)

Lentil Soup (page 194)

Workday Bean Soup (page 195)

Easy Bean and Barley Soup (page 196)

Crock Pot Chicken Gumbo (page 197)

Chicken and Barley Soup (page 198)

QUICK SOUPS:

Chunky Chicken and Pasta Soup (page 203)

Chicken and Chilies Soup (page 204)

New England–Style Fish Chowder (page 206)

INDEX

African soup
  chicken, spicy North African–
    style, 75–76
  curried chicken, West African,
    255–256
  peanut, Gold Coast style, 165–166
Albóndigas (Mexican meatball
    soup), 20–21
Alphabet soup
  beef and vegetable, 54–55
  chicken, 72–73
Apple(s)
  apple-pear soup, golden, 275–276
  apple-wine soup, spicy, 276–277
  butternut harvest bisque, 135–
    136
  mulligatawny, 36–38
  pork soup with, curried, 193–194
  red onion soup with curry and,
    127–128
Apricot soup, 277–278
Artichoke soup, 236–237
Asparagus
  Asparagus-cheese potage, 238–
    239
  cream soup, 111–112
Avgolemono soup, Greek, 43–44
Avocado soup, 256–257

Bacon
  bean soup with, 157–158
  lentil soup, 194–195
  Maryland crab soup, 95–97
  potato-bacon soup, cream of, 131
  tomato bisque with thyme and,
    140–141
Barbecued beef soup with
    vegetables, easy, 190

Barley
  bean soup with, easy, 196–197
  beef soup with, 162–163
  chicken soup with, 198–199
  ham soup, hearty, 62–63
  lentil-barley soup with beef, 158–
    159
  lima bean soup with, 163–164
  meatball and vegetable soup, 55–
    56
  pork rib and cabbage soup,
    country, 63–64
  Scotch broth, 25–26
  soup, hearty, 169–170
  three-meat soup, 59–60
Basil. See Pesto
Beans and legumes, dry
  and barley soup, easy, 196–197
  beef soup with, Eastern European–
    style, 149–150
  beefy minestrone, 51–52
  black bean soup, 154
  black bean soup, Cuban, 170–171
  brown rice and lentil soup, savory,
    161
  cabbage soup Mediterranean
    style, hearty, 116–117
  celery-rice soup, spicy, 164
  chicken gumbo, crock pot, 197–
    198
  chili bean and beef soup, 188
  and corn con carne soup, 19
  corn soup with, easy Mexican,
    175
  garden soup, Italian, 144–145
  ham soup, hearty, 62–63
  lamb and white bean soup, 151–
    152

Beans and legumes, dry (*cont.*)
  lentil-barley soup with beef, 158–159
  lentil soup, 194–195
  lentil soup, East Indian, 177
  pork rib and cabbage soup, country, 63–64
  red bean and sausage soup, 155
  red lentil-tomato soup, 159–160
  Scotch broth, 25–26
  soup, Frankfurt, 27–29
  soup, workday, 195–196
  soup with bacon, 157–158
  soup with pesto (soupe au pistou), 39–41
  split pea and ham soup, 155–156
  three-bean soup, tangy, 172–173
  three-meat soup, 59–60
  turkey vegetable soup, country-style, 77–78
  vegetable-beef soup, Italian-style, 187
  vegetable soup, Spanish-style, 24–25
  vegetarian minestrone, 181–182
  white bean soup, Tuscan, 152–153
Beans, green
  beef and mushroom soup, hunter style, 53
  beef soup with potatoes and, 186
  soup, cream of, 123–124
Beef
  and barley soup, 162–163
  and bean soup, Eastern European-style, 149–150
  beefy minestrone, 51–52
  brown stock, 297–298
  and cabbage soup, sweet and sour, 56–57
  chili bean soup with, 188
  consommé, 303–304
  corn and bean con carne soup, 19
  goulash soup, 17–18
  goulash soup, easy, 189
  and green bean soup with potatoes, 186
  lentil-barley soup with, 158–159
  meatball and vegetable soup, 55–56
  meatball soup, Mexican (albóndigas), 20–21
  and mushroom soup, hunter's, 53
  oxtail soup, favorite, 58–59
  oxtail soup with dumplings, Danish-style, 22–23
  soup with vegetables, easy barbecued, 190
  stock, 295–297
  three-meat soup, 59–60
  vegetable-beef soup, Italian-style, 187
  and vegetable soup, alphabet, 54–55
  and vegetable soup, ground, 191
  and vegetable soup, old-fashioned, 49–51
Beets
  borscht, 257–258
  and cabbage borscht, 173–174
Belgian chicken and vegetable soup (Waterzooi), 33–35
Bermuda fish chowder, 88–90
Bisque
  butternut harvest, 135–136
  garden gold, 143–144
  seafood, creamy, 225–226
  shrimp, 99–100
  summer garden, 271–272
  tomato with thyme and bacon, 140–141
Black bean soup, 154
  Cuban, 170–171
Blenders, 10–11
Bloody Mary soup, 220
Blueberry soup, 282
Borscht, 257–258
  beet and cabbage, 173–174
Bouillabaisse, 82–84
Bouillon, 11–12
  tomato, 307–308
Bouquet garni, 11
Bread
  croûtes, 316
  croutons, 315
  garlic croutons, 315
Broccoli
  broccoli-cauliflower cheese soup, 209–210

broccoli-crab soup, curried, 227–228

broccoli-potato soup, cream of, 112–113

Broth, 11–12
clam-tomato with chives, 308–309
cucumber, 304–305
mushroom, 306
Scotch, 24–25

Browning, 8

Brown stock, 297–298

Brussels sprouts soup, creamy, 210–211

Bulgur wheat, in chicken soup, spicy North African–style, 75–76

Buttermilk
strawberry-buttermilk soup, iced, 285–287
zucchini-buttermilk soup, tangy, 270

Butternut harvest bisque, 135–136

Cabbage
beef soup with, sweet and sour, 56–57
beet borscht with, 173–174
herbed soup, Stonebridge House, 113–114
pork ribs soup with, country, 63–64
soup, Tyrolean, 115–116
soup Mediterranean style, hearty, 116–117

Cajun soup. See Gumbo

Cantaloupe. See Melon

Carrot(s)
beef and mushroom soup, hunter's, 53
carrot-orange soup with ginger, 118–119
cream, winter garden bisque with, 250–252
parsnip soup with, creamy, 128–129
soup, cream of, 117–118
soup with dill, iced, 258–259

Cauliflower
broccoli-cauliflower cheese soup, 209–210
cauliflower-leek potage, 119–120
chicken and vegetable soup with little dumplings, chunky, 68–69
soup with pimiento and cheese, 211

Celery
celery-leek soup, creamy, 120–121
celery-rice soup, spicy, 164
celery-tomato soup, 212
soup, cream of, 174–175
soup, summertime, 259–260

Cheddar cheese soup with tomato, 207

Cheese, 12
asparagus-cheese potage, 238–239
broccoli-cauliflower, soup, 209–210
cauliflower soup with pimiento and, 211
Cheddar soup with tomato, 207
chicken and chilies soup, 204–205
chili-cheese soup, 208
onion soup, French, 41–42

Cherry soup, 279

Chicken
alphabet soup, 72–73
avgolemono soup, Greek, 43–44
and barley soup, 198–199
brown rice and lentil soup, savory, 161
and chilies soup, 204–205
cock-a-leekie, 29–30
and cucumber soup, 205–206
and curly endive soup, 73–75
and green onion soup, Malaysian, 38–39
gumbo, crock pot, 197–198
mulligatawny, 36–38
noodle soup, 65–66
and pasta soup, chunky, 203–204
peanut soup Gold Coast style, 165–166
pimiento-chicken soup with chives, 70–71
rice soup, 67–68
shrimp gumbo with, 100–102
soup, spicy North African–style, 75–76

Chicken (*cont.*)
  soup, West African curried, 255–256
  stock, 299–300
  tortilla soup, 35–36
  and vegetable soup, Belgian (Waterzooi), 33–35
  vegetable soup, Spanish-style, 24–25
  and vegetable soup Provençal, 31–33
  and vegetable soup with little dumplings, chunky, 68–69
Chinese soup
  hot and sour, 45–46
  pork and watercress, 26–27
Chives
  clam-tomato broth with, 308–309
  green soup (potage verf), 244
  pimiento-chicken soup with, 70–71
Chopping, 7
Chowder
  chicken and vegetable, home-style, 71–72
  clam, Manhattan-style, 93–94
  clam, New England–style, 92–93
  corn and potato, 121–122
  fish, Bermuda, 88–90
  fish, New England–style, 206–207
  fish with dill, Scandinavian-style, 90–91
  fish with vegetables, Manhattan-style, 91–92
  potato-corn, Santa Fe, 179–180
  scallop, 103–104
  snow crab and shrimp, 97–98
  Cioppino (fish and shellfish soup), 84–85
Clam(s)
  bouillabaisse, 82–84
  chowder, Manhattan-style, 93–94
  chowder, New England–style, 92–93
  clam-tomato broth with chives, 308–309
  juice, 12
Clear soup
  beef consommé, 303–304
  tomato bouillon, 307–308

wine consommé, 310–311
  see also Broth; Stock
Cock-a-leekie, 29–30
Cold soup
  apple-pear soup, golden, 275–276
  apricot, 277–278
  avocado, 256–257
  borscht, 257–258
  carrot with dill, iced, 258–259
  celery, summertime, 259–260
  cherry, 279
  chicken, West African curried, 255–256
  cranberry madrilène, 284
  cucumber, 261
  gazpacho, easy, 266–267
  gazpacho with marinated shrimp and olives, 267–268
  leek and potato (vichyssoise), 262–263
  lime and cantaloupe soup, easy, 289
  Mandarin cantaloupe soup, iced, 288
  onion-potato, curried, 263
  orange-tomato, 264
  peach with Amaretto soup, fresh, 280
  pimiento, 264–265
  raspberry 'n' cream soup, 285
  summer garden bisque, 271–272
  tomato-vegetable, zesty, 265–266
  watercress, chilled, 269
  watermelon "gazpacho," 289–290
  zucchini-buttermilk, tangy, 270
Consommé
  beef, 303–304
  wine, 310–311
Corn
  and bean con carne soup, 19
  and bean soup, easy Mexican, 175
  chicken and vegetable chowder, home-style, 71–72
  chicken gumbo, crock pot, 197–198
  high summer soup with salsa, 248–249
  and potato chowder, 121–122
  potato-corn chowder, Santa Fe, 179–180

shrimp and chicken gumbo, 100–102

soup, easy, 213–214

and tomato soup, Mexican, 214–215

Country soup
  garden, creamy, 145–146
  pork ribs and cabbage, 63–64
  turkey vegetable, 77–78

Crab
  broccoli-crab soup, curried, 227–228
  fish and shellfish soup (cioppino), 84–85
  seafood bisque, creamy, 225–226
  and shrimp chowder, snow, 97–98
  soup, cream of, 94–95
  soup, Maryland, 95–97

Cranberry madrilène, 284

Cream, 13

Cream soup
  asparagus, 111–112
  broccoli-potato, 112–113
  brussels sprouts, 210–211
  carrot, 117–118
  celery, 174–175
  celery-leek, 120–121
  country garden, 145–146
  crab, 94–95
  cucumber soup, 261
  cucumber and potato soup, 122–123
  fennel and sweet potato soup, 241–242
  fennel velouté, velvety, 239–240
  good wife soup, 246–247
  green bean, 123–124
  green pea, 176
  green soup (potage vert), 244
  leek, 124–126
  lettuce and green pea, 216
  lobster, 228–230
  parsnip and carrot, 128–129
  potato and leek (vichyssoise), 262–263
  potato and parsley soup, 133
  potato-bacon soup, cream of, 131
  pumpkin soup, spiced, 134
  saffron soup, 245–246
  seafood bisque, 225–226

spinach, 217

tomato, 139–140

tomato with chunky vegetables, 218–219

turnip, 142–143

watercress soup, chilled, 269

Creole soup
  lamb, 193
  tomato, 218

Crock pot soup
  barbecued beef with vegetables, easy, 190
  bean, workday, 195–196
  bean and barley, easy, 196–197
  beef and green bean with potatoes, 186
  chicken and barley, 198–199
  chicken gumbo, 197–198
  chili bean and beef, 188
  goulash, easy, 189
  ground beef and vegetables, 191
  lamb, Creole-style, 193
  lentil, 194–195
  pork and apple, curried, 193–194
  veal and vegetables, hearty, 192
  vegetable-beef, Italian-style, 187

Croûtes, 316
  chicken and vegetable soup Provençal, 31–33

Croutons, 315
  garlic, 315

Cuban black bean soup, 170–171

Cucumber
  broth, 304–305
  chicken soup with, 205–206
  good wife soup, 246–247
  and potato soup, 122–123
  soup, 261

Curry
  broccoli-crab soup, curried, 227–228
  chicken soup, West African curried, 255–256
  lentil soup, East Indian, 177
  mulligatawny, 36–38
  onion-potato soup, curried, 263
  pork and apple soup, curried, 193–194
  red onion and apple soup with, 127–128

Danish-style oxtail soup with dumplings, 22–23
Dicing, 7
Dill
  carrot soup with, iced, 258–259
  fish chowder with, Scandinavian-style, 90–91
  green onion soup with, 215–216
Dried fruit and wine soup, 290–291
Dumplings
  chicken and vegetable soup with, chunky, 68–69
  fruit soup, 316–317
  oxtail soup with, Danish-style, 22–23

Eastern European–style beef and bean soup, 149–150
East Indian lentil soup, 177
Easy soup
  avacado soup, 256–257
  barbecued beef with vegetables, 190
  bean and barley, 196–197
  celery soup, summertime, 259–260
  corn, 213–214
  gazpacho, 266–267
  goulash, 189
  lentil soup, East Indian, 177
  lime and cantaloupe, quick, 289
  pimiento soup, 264–265
  pumpkin soup, spiced, 134
  red bean and sausage soup, 155
  strawberry-pear soup, 287
  see also Crock pot soup; Quick soup
Egg noodles, homemade, 317–318
Endive, curly, chicken soup with, 73–75
Equipment, 10–11

Fennel
  and sweet pepper soup, 241–242
  velouté, velvety, 239–240
Fiesta vegetable soup, 220–221
Fish
  bouillabaisse, 82–84
  chowder, Bermuda, 88–90

chowder, New England–style, 206–207
chowder with dill, Scandinavian-style, 90–91
chowder with vegetables, Manhattan-style, 91–92
fish and shellfish soup (cioppino), 84–85
fisherman's pot, Portuguese-style, 86–88
stock, 301
Fisherman's pot, Portuguese-style, 86–88
Food processors, 10–11
Frankfurt bean soup, 27–29
French soup
  bouillabaisse, 82–84
  chicken and vegetable, Provençal, 31–33
  leek and potato (vichyssoise), 262–263
  onion, 41–42
  with pesto (soupe au pistou), 39–41
Fruit soup
  apple-pear, golden, 275–276
  apple-wine, spicy, 276–277
  apricot, 277–278
  blueberry, 282–283
  cherry, 279
  cranberry madrilène, 284
  dumplings, 316–317
  lime and cantaloupe, easy, 289
  Mandarin cantaloupe, iced, 288
  peach with Amaretto, fresh, 280
  plum, 281–282
  pork and apple, curried, 193–194
  raspberry 'n' cream, 285
  red onion and apple with curry, 127–128
  strawberry-buttermilk, iced, 285–287
  strawberry-pear, 287
  watermelon "gazpacho," 289–290
  and wine, dried, 290–291

Garden soup
  bisque, summer, 271–272
  bisque with carrot cream, winter, 250–252

creamy country, 145–146
gold bisque, 143–144
Italian, 144–145
Garlic
croutons, 315
soup, Spanish, 42–43
spinach-garlic soup, 136–137
Gazpacho
easy, 266–267
with marinated shrimp and olives, 267–268
watermelon, 289–290
Ginger, carrot-orange soup with, 118–119
Golden apple-pear soup, 275–276
Good wife soup, 246–247
Goulash soup, 17–18
easy, 189
Greek avgolemono soup, 43–44
Green beans. See Beans, fresh
Green onion(s)
chicken soup with, Malaysian, 38–39
hot and sour soup, 45–46
soup with dill, 215–216
Green pea(s)
lettuce soup with, creamy, 216
soup, cream of, 176
Green soup (potage vert), 244
Gumbo
chicken, crock pot, 197–198
oyster, sausage, and ham, 106–108
shrimp and chicken, 100–102

Ham
bean soup, Frankfurt, 27–29
bean soup, workday, 195–196
country, 12–13
oyster and sausage gumbo with, 106–108
soup, hearty, 62–63
split pea soup with, 155–156
stock, 300
three-meat soup, 59–60
vegetable soup, Spanish-style, 24–25
white bean soup, Tuscan, 152–153

Hearty soup
barley, 169–170
cabbage, Mediterranean style, 116–117
ham, 62–63
veal and vegetable, 192
Herbed cabbage soup, Stonebridge House, 113–114
High summer soup with salsa, 248–249
Hot and sour soup, 45–46
Hunter's beef and mushroom soup, 53

Iced soup
carrot with dill, 258–259
Mandarin cantaloupe, 288
strawberry-buttermilk, 285–287
Ingredients, 11–14
Italian soup
beefy minestrone, 51–52
fish and shellfish (cioppino), 84–85
garden, 144–145
oyster and mushroom, Florentine, 233–234
vegetable-beef, 187
vegetarian minestrone, 181–182
white bean, Tuscan, 152–153

Kale, potato soup with, 132

Lamb
Scotch broth, 24–25
soup, Creole-style, 193
and white bean soup, 151–152
Leek(s), 13
bouillabaisse, 83–84
cauliflower-leek potage, 119–120
celery-leek soup, creamy, 120–121
chicken and vegetable soup, Belgian (Waterzooi), 33–35
cock-a-leekie, 29–30
lobster soup, cream of, 228–230
oxtail soup with dumplings, Danish-style, 22–23
potato and parsley soup, 133
and potato soup (vichyssoise), 262–263

Leek(s) (*cont.*)
  soup, cream of, 124–126
  watercress soup, chilled, 269
Lemon, in avgolemono soup, Greek, 43–44
Lentil(s)
  brown rice soup with, savory, 161
  cabbage soup Mediterranean style, hearty, 116–117
  lentil-barley soup with beef, 158–159
  red lentil-tomato soup, 159–160
  soup, 194–195
  soup, East Indian, 177
Lettuce
  good wife soup, 246–247
  and green pea soup, creamy, 216
Lima bean and barley soup, 163–164
Lime and cantaloupe soup, easy, 289
Lobster soup, cream of, 228–230

Madrilène, cranberry, 284
Malaysian chicken and green onion soup, 38–39
Manhattan-style chowder
  clam, 93–94
  fish with vegetables, 91–92
Maryland crab soup, 95–97
Matzo ball soup, 44–45
Meatball(s)
  soup, Mexican (albóndigas), 20–21
  and vegetable soup, 55–56
Meat soups. *See* names of individual meats
Melon
  lime and cantaloupe soup, easy, 289
  Mandarin cantaloupe soup, iced, 288
  watermelon "gazpacho," 289–290
Mexican soup
  corn and bean, easy, 175
  corn and tomato, 214–215
  meatball (albóndigas), 20–21
  tortilla, 35–36
Minestrone
  beefy, 51–52
  vegetarian, 181–182

Mulligatawny, 36–38
Mushroom(s)
  beef soup with, hunter's, 53
  broth, 306
  hot and sour soup, 45–46
  oyster soup with, Florentine, 233–234
  and shrimp soup under puff pastry, 230–233
  soup, fresh and dried, 242–243
  soup, savory vegetarian, 177–179
  and wild rice soup, hearty, 126–127
Mussel(s)
  bouillabaisse, 82–84
  fish and shellfish soup (cioppino), 84–85
  fisherman's pot, Portuguese-style, 86–88
  soup with saffron, 104–106

New England–style chowder
  clam, 92–93
  fish, 206–207
North African–style chicken soup, spicy, 75–76

Oil
  olive, 13
  vegetable, 14
Old-fashioned beef and vegetable soup, 49–51
Olive(s)
  oil, 13
  and shrimp, marinated, for gazpacho, 267–268
Onion(s), 13
  and apple soup with curry, red, 127–128
  chicken soup, spicy North African-style, 75–76
  onion-potato soup, curried, 263
  soup, French, 41–42
Orange(s)
  carrot-orange soup with ginger, 118–119
  Mandarin cantaloupe soup, iced, 288
  orange-tomato soup, 264
Oriental vegetable soup, 222

Oxtail soup
  with dumplings, Danish-style, 22–23
  favorite, 58–59
Oyster(s)
  gumbo with sausage and ham, 106–108
  and mushroom soup Florentine, 233–234

Paprika
  beef and cabbage soup, sweet and sour, 56–57
  goulash soup, 17–18
  goulash soup, easy, 189
Parsley, 13
  green soup (potage vert), 244
  potato soup with, 133
Parsnip and carrot soup, creamy, 128–129
Pasta
  alphabet beef and vegetable soup, 54–55
  alphabet chicken soup, 72–73
  avgolemono soup, Greek, 43–44
  beefy minestrone, 51–52
  chicken and curly endive soup, 73–75
  chicken noodle soup, 65–66
  chicken soup with, chunky, 203–204
  egg noodles, homemade, 317–318
  soup with pesto (soupe au pistou), 39–41
  spinach-pasta soup with pesto, 180–181
  turkey vegetable soup, country-style, 77–78
  vegetarian minestrone, 181–182
Pastry, puff, shrimp and mushroom soup under, 230–233
Pea(s). See Green pea(s)
Peach soup with Amaretto, fresh, 280
Peanut soup Gold Coast style, 165–166
Pear(s)
  apple-pear soup, golden, 275–276
  butternut harvest bisque, 135–136
  strawberry-pear soup, 287

Pepper, 14
Pepper(s), chili
  chicken soup with, 204–205
  chili-cheese soup, 208
  corn and bean con carne soup, 19
  corn and tomato soup, Mexican, 213–214
  fennel and sweet pepper soup, 241–242
  meatball soup, Mexican (albóndigas), 20–21
  potato-corn chowder, Santa Fe, 179–180
Pepper(s), sweet
  chicken and pasta, chunky, 203–204
  fennel soup with, 241–242
  lamb soup, Creole-style, 193
  meatball soup, Mexican (albóndigas), 20–21
  soup, roasted red, 129–131
  veal soup with, 61–62
Pesto
  chicken and vegetable soup Provençal, 31–33
  soup with (soupe au pistou), 39–41
  spinach-pasta soup with, 180–181
Pimiento(s)
  cauliflower soup with cheese and, 211
  pimiento-chicken soup with chives, 70–71
  soup, 264–265
Pineapple, in curried chicken soup, West African, 255–256
Pistou (seasoning paste), 319
Plum soup, 281–282
Pork
  and apple soup, curried, 193–194
  bean and barley soup, easy, 196–197
  bean soup, Frankfurt, 27–29
  black bean soup, 154
  cabbage soup Mediterranean style, hearty, 116–117
  garlic soup, Spanish, 42–43
  hot and sour soup, 45–46
  potato-bacon soup, cream of, 131
  ribs and cabbage soup, country, 63–64

Pork (*cont.*)
  shrimp and chicken gumbo, 100–102
  and watercress soup, Chinese, 26–27
Portuguese-style fisherman's pot, 86–88
Potage
  asparagus-cheese, 238–239
  cauliflower-leek, 119–120
  vert (green soup), 244
Potato(es), 14
  beef and green bean soup with, 186
  beef and mushroom soup, hunter's, 53
  broccoli-potato soup, cream of, 112–113
  carrot soup with dill, iced, 258–259
  and corn chowder, 121–122
  and corn soup, 122–123
  fish chowder, Bermuda, 88–90
  fish chowder, New England–style, 206–207
  fish chowder with dill, Scandinavian-style, 90–91
  green soup (potage vert), 244
  and leek soup (vichyssoise), 262–263
  onion-potato soup, curried, 263
  and parsley soup, 133
  potato-bacon soup, cream of, 131
  potato-corn chowder, Santa Fe, 179–180
  potato-kale soup, 132
  spinach-garlic soup, 136–137
  swiss chard soup, 137–138
  vegetable and sausage soup, chunky, 64–65
  watercress soup, chilled, 269
Pots and pans, 10
Poultry soup. *See* Chicken; Turkey
Provençal chicken and vegetable soup, 31–33
Pumpkin soup, spiced, 134

Quick soup
  apple-wine soup, spicy, 276–277
  Bloody Mary, 219–220
    broccoli-cauliflower cheese, 209–210
    Brussels sprouts, creamy, 210–211
    cauliflower, pimiento, and cheese, 211
    celery-tomato, 211
    Cheddar cheese with tomato, 207
    chicken and chilies, 204–205
    chicken and cucumber, 205–206
    chicken and pasta, chunky, 203–204
    chili-cheese, 208
    corn, 213–214
    corn and tomato, Mexican, 214–215
    green onion with dill, 215–216
    lettuce and green pea, creamy, 216
    Mandarin cantaloupe soup, iced, 288
    peach soup with Amaretto, fresh, 280
    spinach, cream of, 217
    tomato, Creole, 218
    tomato with chunky vegetables, creamy, 218–219
    vegetable, fiesta, 220–221
    vegetable, Oriental, 222

Raspberry 'n' cream soup, 285
Red bean and sausage soup, 155
Rhubarb, in strawberry-buttermilk soup, iced, 285–287
Rice
  avgolemono soup, Greek, 43–44
  black bean soup, Cuban, 170–171
  celery-rice soup, spicy, 164
  chicken soup with, 67–68
  lentil-barley soup with beef, 158–159
  and lentil soup, savory brown, 161
  oyster, sausage, and ham gumbo, 106–108
  shrimp and chicken gumbo, 100–102
  vegetable soup, fiesta, 220–221
Roasting, 8

Sachet d'épice, 11
Saffron
  bouillabaisse, 82–84
  chicken and vegetable soup,
    Provençal, 31–33
  mussel soup with, 104–106
  soup, 245–246
Salsa, high summer soup with, 248–
  249
Salt, 14
Santa Fe potato-corn chowder, 179–
  180
Sausage
  bean soup, Frankfurt, 27–29
  oyster and ham gumbo with, 106–
    108
  red bean soup with, 155
  vegetable soup with, chunky, 64–
    65
Sautéing, 7–8
Savory soup
  brown rice and lentil, 161
  vegetarian mushroom, 177–179
Scallion(s). *See* Green onion(s)
Scallop(s)
  chowder, 103–104
  seafood bisque, creamy, 225–226
  soup suprême, 235–236
Scandinavian-style fish chowder with
  dill, 90–91
Scottish soup
  cock-a-leekie, 29–30
  good wife, 246–247
  Scotch broth, 25–26
Seafood bisque, creamy, 225–226
Shellfish, *see* names of individual
  shellfish
Seasoning paste (pistou), 319
Shrimp
  bisque, 99–100
  bouillabaisse, 82–84
  and chicken gumbo, 100–102
  fish and shellfish soup (cioppino),
    84–85
  fisherman's pot, Portuguese-style,
    86–88
  and mushroom soup under puff
    pastry, 230–233
  and olives, marinated, for
    gazpacho, 267–268

seafood bisque, creamy, 225–226
  and snow crab chowder, 97–98
Sieving, 9
Simmering, 8
Slicing, 7
Snow crab and shrimp chowder, 97–
  98
Soupe au pistou (soup with pesto),
  39–41
Spanish soup
  garlic, 42–43
  vegetable, 24–25
Spinach
  oyster and mushroom soup,
    Florentine, 233–234
  soup, cream of, 217
  spinach-garlic soup, 136–137
  spinach-pasta soup with pesto,
    180–181
Split pea and ham soup, 155–156
Squash
  butternut harvest bisque, 135–
    136
  garden bisque, summer, 271–
    272
  high summer soup with salsa, 248–
    249
  lamb soup, Creole-style, 193
  zucchini-buttermilk soup, tangy,
    270
Stirring, 8–9
Stock
  beef, 295–297
  brown, 297–298
  chicken, 299–300
  fish, 301
  ham, 300
  vegetable, 302–303
Stonebridge House herbed cabbage
  soup, 113–114
Straining, 9
Strawberries
  strawberry-buttermilk soup, iced,
    285–287
  strawberry-pear soup, 287
Summer garden bisque, 271–272
Summertime celery soup, 259–
  260
Sweet and sour beef and cabbage
  soup, 56–57

Sweet potatoes, in garden golden bisque, 143–144
Swiss chard soup, 137–138

Techniques, 7–10
Temperamental ingredients, 9–10
Three-bean soup, tangy, 172–173
Three-meat soup, 59–60
Thyme, tomato bisque with bacon and, 140–141
Tomato(es)
    bisque with thyme and bacon, 140–141
    Bloody Mary soup, 220
    bouillon, 307–308
    canned, 12
    celery-tomato soup, 212
    Cheddar cheese soup with, 207
    clam-tomato broth with chives, 308–309
    corn soup with, Mexican, 214–215
    gazpacho, easy, 266–267
    gazpacho with marinated shrimp and olives, 267–268
    high summer soup with salsa, 248–249
    orange-tomato soup, 264
    red lentil-tomato soup, 159–160
    soup, cream of, 139–140
    soup, Creole, 218
    soup with chunky vegetables, creamy, 218–219
    tomato-vegetable soup, zesty, 265–266
Tortilla soup, 35–36
Turkey vegetable soup, country-style, 77–78
Turnip soup, creamy, 142–143
Tuscan white bean soup, 152–153
Tyrolean cabbage soup, 115–116

Veal
    and sweet pepper soup, 61–62
    three-meat soup, 59–60
    and vegetable soup, hearty, 192
Vegetable(s)
    barbecued beef soup with, easy, 190
    beef soup with, alphabet, 54–55

beef soup with, old-fashioned, 49–51
butternut harvest bisque, 135–136
chicken chowder with, home-style, 71–72
chicken soup with, Belgian (Waterzooi), 33–35
chicken soup with, Provençal, 31–33
chicken soup with little dumplings and, chunky, 68–69
chunky, creamy tomato soup with, 218–219
country garden soup, creamy, 145–146
fish chowder with, Manhattan-style, 91–92
garden golden bisque, 143–144
garden soup, Italian, 144–145
gazpacho, easy, 266–267
gazpacho with marinated shrimp and olives, 267–268
ground beef soup with, 191
high summer soup with salsa, 248–249
meatball soup with, 55–56
and sausage soup, chunky, 64–65
soup, fiesta, 220–221
soup, Spanish-style, 24–25
stock, 302–303
summer garden bisque, 271–272
tomato-vegetable soup, zesty, 265–266
turkey soup with, country-style, 77–78
veal soup with, hearty, 192
vegetable-beef soup, Italian-style, 187
winter garden bisque with carrot cream, 250–252
see also Vegetarian soup; and names of individual vegetables
Vegetable oil, 14
Vegetarian soup
    barley, hearty, 169–170
    beet and cabbage borscht, 173–174
    black bean, Cuban, 170–171
    celery, cream of, 174–175

Vegetarian soup (*cont.*)
  corn and bean, easy Mexican, 175
  green pea, cream of, 176
  lentil, East Indian, 177
  minestrone, 181–182
  mushroom, savory, 177–179
  potato-corn chowder, Santa Fe,
    179–180
  soup with pesto (soupe au pistou),
    39–41
  spinach-pasta with pesto, 180–181
  three-bean, tangy, 172–173
  see also Vegetable(s)
Velouté, velvety fennel, 239–240
Vichyssoise (potato and leek soup),
  262–263

Water chestnuts, in avgolemono
  soup, Greek, 43–44
Watercress
  good wife soup, 246–247
  green soup (potage vert), 244
  pork soup with, Chinese, 26–27
  soup, chilled, 269
Waterzooi (Belgian chicken and
  vegetable soup), 33–35
Wild rice, hearty mushroom soup
  with, 126–127
Wine, 14
  apple-wine soup, spicy, 276–277
  apricot soup, 277–278
  beef and mushroom soup,
    hunter's, 53
  blueberry soup, 282

celery-leek soup, creamy, 120–
  121
chicken and vegetable soup,
  Belgian (Waterzooi), 33–35
chicken and vegetable soup
  Provençal, 31–33
consommé, 310–311
cranberry madrilène, 284
fish and shellfish soup (cioppino),
  84–85
fisherman's pot, Portuguese-style,
  86–88
fruit soup with, dried, 290–291
goulash soup, 17–18
lobster soup, cream of, 228–230
mussel soup with saffron, 104–
  106
pimiento-chicken soup with
  chives, 70–71
plum soup, 281–282
saffron soup, 245–246
shrimp bisque, 99–100
sweet red pepper soup, roasted,
  129–131
tomato bouillon, 307–308
tomato-vegetable soup, zesty, 265–
  266
veal and sweet pepper soup, 61–
  62
Winter garden bisque with carrot
  cream, 250–252
Workday bean soup, 195–196

Zucchini-buttermilk soup, tangy,
  270